PRACTICAL METHODS IN SPEECH

PRACTICAL
METHODS
IN SPEECH

BY HAROLD BARRETT

Compton College

HOLT, RINEHART AND WINSTON
NEW YORK · CHICAGO · SAN FRANCISCO
TORONTO · LONDON

Copyright © 1959
by Holt, Rinehart and Winston, Inc.
7 8 9
Library of Congress Catalog Card Number: 59-14263
2047009
Printed in the United States of America

To those lovable consultants:

MY WIFE, CAROL

AND OUR BOYS - JOE, PAT, AND EDDIE.

Preface

  This textbook is designed to meet a need for a teaching aid in speech courses that is adapted to students of differing abilities and backgrounds. An attempt has been made to present the accepted principles of oral communication in a relaxed and readable style, and to provide numerous and varied assignments and exercises that will help the student to apply the methods drawn from those principles.

  A major goal was to explain the methods of speech in order to minimize the amount of class time necessary for lecturing. First- and second-semester students need a maximum number of speaking experiences, and if theory is mastered chiefly through reading the text, more time can be devoted to oral performance.

  Practical Methods in Speech is divided into three parts. Part I, Rudimentary Methods, treats basic methods that are covered in most beginning courses: choosing a subject, wording a purpose, organizing, using various aids and materials to strengthen and support ideas, using the extemporaneous style, and so forth.

  Part II, Complementary Methods, includes chapters on language, delivery, and listening. This is a resource section which allows a teacher to introduce any one of the three chapters at any point during the course—whenever he decides that the application of basic methods should be complemented with instruction in using language, deliverying ideas, or listening.

  Part III, Supplementary Methods, can serve as the core of

the second-semester class; though some teachers may wish to utilize its chapters in a one-semester course. Each chapter is an independent unit and may be used in any order.

Although this is the first edition of *Practical Methods in Speech,* our method of preparation has provided for pretesting its worth. Working very closely with me were three speech colleagues—Peter Altpeter of Ventura College, Charles Guss of Stockton College, and Sheldon Hayden of Santa Monica City College. They assisted in planning the scope of the work, providing materials, criticizing various drafts, using the preliminary edition (1958) in their classes, offering suggestions for revision, and giving the encouragement that one needs to carry out such a project. Credit for whatever merit this textbook may have belongs in large part to them.

For inspiration and academic training, I shall always be indebted to many people who have helped to lay key stepping stones which have led directly or indirectly to the publication of this book. A particular expression of gratitude I offer to the following:

Charles M. Guss and John M. Fanucchi, whose friendship and teaching excellence recruited a speech teacher;

Roy C. McCall, whose wisdom and art have been a constant source of direction for many years;

Those other trusty guides: Granville Basye, K. C. Beighley, Edward S. Betz, Fleda M. Brigham, John Crabbe, William B. McCoard, Howard L. Runion, Edwin R. Schoell, Forrest L. Seal, and Glenn Starlin;

To Howard Chandler, Orvell K. Fletcher, Earl F. Osborne, and Win Kelley, whose counsel is respected by all who have had the good fortune of knowing them;

To my wife, Carol, whose many contributions are beyond measure.

H. B.

August 1959
Compton, Calif.

Contents

PART I

RUDIMENTARY METHODS

1. Approaching the Speech Class   3
2. Getting Started   15
3. Organizing Your Thoughts   31
4. Strengthening Your Thoughts   54
5. Developing Your Thoughts with Physical Materials   70
6. Developing Your Thoughts with Verbal Materials   82

PART II

COMPLEMENTARY METHODS

7. Using Effective Language   107
8. Refining Speech Delivery   121
9. Improving Listening Skills   144

PART III
SUPPLEMENTARY METHODS

10. Participating in Group Discussion   157
11. Applying Parliamentary Law   182
12. Speaking to Persuade   198
13. Preparing for Various Occasions   225
14. Reading Aloud   236

PART IV
APPENDIXES

A. Practical Methods Applied: Model Speeches   273
B. Readings in Speech   301
    Index   321

I

RUDIMENTARY
METHODS

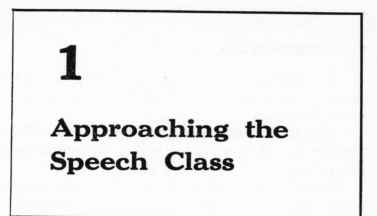

1

Approaching the Speech Class

YOUR CHIEF BUSINESS

Whoever you are, wherever you go to school, whatever you hope to do with your life, you now find yourself enrolled in a speech class. You may have made an independent decision to study speech, or a counselor may have recommended it. Friends who have had the course might have suggested that you take it, or speech may be a required subject for you. Whatever the reason, either you or someone who has an interest in you recognizes the wisdom of a remark made by one of our most perceptive American authors, Walt Whitman, who said, "The first duty of a man is to speak, that is his chief business in the world."

Whether your goal is commercial, technical, professional, or still undefined, you have taken the first step toward gaining increased proficiency in an art and skill which is your "chief business in the world."

THE SPEECH CLASS

If you have never had a course in speech, you will find that your experiences this semester will be different from those in most other classes.

First of all, the greatest part of your work will be oral. This fact is surely no revelation to you. We learn to speak well by speaking.

Secondly, speech is to a considerable extent subjective in nature. That is, it is a human activity and related to the "feeling" side of man's make-up as well as to his intellectual side. Machines have been invented which can produce "speech," but no machine will ever be devised which can convey even a portion of the warmth, feeling, and beauty of human oral communication. No, we shall not treat speech as a mechanical activity. In the speech class we are concerned with people; we are concerned with *you* and *your speech*.

A third distinguishing feature of the speech class is that it is necessarily a social situation—one in which you will have relationships with others. You speak to the class; you may get suggestions from the class; you in turn may give suggestions to class members. In short, you do not learn to speak merely by reading a book or by speaking in an empty room. A social unit, the class, will provide for you the needed motivation and justification for speaking, and it will act in different ways as a sounding board to answer your vital question, "How am I doing?"

Speech is different from other courses in at least one other way. One speech student summed it up quite well when he said, "In this course you really learn more than how to be a better speaker. You have a chance to learn about people and their thoughts and experiences. By hearing them express themselves, you seem to develop a greater respect and appreciation for them." Speech improvement will help you to make your life a better one.

IN YOUR PERSONAL LIFE

People get along better with themselves if they like themselves, if they consider themselves worthy, if they respect themselves.

It follows that if you improve yourself you will have more reason to increase your self-respect. This is certainly true in the case of speech improvement. Speaking characteristics are a central and vital part of personality, and when the part is strengthened, the whole is strengthened. When you grow in your ability to communicate orally, your total personality grows and develops. You can expect, then, to work for personality development in this course.

Another phase of increasing one's self-respect involves the handling of fear. Let us face it; people—you, the author of this book, everyone—experience fear. The majority of the fears in speaking arise from a person's need to safeguard his ego, to protect his self-concept. He is concerned that something will happen to deflate his ego and thus damage or embarrass him in the presence of others.

So it is in a speaking situation. Speakers become fearful because they know that they are being observed. They cannot "pull down the shade" or isolate themselves in a room or talk to a tree on some distant hill. In the speaking situation there is always an audience, always at least one observer.

Now in the speaker's mind, observers exert pressure, and they cause him to respond in different ways. For example, he may feel inspired by his audience and give a successful speech because of them, or he may be so affected by their presence that he fails to use his capabilities and, therefore, does not succeed. In other words, fear is both constructive and destructive, and the emphasis on one or the other depends upon how the speaker looks at himself in the speaking environment. Does he feel reasonably confident, secure, and thankful for the opportunity, or does he feel out of place, embarrassed, inferior, ashamed, or fearful of making a mistake?

Speech instruction helps him to realize that he is worthy,

that he can be successful, that he does have a right—in fact, an obligation—to share his ideas with others. He will take a big step toward improving his personal life when he comes to the realization that a residue of fear can spur him on, while blind, unattended fear can hold him back. He will attend to the blind fear which retards and causes loss of effectiveness, and he will allow the remaining fear to act as a stimulus for doing well.

IN YOUR SOCIAL LIFE

Now, it is impossible to separate personal life from social life—at least for very long. There are very few hermits these days, and as one person recently said, "There is no place to hide anyway." For better or for worse, we put ourselves into a society, into a variety of societies. We belong to family social units, clubs, school classes, churches, and, of course, we find ourselves in an infinite number of less intimate, ever-varying social locales.

When we accept the thought of John Donne that no man is an island, that people must relate themselves to other people, we then begin to ponder how to acquire more social effectiveness. How can we get along in this world full of people? How can we understand others and be understood by them? How else than by communication? In fact, one definition of "to communicate" is "to create understanding." Perhaps the most urgent need today is for better communication among people.

In speech you will study communication, how to be understood and how to understand. From such activity, when extended and applied outside of the speech classroom, you can expect to become a socially more effective person.

IN YOUR VOCATIONAL LIFE

Can you think of an occupation or profession which does not involve the oral exchange of ideas? It is true that some fields seem to call for more speaking than others. We immediately think of law, selling, politics, radio and television, teaching, the ministry, personnel work, and public relations as careers which emphasize the need for skillful speaking; however, we should not overlook the value of the spoken word in accounting, medicine, art, library work, social service, forestry, and engineering. The fundamentals of speech that you will learn and apply in your class are applicable to the speaking activities in which you will engage in your business life.

We once made a study of the speaking methods of twenty-seven leading business and professional people in a medium-size American community. The purpose was to determine the extent to which these citizens used speaking methods similar to those taught in the classroom. We asked them such questions as: "Do you limit your subject?" "Do you consider it necessary to analyze the audience and the occasion?" "Do you outline your speeches?" "What do you plan to accomplish in your introduction?" It is difficult to chart the results statistically; however, at least 85 percent of those interviewed indicated on most of the questions that their most effective methods were the same ones taught in speech classrooms.

Where did the twenty-seven interviewees learn their speech methods? Undoubtedly their speaking experiences since leaving school helped them to refine and perfect their methods, but it is interesting to note that twenty-six of the twenty-seven had had a speech course of one kind or another.

Your conscientious study and practice of the time-tested principles of speaking will help you to succeed no matter what vocation goal you may pursue.

THE GOALS

In order to meet your personal, social, and vocational speaking needs, we shall strive for the achievement of the following goals.

1. *To develop ease in the speaking environment.* This is a necessary first and continuing order of business. Effective participation in any activity is based upon familiarity with the environment. One cannot be free to respond to the limits of his capabilities until he feels at home, until he is adjusted to his surroundings. He needs to feel reasonably secure and also to realize, as improbable as it may appear, that others have similar emotional problems in speaking.

2. *To master the time-tested techniques of speech composition.* Most of the basic principles to be covered in this course are by no means new. They were originated and taught by great minds hundreds of years ago—Aristotle, Quintilian, Cicero, and many others. We of the twentieth century have merely revised them for modern usage. Though ancient in origin and few in number, they are the cornerstones of effective oral communication today.

3. *To discover and refine a proper individual style for presenting ideas orally.* If you are diligent and have a sincere desire to do something for yourself, you may discover your *individual* manner for presenting your thoughts early in the semester. Then, along with mastering the other speaking principles, you may devote the balance of the term to sharpening and vitalizing your delivery. In any event, you will want to find what is *yours; your* style, *your* best means of expression.

4. *To develop greater skill in the use of language.* The vocabularies of most people can be strengthened. Mistakes in pronunciation can be corrected. One can learn to avoid usage errors. Looking at the matter of using language broadly, we shall work toward including elements which help express the idea and toward avoiding those which detract from the idea.

5. *To become a more effective listener.* Probably the majority of people believe that they are good listeners—when they want to be. While it is true that wanting to be a good listener helps one to listen, it is also true that most untrained listeners are rather inefficient. Good listening can be learned, and we shall strive toward this end.

YOUR RESPONSIBILITIES

As is the case with accomplishing most of life's goals, the five aims explained above are demanding. They ask you to make a personal investment of thought and effort and to offer your best in terms of self-reliance and self-discipline. We cannot disagree with the old man who told his grandson, "Get an education, lad; that's something no one can take away from you." We can add, however, that "the getting" requires much of the "getter."

Be True to Yourself

1. *Be yourself.* Allow the most creditable personal assets you possess to come forth. For some people, these are "frozen assets," now lying dormant and not allowed to circulate. The best thing you can do for yourself is to resolve at the outset that you will make a determined attempt to free the worthwhile thoughts and feelings which you have been reluctant to express heretofore.

Then, too, you want to avoid the artificial, that which is *not* yours. Somewhere along the way (and why not now?), those who have borrowed a vocal quality or physical characteristic from a movie star or some other admired person must emancipate themselves from such bondage.

Be free, and be an individual.

2. *Take advantage of this opportunity.* Make the most of your time by assuming the responsibility of having assignments ready on time, being regular in attendance, and being prompt.

Know that the successful application of nearly any principle is based on a knowledge of that principle. This fact is especially relevant to speech training. In some areas the dispute goes on over such questions as "Which came first, the chicken or the egg?" or "Which is the stronger influence, heredity or environment?", but we in speech do not debate the question, "Which is more important, theory or practice?" We know that both are necessary. One is linked to the other.

What does this say to the student in a speech class, to you? Obviously, it indicates the need to learn the theory first; therefore, as a basis for speech making you will need to study the reading assignments, take notes on lectures and discussions, and listen attentively to the other speeches.

3. *Develop an attitude for accepting helpful criticism.* No phase of your program for developing greater speaking proficiency is more vital than the part devoted to criticism. You will be criticized, and perhaps at some time during the semester, you will be expected to offer criticisms.

Now what is criticism? First, like a coin, it has two sides. There is criticism which refers to the strengths of the speaking effort and criticism which refers to the points needing improvement. Too often we think of criticism as only negative, whereas good criticism is positive and constructive.

You can expect to be criticized in several ways. The instructor may make comments directly to you either orally or in written form. When the instructor analyzes your speech orally, it may help him to teach the entire class. Again, he may be referring to you incidentally when he discusses the class efforts as a whole. When he is talking about another student's speech, some of the items covered may pertain to your own. Finally, you may have an opportunity to be criticized by your class members.

The remarks about your speaking are intended to be positive and helpful, that is, designed to further your speech development. In receiving criticism, you, too, should have a positive point of view, a willingness to help yourself by accepting the considered observations of others.

Specifically:
(a) Listen to and read the criticisms offered.
(b) Ask for clarification of any remark which is not meaningful to you.
(c) Be objective; take criticism maturely.
(d) Follow the considered suggestions made to you.

Be True to Your Class

If you are true to yourself, it is likely that you can *be true to your class*. The words of Shakespeare from *Hamlet* support us:

> To thine own self be true,
> And it must follow, as the night the day,
> Thou canst not then be false to any man.

1. *To be true to your class, you must accept the fact that your active participation is needed.* Become a part of the class. Listen thoughtfully and courteously to the other speakers. Enter into general class discussions, and be able to offer reasoned observations when called upon.

2. *Observe the time limit set for each speaking assignment.* The instructor has a number of activities and experiences he would like you to accomplish, and perhaps he wishes that he could allow you to speak as long as you desire on any given subject. Realistically, for your benefit and for the general welfare of the class, he will have to limit your speaking time. So, in observing the time limits established, you will show consideration for others and for yourself. Actually, the discipline of planning to conform to the dictates of a "tyrant time clock" is a very beneficial and desirable part of speech education. It might help to bear in mind the words Will Rogers spoke after a lengthy speech: "Gentlemen, you have just been listening to that Chinese sage, On Too Long."

Be True, too, to Society

By society, we mean all the people with whom you will be speaking throughout your entire life.

1. *Recognize the power of the spoken word.* Speaking moves people. Much of what we buy, how we vote, and what we do and think can be traced back to the influence other

people have had on us, and they have relied to a great extent on speech.

Does it not follow that *you* are an influencer, that you, too, change people's lives? Does it not follow that with increased speaking proficiency you will strengthen your power to influence others? Keep these questions in mind, and as the semester unfolds, notice the effect that you and your fellow speakers have on the class. Notice audience reactions, the evidence of the power of the spoken word.

2. *If speaking moves people, it is an absolute necessity that those who speak be responsible for what they say.* The man with a permit to carry a gun or drive a car has no greater responsibility to society than the man who has the power of speech. A gun, an automobile, or speaking ability can be used to accomplish destructive or constructive ends. It is up to the user to determine what he will do with the tool or ability he possesses. If he is responsible, he will use the gun or automobile skillfully, wisely, and for laudable purposes. If he is responsible he will use the power of speech skillfully, wisely, and for laudable purposes; skillfully to be effective, wisely to have something to say, and with laudable purpose to fulfill his obligations to his fellowmen.

LET US SUMMARIZE AND LOOK AHEAD

Up to this point we have considered the values and characteristics of speech training, the goals to be worked for, and the accompanying responsibilities. Before we get into the work of making speeches, let us preview what is to follow.

This course, guided by your instructor whose field is oral communication, is designed to take you in a step-by-step movement toward speaking proficiency. The plan of assignments calls for starting with a basic principle and for proceeding by introducing one or two new principles into each successive assignment. You might call it the one-thing-at-a-time or stone-upon-stone approach. After practicing one element of speech making, you will add to it another element and then another. This building process goes on until all of the basic ingredients of speaking have been successfully integrated into your oral efforts.

For some, the development will be more rapid than it will be for others. Whatever is your lot, be patient. Remember that the rate of development does not always indicate the quality of development. Work hard; take first things first; and keep the words of an eminent Roman speech teacher, Quintilian, in mind:

> Nature has herself appointed that nothing great is to be accomplished quickly, and has ordained that difficulty should precede every work of excellence.

FOR FURTHER STUDY

Dickens, Milton, *Speech: Dynamic Communication* (New York, Harcourt, Brace, 1954), Ch. 1, "Why Study Speech?"

Norvelle, Lee, Smith, Raymond G., and Larson, Orvin, *Speaking Effectively* (New York, Holt-Dryden, 1957), Ch. 1, "The Approach."

Oliver, Robert T., Dickey, Dallas C., and Zelko, Harold P., *Communicative Speech* (New York, Holt-Dryden, 1955), Ch. 1, "Speech in Twentieth-century America."

BASIC ASSIGNMENT NO. 1

Prepare to give a very brief and informal "This I Believe" talk on one of the topics listed below. Express your personal views frankly and freely.

1. Developing Ease in the Speaking Environment
2. Individual Style
3. Use of Language
4. Effective Listening
5. A Speaker's Responsibilities to Himself
6. A Speaker's Responsibilities to His Class
7. A Speaker's Responsibilities to Society

SUGGESTED EXERCISE A

To give your instructor information about your speech experiences and needs, answer the following questions carefully and completely.

1. Have you ever had a course in speech? When and where?
2. Have you ever participated in debate, discussion, extemporaneous speaking, student congress, radio, dramatics, oratory, or other such oral activities? When and where?
3. Have you ever had a speaking or hearing defect? If so, explain.
4. Are you nervous when you talk to people? When and with whom?
5. Are you dissatisfied with any of your present speaking habits or characteristics? Which ones?
6. What types of speaking are demanded by your chosen occupation?
7. What are several topics on which, with preparation, you could speak briefly? List a few.
8. What are several topics on which you would like to hear other class members speak? List a few.

SUGGESTED EXERCISE B

Prepare a brief statement on one of the following topics designated by your instructor.

How I Expect Speech to Play a Part in My Life

Values of Good Speech

How I Have Learned to Accept Criticism

What Do Instructors Have a Right to Expect of Us as Students?

How I Have Learned to Handle Fear

Your instructor may wish to ask you to put these ideas down in the form of a simple outline for later presentation in a speech or group discussion.

2

Getting Started

FIRST THINGS FIRST

The first, and sometimes most difficult, phase of speech preparation is finding a subject. "What shall I talk about?" probably is the question most frequently heard in the speech class.

From the other side of the desk, the answer most frequently given to this query is, "Talk about what you would like to talk about." In the final analysis, the subject choice is *yours*, and there are three factors by which you should be guided in making such a choice.

THREE FACTORS

YOURSELF

What do *you* want to talk about? What are your interests? What are your favorite subjects of conversation? When you have a bull session, what subjects seem to stimulate you and mean something to you? What are the areas which matter most in your life?

The answers to such questions will remind you of where you should start your thinking in this business of finding an idea for a speech. Talk about what you like to talk about. For instance, a jazz fan has many possibilities

The Origin of Jazz
The Contributions of W. C. Handy to Jazz
The Instruments of Jazz
Why I Like Jazz
How to Appreciate Jazz
The Best Jazz Recordings
Why Jazz Will Never Die
The Relationship of Jazz to Other Types of Music

We could go on and list scores of potential speech topics from this one field. Let us take another area, say, football, and imagine what an interested person could explore:

The Defense in Football
Football's Offense Formations
Blocking Techniques
Tackling Techniques
How to Watch a Football Game
Physical Conditioning for Football
A Great Football Player
The Contributions of Coach Bud Wilkenson

Literature may be your main interest. If you let your imagination wander, you might think of such topics as the following:

Why Edgar Allan Poe Wrote as He Did
Shakespeare, Fraud or Genius?
Elements of the Short Story
Homer, The One Who Started It All
What Is Literary Art?
The Importance of Literature
You *Can* Like Poetry

Do you have an interest in the mechanical world of engines, tools, electrical devices, electronics, and so forth? If so, you have a wealth of prospective subject matter:

What Is a Spark Plug?
How You Can Increase Your Car's Horsepower
What Every Driver Should Know About His Automobile
The Principles of Flight
What Is a Rocket?
What We Owe to Marconi
Safety Features on New Cars

What are your interests? People? Professions? Places? Politics? Penology? Pachyderms? Decide that first, then ask yourself how much you know about a possible subject. It is very likely that a subject which you find interesting will be one about which you have considerable information. Probably we are safe in saying that if you like it, you know enough about it to discuss it in a short speech.

Another important consideration arises here. You are concerned with the matter of stage fright now, to some degree at least, and an appropriate subject choice can help you avoid some of that fear. Speaking on an interesting and familiar subject allows one to be more comfortable and confident than he would be if he were talking about something he did not like or did not know. It stands to reason that everyone is more at home in his own backyard. When dealing with stimulating and known ideas we are more efficient and relaxed.

Then, too, a little bit of the appealing and the familiar helps us to adjust to new situations. When we are traveling, what great pleasure we derive from meeting someone from back home. The foreign setting does not seem as foreign. A familiar element has helped us to adjust to and accept the new surroundings. So it is with the new surroundings of the speaking situation. Bring your knowledge and your interests into the speaking environment to help you adjust to that situation.

YOUR AUDIENCE

What does your audience want? Do they want a political address equal to those presented by one of our Presidents? Do they expect to hear a Daniel Webster or a Franklin D. Roosevelt? If your subject is law enforcement, do they expect you to be as well informed as J. Edgar Hoover? No, your listeners have no such desires or expectations. They know that this is a speech class, a laboratory, a learning situation. Everyone expects you to do your best, but no one expects you to have all the information related to a given area.

Now you may be an expert in some field, but no one is going to condemn you if you are not. A speech instructor was very pleased one semester when a student confidently delivered a talk on "How to Pitch a Baseball." He never faltered or apologized at any time, even though he knew that one of the class members was a young man who had been an eight-game winner in the Pacific Coast League during the past season.

Your audience, too, wants you to present familiar and personally appealing ideas. This is important for you to accept, especially in the early stages of your speech growth. Remember that interest is contagious. If you have feeling for what you say and express it, the listeners will catch your enthusiasm.

Later, when you are more confident, you will begin to analyze audiences more thoroughly and make planned attempts to choose areas for discussion which can be closely adapted to them. Then, you will examine the age characteristics, sex distribution, backgrounds, and possible interests of the audience, and in planning you will ask questions about each of these factors.

Age

How old are my prospective listeners?

Are they children? Adolescents? Adults? Mixed?

Sex

Are they predominantly male or female? Mixed?

Backgrounds

> What are their probable educational, social, political, and religious backgrounds?
>
> What subjects will appeal and what subjects should I avoid?

Interests

> What subject will appeal to their interests?
>
> What subjects, even though not appealing to their interests, do I have an obligation to discuss with them?

THE OCCASION

What subject does the occasion demand? In the speech class the occasion probably remains about the same unless your instructor chooses to vary it. Therefore, the greatest demand is the same as that imposed by any social situation. Choose an idea that will be appropriate for the "society" in which you are speaking. Use good taste and avoid embarrassing yourself or your audience. You have freedom, true; however, a certain amount of discretion is called for when dealing with people. A former chief justice of the Supreme Court, Charles Evans Hughes, expressed a similar thought: "Freedom of expression gives the essential democratic opportunity, but self-restraint is the essential civic discipline."

On future occasions your speech may be restricted by the purpose of the gathering, the season of the year, or the time of day; however, these demands are not meaningful to us now. (See Chapter 12 for a further discussion of audience analysis.)

TO WHAT END?

What effect do you wish to have upon your listeners? In the speech class you will be completing assignments, true, but in doing them, you will be taking advantage of an opportunity to influence people. Along with choosing a subject, it is necessary to determine the general end toward which you will speak. Hugh Blair, who wrote about communication in the eighteenth century, puts it aptly.

> Whenever a man speaks or writes, he is supposed as a rational being, to have some end in view: either to inform or to amuse or to persuade, or, in some way or other, to act upon his fellow creatures.

The equally esteemed critic, George Campbell, agrees: "In speaking, there is always some end proposed, or some effect which the speaker intends to produce in the hearer."

Ask yourself when preparing every speech, "How do I wish to act upon my 'fellow creatures'?" "To what end am *I* speaking with *this audience* on *this* subject?" Decide if your general end is to inform, to persuade, or to entertain.

TO INFORM

Perhaps most of the speeches to be given in your class will be designed to give information. Talks with this general end are the most common ones. When informing, the speaker's purpose is to enlighten the audience, to tell the listeners how to do something, to explain the nature of some person, place, or thing, and so forth. For example, the following general ends are essentially informational:

> To give a character sketch of Sid Caesar
> To define psychology
> To describe the Grand Canyon
> To relate the elements of student government
> To clarify the nature of modern art
> To explain styles of high jumping

TO PERSUADE

Persuasion is the highest form of oral expression and the most challenging. It involves not only giving information but also establishing beliefs, and sometimes it causes the audience to act. When you persuade, you convince people to believe something or to do something. Now not all of the audience may be moved to believe, nor may any action be immediate; nevertheless, the speaker's goal is to convince or to secure action at once or for some future time. These ends are persuasive:

> To show why Ray Barton should be elected student body president
> To develop an appreciation for the customs of foreign people
> To give reasons for the necessity of taking a math course
> To present the values of military experience
> To explain why everyone should contribute to the Red Cross
> To show why every citizen should study the history of his country
> To present a case for attending basketball games

TO ENTERTAIN

Any speech, regardless of its general end, may have elements of entertainment, of humor. There are speeches, however, that are planned solely for entertainment. These are not as common in the speech classroom as are informative and persuasive speeches. Talks to entertain are difficult, and it takes a special flair to be able to sustain humor and carry it off well. Then, too, many speech educators believe that speech training will be more profitable if the oral assignments are completed with more serious goals in mind. Nonetheless, you may wish to try an entertainment speech sometime during the semester. The following might represent such aims:

> To ridicule the do-it-yourself craze
> To show how to get rid of friends in three easy lessons
> To characterize "Joe College"
> To discuss a typical student's most embarrassing moments
> To describe hair styles of the future
> To poke fun at vulnerable human characteristics

Determine what your primary general end will be, then, but be aware of the fact that any speech may involve the development of minor ends which will help you to achieve your major goal. This would be true, for example, in persuasion. Undoubtedly you would include information and perhaps use some humor, even though your chief aim is to persuade.

In selecting the initial idea, satisfy yourself first; that is, consider your reservoir of knowledge and experience and your desires. Such careful consideration will go a long way toward satisfying the audience and meeting the demands of the occasion.

> Suit your topics to your strength,
> And ponder well your subject, and its length;
> Nor lift your load, before you're quite aware
> What weight your shoulder will, or will not bear.
>
> —BYRON

NARROW YOUR SUBJECT

What would be your reaction to a speaker who announces, "Today I shall discuss the state of California"? Would you believe he could do it? Is it possible to discuss California, or even Rhode Island for that matter, in a single speech? Of course not. The subject is too broad. Thousands of books have been written about California, and hundreds of motion pictures and magazine articles have treated the subject. What confidence it would take for a speaker to say that he will handle it in five minutes—or even five hours.

It is apparent, is it not, that subjects need to be limited, cut down to size to comply with the limitations of time and purpose. After selecting your basic idea, then, study its breadth and ask yourself these questions about it:

1. Can I cover it in the time allowed?
2. Can I cover it without having to hurry?

If your answer to either question is in the negative, there is but one solution: *narrow your subject.* In other words, break the subject down into parts, and use one of the parts as the area to be covered in your speech. Let us take California as an example and imagine that we have a large box labeled "California." In the box there are compartments, and in the compartments are smaller compartments, and so forth. A side view might look like this.

RIVERS	EARTH FAULTS	UNIVERSITIES	JUNIOR COLLEGES
GEOGRAPHY		SCHOOLS	
MOUNTAINS	BEACHES	HIGH SCHOOLS	ELEMENTARY SCHOOLS
MOTION PICTURE	AGRICULTURE	DESERT DWELLER	MOUNTAIN DWELLER
INDUSTRY		PEOPLE	
MANUFACTURING	FISHING	VALLEY DWELLER	COAST DWELLER
SAN FRANCISCO	SACRAMENTO	RUSSIAN EXPLORATIONS	SPANISH SETTLEMENTS
CITIES		HISTORY	
LOS ANGELES	SAN DIEGO	ENGLISH EXPLORATIONS	MEXICAN PERIOD
CALIFORNIA			

We know the foolishness of trying to discuss California, therefore, we might consider the "Industry of California." Even this subtopic is too bulky, and so we look into the "Industry" compartment for a more limited part and select "Agriculture," possibly. This *could* be our topic, but even now we must ask ourselves "Is this topic sufficiently limited?" If not, the break-down process must go on until we have found an area to which we can do justice in the time allowed.

Let us look at some other examples:

1. *Subject:* Animals
     Subtopic: Dogs
          Subtopic: Caring for dogs
2. *Subject:* People
     Subtopic: People's habits
          Subtopic: Reading habits
3. *Subject:* Speech
     Subtopic: Choosing a subject
          Subtopic: Narrowing the subject
4. *Subject:* Philosophy
     Subtopic: A philosophy of life
          Subtopic: The need for a philosophy of life

WORD YOUR PROPOSITION

With your topic in mind, your next task will be to write your specific purpose. The specific purpose or *proposition,* as we shall call it, is a sentence employed to indicate to your audience what you desire to discuss. It makes known your intent, the ground you will cover, where you are going. To prevent misunderstanding and vagueness, the proposition must be a complete sentence and include only one idea. Further, it should be stated briefly and designed for audience acceptance.

Let us digress momentarily in order to put the all-important proposition in its place as a member of a "four-man speech team." As we will explain in Chapter 3, a speech is made up of an introduction, a proposition (specific purpose), a body, and a conclusion. Each has a vital function. The introduction leads up to the objective of the talk; the proposition states the objective; the body works to attain that objective; and the conclusion clinches the attainment of the objective. Is it not evident that the objective, the proposition, is the heart of the speech? It is the theme or central idea.

Little wonder it is, then, that the proposition requires so

much care in phrasing. An error here can cause the entire effort to be faulty. Note the weaknesses of these propositions:

1. Dress styles of the 1920s.
2. May I acquaint you with a crystal radio set and tell you how to test tubes?
3. It is my purpose to explain the various functions of an internal combustion engine which is designed to offer maximum efficiency when the spark plugs have been thoroughly cleaned or replaced with the best on the market today.
4. Sensible people, those who matter in the first place, do not buy houses in developments.

Do you observe the faults of these propositions? No. 1 is incomplete. We might ask, "What about the dress styles of the 1920s?" Is it the speaker's aim to evaluate the styles? To describe them? To show that they are coming back into fashion? We just do not know, and the wise speaker will prevent such a problem from occurring by telling the audience his goal—in a complete sentence.

No. 2 is a full sentence but decidedly vague. What is the purpose? Actually, this proposition is two-headed; it indicates two purposes. The speaker employing this purpose statement would be ambitious, indeed, if he were to suppose that both aims could be accomplished. It is enough of a task to realize *one* objective. When confronted with a two-headed proposition, discard one of the ideas, or save it for another speech.

No. 3 is ambiguous because of its extreme length and involvement. It should stop after "engine." Explanations and qualifications can come at a later point in the speech. The job at this point is to state the exact purpose, briefly and simply.

No. 4 will alienate the audience. The speaker may have some good reasons for not liking tract houses, but he needs listeners before he can do any convincing. With such a desired goal he might do better to employ a less direct proposition. For example, "Here are some points to consider in buying a house in a development."

A well-phrased proposition, we see, gets the speaker off to a good start by definitely specifying his objective. Remember:

It must be a complete sentence.

It must include a single idea.

It must be uninvolved and reasonably brief.

It must be designed for audience acceptance.

USE THE EXTEMPORANEOUS STYLE

Chapter 8 treats speech delivery rather completely, but for now let us single out for discussion the style of presentation.

There was a time when speeches were memorized, and some of the most effective speakers were those with the best memories. Fortunately, times have changed (especially for those with poorer memories), and today we hear memorized speeches infrequently. There are good reasons for the change. Few people can deliver a speech which is committed to memory without "having it show." Too often such a talk is stilted, stiff, and held at a distance from the audience. There is also the ever-present fear of forgetting, and this causes the speaker to be on his guard and in dread of missing one word, one word which may throw the whole effort awry.

Another method of presenting ideas is manuscript style or reading. This system is used considerably by politicians, government officials, some business executives, and some clergymen. When done well, it can be effective; when done poorly, communication does not take place. Too often the speaker never gets his speech off the page and out to his audience. Too often there is no meeting of the eyes and, it follows, no meeting of the minds. Eugene Smith expresses the thought cleverly.

I always dislike using a manuscript in making a speech. It's like courting a girl through a picket fence. Everything that is said can be heard, but there isn't much contact.[1]

---

[1] Eugene Smith, *Quote Magazine*, May 19, 1957.

Because of the possible hazards inherent in memorization and manuscript reading, we shall emphasize the *extemporaneous style*. Do not associate this use of the term with the "extemporaneous" speaking contest which allows a participant forty-five minutes or an hour for preparation.

When you use the extemporaneous method, you prepare, certainly, but you do not memorize your speech nor do you write it out word for word. You will benefit from the experience of thousands like yourself, if you follow five key steps:

1. Select familiar and interesting ideas, ideas you have a *desire* to communicate and *want* your listeners to hear.
2. Use an outline, either mental or written. Avoid cluttering it with so much detail that it becomes a verbatim representation of your speech. Include the skeleton of your talk and key details, just enough to help you carry the thought along.
3. Let your speeches take shape gradually. Start preparing well ahead of your speaking date, and allow the ideas to sift through your mind. Some thoughts you will discard, others you will keep, and you will add new ones as they occur to you. The retained ideas will become a part of you, and there will be no cause to want to memorize or read the speech.
4. Practice! Practice aloud in seclusion. Practice before family or friends, and try out ideas in dinner-table conversation. Practice to get that confident feeling which comes from knowing what you are saying and where the thought is going. Practice purposefully—with your goal in mind. Practice as often as necessary to get yourself ready to communicate your ideas.
5. Speak naturally and conversationally with your audience. *Talk* with them. They are human, you are human, and both of you are engaging in a human activity. Keep it that way—an unmechanical, human exchange of thought.

Grove Patterson, an exceedingly popular American speaker, has a pertinent thought.

There is no general rule applicable to all men and women who speak in public, except one: You must be natural, be yourself, and be friendly to your audience. Your technique may not necessarily be the best technique for another speaker.[2]

Now, Grove Patterson has had the advantage of many years of speaking experience, having started making speeches at the age of 15, so do not be discouraged if your first or second or third speech falls short of the standard. But above all, recognize the standard and work toward that end.

LET US SUMMARIZE

In getting started, then, put forth your best.
1. Choose an appropriate subject.
2. Determine the general end.
3. Narrow the subject.
4. Word your proposition carefully.
5. Use the extemporaneous and conversational style.
6. Practice! Practice! Practice!

Put forth the best that you have to offer, and remember that the single most vital element in speaking is the personal element—*you* and how the audience is disposed toward *you*. Show your interest in the well being of the audience, and your desire to communicate something worthwhile to them. People will be prepared to listen to a speaker who is sincere, of good character, and well prepared.

FOR FURTHER STUDY

Baird, A. Craig, and Knower, Franklin H., *General Speech* (New York, McGraw-Hill, 1957), Ch. 3, "Choosing Your Subject and Purpose."

---

[2] Grove Patterson, *Look*, June 2, 1953.

Barnes, Harry G., *Speech Handbook* (Englewood Cliffs, N. J., Prentice-Hall, 1941), pp. 27-35.

Brigance, William Norwood, *Speech Communication* (New York, Appleton-Century-Crofts, 1955), pp. 25-29 and 39-42.

McCall, Roy C., *Fundamentals of Speech* (New York, The Macmillan Co., 1949), Ch. 2, "Subject-Topic-Thesis-Title."

Smith, Raymond G., *Principles of Public Speaking* (New York, Ronald, 1958), Ch. 4, "Selecting the Speech Purpose, Topic, and Title."

BASIC ASSIGNMENT NO. 2

Prepare a short speech. You need not include an introduction or conclusion. Merely state a carefully prepared proposition, and develop it. In other words, stand before your audience, announce your goal, and speak toward that end.

Reminders:

1. Choose a narrowed subject that is interesting and familiar to you.
2. Do not memorize or read your speech.
3. Plan carefully in order to achieve your goal in the allotted time.

SUGGESTED EXERCISE A

Write five propositions which are sound in every way, and label each with the general end it suggests.

SUGGESTED EXERCISE B

Listen to two speeches (lectures, sermons, political addresses, and so forth). Summarize each in a paragraph. State the general end and specific purpose of each.

SUGGESTED EXERCISE C

Select a limited subject (one which could be covered in a four-minute speech) for each of the following broad areas:

1.	Aviation	4.	Philosophy
2.	Politics	5.	Medicine
3.	Customs	6.	Language

7. Science
8. Dancing

9. Music
10. Economics

SUGGESTED EXERCISE D

Students frequently say that the most difficult aspect of speech preparation is choosing a subject. Is this true for you? If so, have you really thought about it objectively? Do you *really* believe that you have nothing worthwhile to say? Are you one who believes that everyone else in the class knows more about *any* subject than you do?

Let us try the positive approach. List two topics of interest to you, and explain why *you* are well qualified to speak on them.

3

Organizing Your Thoughts

ORDER VERSUS CHAOS

Imagine yourself turning the pages of the daily newspaper. Start with page one, and notice the headline, DISORGANIZED TROOPS ROUTED, and down the page a bit, FIRE CAUSES PANIC. Turn to the sports page, and read a heading CONFUSED TIGERS LOSE TO TECH. In the second section you find an article titled HOW NOT TO BE THE MUDDLED HOSTESS, and finally you see on the financial page UNSYSTEMATIC SPENDING HARMFUL TO BUSINESS.

What is the key thought suggested in all these newspaper headings? Worded positively, the key thought is that in most human endeavors organization is necessary for success. In other words, the elements having to do with purposeful action must be handled systematically, and when we think of a *system*, we think of order, planning, arrangement, and method. Down through the centuries, men have expressed the need for order in many ways. For example:

> Order means light and peace, inward liberty and free command over one's self; order is power.
>
> —AMIEL

A place for everything, everything in its place.

—Benjamin Franklin

Set all things in their own peculiar place,
And know that order is the greatest grace.

—Dryden

Whether it is in flower arranging or in election campaigning, order cannot be neglected. The human activity of speech making is no exception. To speak well is to do more than stand and talk; to speak well is to stand and talk purposefully, using a plan which will help you to accomplish your purpose. You have chosen your subject, trimmed it down to size, and worded your specific purpose. It now becomes necessary to plan the course for achieving your purpose.

BENEFITS OF ORGANIZATION

A river can be directed into channels to provide the greatest good for all people, or it can be allowed to run at will. So it is with the speech. When a speaker's ideas are arranged and directed, listeners have a good chance of understanding the ideas. They can know what the speaker is saying because he is saying it in an orderly fashion, first things first and part by part.

The speaker benefits because the audience is understanding his ideas, or further, because he is able to inform or persuade his audience. Organization has helped him in his own thinking about the content of his speech and has given him confidence from knowing just how he will progress in delivering the content. As a result we have communication.

OUTLINING

The basic representation of a speech plan is an outline. It is the framework of the entire speech which shows the principal points to be covered and the order in which they will be covered.

Coordinate Points

Outlines consist of coordinate points and subordinate points. The coordinate heads in an outline are those of equal weight, those of the same approximate value or nature. For example, the following means of transportation:

1. Aircraft
2. Automobiles
3. Trains

Or these headings, for instance:

1. Organized crime may be centered in a single city.
2. Organized crime may be national in scope.
3. Organized crime may be international in scope.

Subordinate Points

Divisions of larger points are called subordinate points. They are secondary to and parts of the larger ones and either explain the larger heading or show the contents of it. A leg (subordinate) is a part of a man (larger point). *Room* is subordinate to *house*. Subordinate headings under the previously mentioned modes of transportation could be the following:

1. Aircraft
   a. Propeller driven
   b. Jet-propelled
   c. Rocket
2. Automobiles
   a. Four-cylinder
   b. Six-cylinder
   c. Eight-cylinder
3. Trains
   a. Steam
   b. Diesel

    c. Electric

    d. Diesel-electric

In organizing ideas, we find that every point *can* have a subordinate point, and every subordinate point can have a point subordinate to it. This is illustrated by the children's song, *And the Green Grass Grew All Around.* Do you remember it? In part, it goes:

> In the woods there grew a tree; on this tree there was a limb; on this limb there was a branch; on this branch there was a bough; on this bough there was a twig; on this twig there was a nest; in the nest there was a bird. . . . .

Each succeeding part is subordinate to the preceding one, and we observe a movement from the general to the specific. That is outlining. We have general headings and specific subheadings under them. Overextended though it appears, here is an outline of the *Green Grass* excerpt.

  I. Woods
    A. Tree
      1. Limb
        a. Branch
          (1) Bough
            (a) Twig
              1. Nest
              A. Bird

Symbols for Headings

Numbers and letters are used alternately in outlining (as we see above) to indicate points and divisions of points. We start with Roman numerals and show progressive subordination with capital letters, followed by arabic numerals, followed by small letters, and then by an alteration of arabic numerals and small letters in parentheses. That is the system, but remember that rarely will any point in a practical speech outline be broken down beyond the small letter stage.

THE SPEECH OUTLINE

In the fourth century B.C., Plato has Socrates say in the dialogue, *Phaedrus,* about the speech outline:

> ... every speech ought to be put together like a living creature, with a body of its own, so as to be neither without head, nor without feet, but to have both a middle and extremities, described proportionately to each other and to the whole.

Today, in the twentieth century, we still accept this ancient "figure of speech." The main section of a speech is the body. Attached to it are the head (introduction) and the feet (conclusion). We merely add one additional part—the specific purpose which, as you recall from Chapter 2, we call the proposition.

Let us analyze the functions of each part.

The Introduction

This is the beginning of your speech, and you will use this introductory phase to accomplish two important goals.

1. *Capture attention and develop interest.* Put your listeners in a receptive mood. Give them reason to want to listen to you. You may begin by referring to an incident or coming event which is meaningful to them. Perhaps there was a campus event that can be tied in with your topic and thus serve as an example for launching your talk. As a case in point, let us say that you plan to discuss "Ways to Use the Library" and that everyone knows about the recent invasion of the library by three dogs. Use your imagination here. You might start with, "Everybody—and thing—uses the library."

You can start your speech by making a reference to a previous speaker. Use some of the steam generated by a classmate to assist you in getting started. If on Wednesday Bob showed the advantages derived from a college education and on some future day you plan to talk on "Improving Listening," you might open your speech by saying, "On Wednesday, Bob told us why we need a college education, and today I would like to analyze one of the means for achieving this education."

Sometimes a startling statement, question, or statistic can arouse interest. If your purpose is to encourage the listeners to be careful of their hearts, you can start by announcing, "More people die from heart ailments than from any other single cause." Your topic might be traffic safety, and you might begin with statistics. "Did you know that last year 40,000 people lost their lives on America's streets and highways?" A word of caution should be offered about using startling statements. Use discretion, and avoid a shock which might mean the loss of attention. In one campus speech contest an enthusiastic speaker, desiring to get attention at the outset of his speech, pulled out a track pistol and fired it. Needless to say, it produced a shock, so much of a shock that no one was able to listen for the balance of the program.

Whether you use examples, statistics, quotations, humor, definition, or some other aid, start your speech positively, and make the audience desire to listen.

2. *Guide the audience to the proposition.* After you get attention, lead your audience to the proposition. You must prepare them for the announcement of your purpose. Avoid stating the proposition before you have unfolded preliminary background or explanatory material. After all, you want your listeners to accept the proposition, and you need to justify its worth or importance by building up to it. If your purpose is to discuss the need to increase property taxes, it may be necessary in the introduction to work at dispelling negative feelings that people may have about taxes. If you are advocating a compulsory class in biology, a careful build up before presenting your purpose will be needed. Almost all topics, but especially controversial ones, require some kind of preparatory setting of the scene.

The Proposition

The proposition stems naturally from the introduction. It is what you have been working toward and leading up to in the introduction. After a good introduction, the proposition will fall in place and take a position of central importance.

Recall from Chapter 2 that your proposition must be a complete sentence which states your objective. Further, it must include only one idea, be short, and be designed for audience acceptance. Here are three samples:

> Allow me to point out the advantages of going away to college.
>
> My purpose today is to discuss four features of the republican form of government.
>
> These are my reasons for saying that everyone should be a radio and television critic.

The Body

The body is a discussion of the proposition and is composed of the main ideas to be presented. In this section you develop your purpose, that is, you tell your audience what you told them you would tell them.

But how do you tell them? First of all, you tell them in an orderly manner. It is folly in speaking to stand and cast ideas in all directions with the hope that by some mysterious means your listeners will pick up your thoughts. Speech is too important to be treated so haphazardly. You must be more purposeful and scientific about it and proceed step by step.

1. *Analyze your proposition, and determine its contents.* What are its inherent parts? What sections or divisions of thought does it contain? It is made up of pieces of thought. What are they? These divisions of the proposition will be the chief points in the body of your speech. We call them *main heads*. Let us look at some sample propositions and main heads.

> *Proposition:* It is my purpose to discuss the extent of our basic national defense planning.
>
> *Body*
>   A. We are ready to meet land attacks.
>   B. We are ready to meet air attacks.
>   C. We are ready to meet sea attacks.

Proposition: Allow me to plan for you one day's menu of nutritious and wholesome food.

Body
- A. Start the day with a hearty breakfast.
- B. Do not neglect an ample lunch.
- C. Complete your daily eating with a delicious dinner.

The main heads are parts of the proposition. The proposition is like a pie and the body is made up of pieces of the pie. In the first example, the three "pieces" (or subareas) of national defense plans deal with land, air, and sea defense. The second case shows that breakfast, lunch, and dinner are the logical points from which to consider the planning of a day's menu.

What does such analysis do for the speaker? First of all, it helps him to get his thinking straight. By planning and studying, he determines what his chief ideas will be, what main points he wants to present to the audience.

Secondly, a careful analysis of the proposition makes for audience understanding. How much communication would take place if the speaker threw the whole pie at the audience without giving thought to arrangement and purposeful distribution? Actually, very little. On the other hand, when the speaker announces what the whole pie will be, and then proceeds to distribute it piece by piece, there is an absence of confusion. The process is an orderly one because ideas are being presented one at a time, part by part. It is easier for a listener to handle thought when it is given to him in bits. He can understand smaller pieces of information better and is able to see how each relates to the whole.

2. *Choose only two, three, or four main heads.* Divide your proposition into at least two parts. There are many propositions, in fact, which lend themselves to just two main heads. You have heard speeches, for example, that have dealt with the "pros and the cons," the "advantages and the disadvantages," the "right and the wrong," the "east and the west," "before and after," and so forth.

Only in rare cases should you have more than four main parts. We must be realistic and recognize that listeners can assimilate only a few thoughts at one time. A point of diminishing returns can be reached in speaking, a point at which the listener can absorb no more new ideas. It is like shoveling gravel on the flat bed of a truck. You reach a point when it is useless to continue. The added gravel merely rolls down from the high pile as fast as it is shoveled on.

Consider your audience and purpose, and choose only two, three, or four main heads.

3. *Check your main heads for balance.* After analyzing your proposition, test the chosen main heads. Determine if they are coordinate.

You will remember in discussing outlining earlier in the chapter that we defined coordinate points as those equal in weight or nature. Now, since main heads are the primary parts of the proposition, they must be coordinate. Each one must be parallel to the other. Notice the balance and parallel structure in the following set of main heads.

A. One way to learn is to read.
B. One way to learn is to listen.
C. One way to learn is to experiment.

Here is an upsetting of the balance, an upsetting of coordinate relationships:

A. One way to learn is to read.
B. One way to learn is to listen.
C. To learn is difficult.

Do you see what happened? A and B refer to specific means for learning while C comments upon the difficulty of the process. C does not belong because it is of a different nature. In handling such a problem, the speaker must make a choice as to what unifying characteristic he wants his main heads to have, and then make certain that each one takes on that characteristic.

4. *Check your main heads to see if there is any overlap-*

ping. Each unit of the proposition should be mutually exclusive of each other unit; that is, it should be concerned with a single and separate point of its own. Overlapping indicates that one main head is a part of another, and the outline should be arranged with that part shown to be subordinate. In the following example, C does not deserve main head status.

    A. A good salesman believes in himself.
    B. A good salesman believes in his product.
    C. A good salesman chooses a product in which he can believe.

A better arrangement would be:

    A. A good salesman believes in himself.
    B. A good salesman believes in his product.
        1. He should choose a worthy product to sell, first of all.

Here is another example of overlapping.

    A. Psychology is a study of human behavior.
    B. Psychology is a study of human experience.
    C. Psychology is a study of human reaction.

What is the difficulty here? A and C are very closely related, and since *reaction* is a type of *behavior*, C should be subordinate to A, and placed as a subhead to A.

Be wary of overlapping. It can happen quite easily if you are not alert.

5. *Keep in mind five distinct forms that your main heads may take.* If your main heads are balanced and unified they may involve either time order, space order, reason order, topic order, or problem-solution order.

When ordered according to *time*, the main ideas of the body suggest something to do with the clock, the calendar, or periods, eras, seasons, decades, and so forth. You will choose this frame of reference if you consider elements of time as the key thoughts to emphasize. For example:

    Proposition: I'd like to contrast the two periods of last week's championship basketball game.

Body
   A. During the first half, we saw skillful defensive play.
   B. In the second half, the offenses sparkled.

Proposition: It is my desire to show briefly at what points our specific social abilities develop.

Body
   A. In childhood we begin our development.
   B. In adolescence we experiment.
   C. In adulthood we refine our social skills.

To unify your main heads in terms of *space* means that you wish to focus on areas, regions, districts, zones, or locations. Space may refer to an area microscopic in size or to the whole universe.

Proposition: May I recommend four popular American vacation states to you?

Body
   A. Go to California's beaches for a sun tan.
   B. See the historic sights of Massachusetts.
   C. Relax at a dude ranch in Arizona.
   D. Fill your creel in Michigan's lakes.

Proposition: Let me relate the main floor-plan features that I shall include when I build my ideal house.

Body
   A. The kitchen will be spacious.
   B. The bedrooms will be convenient to bathrooms.
   C. The living room will be out of traffic paths.
   D. The den will be isolated.

You may use *reason* order to arrange your main heads when you plan a speech designed to uphold a point of view. In this case word your proposition to state your point of view, and each main head becomes a reason for your stand. Each main head, each argument for your case, conceivably could start with "because."

Proposition: I believe that everyone should join some worthwhile organization.

Body

    A. (Because) Everyone needs to belong to something.

    B. (Because) Everyone should learn to work with others.

Proposition: Allow me to tell you why I feel that each person should develop his strong individual characteristics.

Body

    A. (Because) He will like himself better personally.

    B. (Because) He will be more capable socially.

    C. (Because) He will be advanced further vocationally.

When you divide your proposition *topically*, you select the mere "neutral" parts of the proposition, parts not tinged with a time, space, or reason character. Topic order is probably the most common, and we might define it best by saying that it is what other patterns are not.

Proposition: Every good teacher has three major strong points.
Body

    A. He knows his subject.

    B. He knows teaching techniques.

    C. He knows people.

Proposition: It is my purpose to describe the functions of several common office machines.

Body

    A. First, let us consider calculating machines.

    B. Next, there are recording machines.

    C. Finally, we should discuss duplicating machines.

A fifth pattern which might be assumed by your main heads is *problem-solution* order. If this form suits the potential development of your proposition, you will have only two main heads. The first main head discusses a problem, and the second presents one or more solutions. Of course, you would use the problem-solution order only if your purpose were to present a problem and to solve it.

Proposition: The matter of marriage failure should concern all of us.

Body
    A. The problem is serious.
    B. There are solutions.

Proposition: Control of your weight is important to your health.

Body
    A. Let us examine the nature of the problem.
    B. Let us analyze possible solutions.

It is necessary, then, to check the relationships of your main heads to be sure that they are balanced and coordinate. Develop your proposition with a time, space, reason, topic, or problem-solution emphasis, but be consistent. If you start with time, stay with it, and word all of your main heads in terms of time. Avoid mixing elements, and you will do much toward avoiding audience confusion.

The Conclusion

The conclusion, of course, is the final phase of the speech. This is your last opportunity to accomplish your purpose. Your speech may have an arresting introduction, a worthwhile and clearly stated proposition, and a well-developed body, but without a carefully planned conclusion, it is not ready to be presented.

1. *Summarize your main heads.* Remind the audience of the main points you have covered. People forget more readily than many of us realize, and it is a wise speaker who does not take it for granted that his listeners have retained all he has said.

In addition, remember another human characteristic, this one about words. Words have different meanings for different people. You can express a thought in one way and get very little response, while the same thought expressed in different terms may cause a noticeable reaction. When you summarize the main heads, choose new wording. If only one listener has been enlightened as a result, you can consider it worth the effort.

As the semester progresses, employ various summary techniques. Some student speakers have been successful with example summaries. For instance, one speaker, after discussing three baseball skills, summarized by citing Mickey Mantle of the Yankees as an outstanding example of a player who possesses all three skills. You might employ an effective quotation to remind the audience of what you have covered. If you have "Freedom in a democracy" and "Control in a democracy" as your two main heads, this quotation of George Sutherland might provide a meaningful summary: "Liberty and order are the most precious possessions of man, and the essence of the problem of government is reconciliation of the two."

2. *After you have summarized and, in so doing, reemphasized your main thoughts, make an appropriate ending.* Round out your speech to give a feeling of completeness. Avoid both abrupt and drawn-out endings, and never make apologies. Above all, finish on a note which is consistent with your purpose. Your purpose may indicate that you should make an appeal at the end, or possibly you should leave the audience with a challenge or with a provocative thought.

Once again it may be appropriate to end with a fitting story or example or with the well-chosen words of an authority in the field. Remember that your job is to adapt your ideas to the lives of your listeners. This fact should dictate your choice of closing content.

LET US SUMMARIZE

1. Recognize the need for and benefits of organization.
2. Continue to improve your outlining skill.
3. In the introduction, capture the listeners' attention, and guide them to the proposition.
4. State your proposition clearly and precisely.
5. Select for the body two, three, or four coordinate main heads which do not overlap.

6. In the conclusion, summarize, emphasize, and make appropriate final remarks.

SPEECH IDEAS

Your reservoir of knowledge and experience constitutes your best source of speech ideas; however, the following general topics may be consulted during the semester—at least to stimulate your thinking.

The problem of juvenile delinquency

Liberal education or specialized education?

Armed service experiences

The values of an education

Rearing children

Student life and student government

Arts, crafts, hobbies, pets

People: Habits and characteristics

Finding a philosophy of life

Hunting and fishing

Cooking and eating

Music and musicians

Athletics

Airplanes and flying

Speaking and listening

Manufacturing and construction

Travel and places

Writing, literature, drama

History, world affairs, politics

Communities: Agencies and problems

Personal adventures and experiences

Photography

Boating and water skiing

Religions of the world

A sense of humor

Salesmanship

Study methods

Ambitions and ideals

Astronomy

Fads and fashions

Police science, ballistics, fingerprinting

Choosing a major

Flying saucers and space travel

Skin diving and spear fishing

Skiing and tobogganing

Words and meanings

Family life

Agriculture

Alcohol and narcotics problems

Student-teacher relationships

Customs and mores of other peoples

Dancing

Mining

The United Nations

Hypnotism

FOR FURTHER STUDY

Baird, A. Craig, and Knower, Franklin H., *General Speech* (New York, McGraw-Hill, 1957), Ch. 5, "Organization and Outlining."

McCall, Roy C., *Fundamentals of Speech* (New York, The Macmillan Co., 1949), Ch. 3, "The Four-part Speech, Mainheads, and Examples."

Nichols, Ralph G., and Lewis, Thomas R., *Listening and Speaking* (Dubuque, Ia., Brown, 1954), Ch. 3, "Detecting Patterns of Speech Composition."

Norvelle, Lee, Smith, Raymond G., and Larson, Orvin, *Speaking Effectively* (New York, Holt-Dryden, 1957), Ch. 3, "The Over-all Plan of a Speech."

White, Eugene E., and Henderlider, Clair R., *Practical Public Speaking* (New York, The Macmillan Co., 1954), Ch. 5, "Organizing the Discussion."

SAMPLE SPEECH OUTLINE 1

(In sentence form)

WANTED: THE RIGHT JOB

I. *Introduction*
  A. It seems that if you want to eat, you have to work.
    1. My friend, Roger Dellson, found this out. (*Example*)
    2. Uncle Fred learned the hard way. (*Example*)
  B. Finding the right occupation is a problem.
  C. There are helpful guide lines, however, which can be of value to you.

II. *Proposition:* Here are three proven rules that you can use in determining your lifework.

III. *Body*
  A. Select an occupation that fits your interests.
    1. For example, Sharon did not like office work but tried it because all her friends were office workers. (*Example*)
    2. There are many people who do not like what they are doing.

B. Select an occupation that fits your abilities.
  1. Ask yourself if you have the required aptitudes.
  2. Darrell, because of poor physical coordination, was not suited for his job of assembling small machine parts. (*Example*)
C. Select an occupation that is rewarding.
  1. Financial rewards must be taken into account.
  2. Do not ignore the more lasting rewards as James did; he made money as a salesman but felt the absence of genuine satisfaction. (*Example*)

IV. *Conclusion*
  A. Choose a field, then, which suits you in these three ways.
    1. You must like to do it.
    2. You must be able to do it.
    3. You must be satisfied in doing it.
  B. Great satisfaction can come from a wise decision.
  C. The words of George Moore can give us some solace: "The difficulty in life is the choice." (*Quotation*)

SAMPLE SPEECH OUTLINE 2

(In topic form)

LINGUAL LOGIC

I. *Introduction*
  A. An American strength: Good government
    1. Democratic
    2. Functional
  B. An American weakness: Scant knowledge of languages
    1. Cannot communicate with foreign visitors
    2. Cannot communicate abroad
      a. An American mayor's trouble in Brussels (*Example*)
      b. An Olympics athlete and a Finnish girl (*Example*)

II. *Proposition:* Consider with me reasons why everyone should be able to speak at least one additional language.

III. *Body*
  A. Increased foreign travel
    1. Social embarrassment
    2. Shopping problems (*Example*)

    B. Expanded international business
      1. Loss of goodwill
      2. Loss of immediate business
        a. Experience of one sales representative (*Example*)
        b. Estimated over-all loss (*Statistics*)
    C. Greater need for diplomacy
      1. The diplomatic corps
      2. The private citizen as a diplomat
        a. Loss of prestige in Copenhagen (*Example*)
        b. The case of a traveler in Madrid (*Example*)
      3. Servicemen as diplomats
IV. *Conclusion*
    A. The shrinking world
      1. Travel
      2. Business
      3. Foreign affairs
    B. Must understand others and their cultures
    C. Army language school proves practicability (*Example*)

BASIC ASSIGNMENT NO. 3

Prepare a speech using the plan explained in this chapter: Introduction, Proposition, Body, and Conclusion. Use an example (anecdote, case in point, meaningful story) to support each main head.

Develop your introduction and conclusion by employing the methods suggested in this chapter which seem appropriate for your particular case.

Make two speaking outlines, one for your use and one for the instructor's benefit.

Reminders:

1. Arrange your ideas carefully in order to help your audience to understand your ideas and their relationships.
2. Continue to improve your extemporaneous style by practicing the talk aloud several times before the day of presentation.
3. You can lessen stage fright by choosing a subject which is interesting and well known to you.

The following speech bodies are in some way poorly organized. Each one contains a major flaw. First, diagnose the difficulty; then, do the necessary rearranging.

SAMPLE 1.

II. *Proposition:* Consider with me the ways in which television production has improved in the last ten years.

III. *Body*
    A. The programing is better.
       1. There is more variety.
       2. There is better quality.
    B. The technical aspects are better.
       1. Improved use of sound can be noted.
       2. More appropriate lighting methods are used.
       3. Refined camera techniques are used.
    C. The performers are better.
       1. The acting has improved.
       2. Announcers are more proficient.
       3. There are better musicians.
    D. Even the commercial announcers are better.
       1. They are more natural.
       2. They are less antagonistic.

SAMPLE 2

II. *Proposition:* Our last fishing trip was something less than a success.

III. *Body*
    A. We were up at 4:30 A.M.
       1. We awakened the neighbors.
       2. Ben couldn't find the car key.
    B. We were fishing by 7:30 A.M.
       1. I broke an expensive rod.

       2. We lost most of the bait.

       3. We caught only one small fish.

   C. We had a flat tire coming home.

       1. We started home at 2:30 P.M.

       2. Ben had no spare tire.

       3. We hitchhiked home.

SUGGESTED EXERCISE B

Outline these speech introductions and conclusions.

SAMPLE 1

I. *Introduction*

Last Thursday, while watching our basketball team practice in the gym, I started to think about the importance of physical education.

Strong bodies and teamwork are needed in almost all phases of living. We work; we play; sometimes we defend our country.

But down there on the court I saw only ten active people out of a student body of 2000. Where were the other 1990 getting their training? In physical education classes? Yes, and I learned later that several hundred take part in intramural athletics—organized, on-campus team competition.

Are you, too, interested in developing physical skills, learning how to work better with others and having fun?

II. *Proposition:* Let me tell you how to take part in the intramural athletic program.

III. *Body*

IV. *Conclusion*

So you see it isn't difficult at all. Just register with the director of activities, join a team or form one, and schedule your games.

Everyone can play and have a good time. You may not be a Joe DiMaggio or a Bob Cousey of basketball fame, or an Eddie Le Baron, but you will profit from the experience, especially if you remember the words of Grantland Rice: "For when the One Great Scorer comes to mark against your name, He writes—not that you won or lost—but how you played the Game."

SAMPLE 2

I. *Introduction*

Remember the story of King Midas? Everything he touched turned to gold, and he was very happy until he found that his food, too, turned into indigestible chunks of gold. He was greedy, and his greed caused him no end of displeasure.

Now there are other more desirable types of the golden touch that can bring pleasure and satisfaction to us all.

Would you like to have a golden touch that would allow you to make one of the greatest contributions to humanity?

I'm speaking of a very constructive kind that seems so necessary these days, the touch that has somehow been lost by so many—raising children properly.

II. *Proposition:* Here is how you can begin to acquire this golden touch for able parenthood.

III. *Body*

IV. *Conclusion*

"As the twig is bent, so is the tree inclined." Give your children a proper start. Remember to love them, guide them, and provide for their physical needs.

The golden touch isn't so magical after all, is it? There is no magic wand or secret formula. If any secret exists at all, it exists in the hearts of each parent and each prospective parent. The means to the end are there to be developed. Can you think of any more important end of human endeavor?

SUGGESTED EXERCISE C

Each of the following series of main heads has a special characteristic (either topical order, time order, space order, or reason
order). Label each in the series.

SAMPLE 1

    II.   *Proposition:* I want to describe what I consider to be a
               student's typical day.

    III.   *Body*
        A.   First, we look at the morning hours—classes.
        B.   The afternoon hours are just as unexciting.
        C.   The evening hours are taken up with quiet study.

SAMPLE 2

    II.   *Proposition:* Consider with me three important safety
               features found on many modern automo-
               biles.

    III.   *Body*
        A.   Safety glass is used in almost all cars.
        B.   Seat belts are optional equipment.
        C.   Padded dashboards are becoming more common.

SAMPLE 3

    II.   *Proposition:* It is not really difficult to understand why
               people act like people.

    III.   *Body*
        A.   They do so because of their heredity.
        B.   They do so because of their environment.

SAMPLE 4

    II.   *Proposition:* Come along with me, and let us explore
               what many consider to be the most exciting
               sections of Disneyland.

III. *Body*

    A. Frontierland will take you back to early America.

    B. Tomorrowland will take you into the future.

    C. Adventureland will take you to foreign settings.

SUGGESTED EXERCISE D

Write two, three, or four coordinate and nonoverlapping main heads for the following propositions:

1. These are my arguments, then, for urging you to read at least one good book a month.
2. I would recommend certain changes in our national election procedures.

SUGGESTED EXERCISE E

In a brief talk, tell how the lack of organization thwarted some human effort. Your case need not refer to the speech field specifically. Consult your own experience or books, magazines, and so forth.

SUGGESTED EXERCISE F

Shorten and make more concise one of the two sample outlines on pages 46-48. Rewrite it in the form of a speaking outline as specified by your instructor.

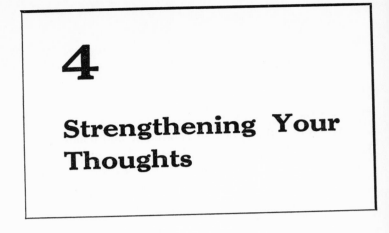

4

Strengthening Your Thoughts

> . . . speech is a joint game by the talker and the listener against the forces of confusion.
>
> —NORBERT WIENER [1]

The wisdom reflected in this quotation is surely nothing new to you at this stage of your speech work. Look back to your earlier class activities. Why is it necessary to use a proposition which states your purpose in a complete sentence? Why should it express only one idea? Why should it be stated briefly? Why is it necessary to organize your ideas? You know the answers: You must do these things in order to transmit your ideas clearly and with certainty. In order to communicate and to conquer the forces of confusion, you must help the listener understand your thoughts and let him know the direction they are taking.

Initially, then, you can work toward communication by being clear in purpose and sound in arrangement. Also, there are factors besides the speech itself with which the speaker must cope if he is to avoid confusion and lead listeners.

---

[1] *The Human Use of Human Beings*, New York, Doubleday, 1956, p. 92.

THE AUDIENCE

That person or group of people with whom you speak, the audience, is made up of an ever-changing, highly complex combination of elements. Imagine a speech situation, possibly your own class. It is Monday, and the first speaker of the day walks up to the front of the room. He looks out at the audience. What does he see? Does he see a group of robots each of whom is assuming exactly the same appearance and position? Of course not; he sees a diverse array of individual persons manifesting a variety of outward characteristics. Some are sitting up straight in their chairs; some are semireclining; some are looking out the window, at the wall, or at a neighbor. He sees smiles and frowns, looks of anticipation and looks of lassitude, appearances of happiness, and appearances of unrest.

The speaker begins to speak, and he soon observes changes in his audience. The one in the third row who seemed rather gloomy before now smiles at one of the speaker's comments. The fellow who was slouching down is now sitting more erectly. The blond girl in the back is looking out the window. Things are happening, but only the outward evidence of the happenings can be noticed by the speaker.

What does he not know? What can he not see? Like viewing an iceberg, only to an enormously greater degree, the speaker sees but a fraction of the audience dynamics. He does not know that one of his listeners worked all night and is plagued by drowsiness, that another is worried about failing a history test, that another is thinking ahead to tonight's game, that another is remembering the appointment he forgot, and that another has broken up with her boy friend. It would be absurd to expect you as a speaker to know all such details about your audience, but it is imperative that you have a general realization of the "forces of confusion" with which you are dealing.

THE PHYSICAL ENVIRONMENT

In addition to the human element, every speaker needs to be aware of his physical surroundings, especially those which compete with his efforts to communicate. Let us go back to the speaker in front of his audience. As he talks, someone drops a book, and some attention is lost. An airplane flies low overhead. Carpenters are working next door. Someone comes into the room. The room is stuffy, or the room is too cold. The seats are uncomfortable and poorly arranged. Once again, we recognize forces of confusion at work; this time they are physical forces which challenge the speaker's attempts to communicate.

THE ORAL MODE

Is it any wonder that speaking, with all its variables, is such a demanding activity? Now, in written communication the problems are quite different in some ways. The contact between originator and receiver is indirect, and the receiver of the message controls the experience. If distracted by an emotional or physical factor, the reader can reread a sentence or a paragraph. He can transport himself to a better environment, but a listener usually must stay where he is. If he is tired, the reader may put his book aside and go back to it at a later time; the fatigued listener has only the present opportunity to receive the message.

In oral communication, you, the speaker, are the one who makes decisions about how fast to go and when to review. You have ideas that you want to get across, and in order to do so, you must anticipate and contend with the various emotional and physical distractions. You must find ways to keep your listeners ever mindful of your "whereabouts," to clarify what you are saying, and to enforce your thoughts. How can you bring a wayward listener back into the stream of your thought?

What methods can you use to compete with the great variety of distractions that are always present? At this time, let us discuss three aids which are at your disposal: the transition, the restatement, and the definition.

THREE AIDS

Transition

One way to provide for clarity and certainty in the expression of ideas is to show the relationships of your ideas by connecting your thoughts as you move along during the presentation of a speech. To keep your audience continually aware of what you are saying and where you are taking them, link new thoughts to those previously offered. Connect and integrate the new parts as you add them to the whole. To illustrate, let us assume that you are discussing propaganda techniques, and you have just finished describing "the bandwagon approach." You should not take up another point without making some connection between the new point and the last point. As you introduce your second point, you should fit it in with the developing pattern of ideas. For example.

> Now we can see that propagandists use the bandwagon approach to ensnare those who are easily influenced by what others do. Next, let us consider a language trick that fools the unthinking—the use of glittering generalities.

Then you would go on in your development of the second main head, aware of the possible need for tying together subpoints under the main head. Your next *major* connection, however, should be made at the third main head.

> If they haven't put you on the bandwagon or captivated you with their high-sounding generalizations, they may try card stacking.

The body is not the only section of a speech requiring the

aid of transitions. Actually, in order to compete with the emotional and physical forces of confusion, you should guide your audience with the assistance of transitions through the entire talk.

1. *From introduction to proposition.* Lead up to the proposition so that it seems to fall in place and seems to be the next logical thing to say. For example:

> We can see, then, that there are many people and agencies active in our society with an intent to influence us in one way or another. Some want our allegiance; some want our vote; some want our money. We come in contact with their methods every day. *Allow me to describe three techniques of the propagandists.* (*Proposition*)

2. *From the proposition to the first main head.* Here you merely repeat the essence of your proposition as you present the main head statement.

> The first method of propaganda that I shall discuss is called the bandwagon approach.

3. *From subhead to subhead.* Usually, these are brief and oftentimes nothing but one-word conjunctions. We use transitions, including those to link subheads of thought, many times a day without realizing it. Notice the simple use of "and" to connect these two minor thoughts. "Most people want to be with the majority, *and* they are moved when told that they, too, should get on the 'bandwagon.'"

4. *From main head to main head.* We illustrated this point earlier (p. 57). Considerable confusion can be avoided if you keep your listeners aware of your main points. Let them know where you have been and where you are going. When you approach a new main head, show your audience how it relates to the other main heads. You may be able to make the connection with a few words or a sentence. Other times you may need a full paragraph to integrate the ideas.

5. *From the last main head to the conclusion.* In connecting the body to the conclusion, many speakers seem to be

hard pressed for words. How many times have you heard the trite phrase, "In conclusion . . ."? It is easy to avoid such over-used expressions if you will allow your purpose to dictate your wording. Ask yourself what thoughts and feelings you want to convey with your closing remarks. "What parting tone will help me to realize my goal?"

If propaganda is the subject, again, and your purpose is to inform, you could move from the last main head into the conclusion in this manner:

> These, then, are but three of the weapons used to reach you— the bandwagon, the glittering generality, and card stacking.

The connection between body and conclusion might be quite different if your aim is to persuade.

> Well, now, what can you do to combat the propagandist? How can you avoid landing on the bandwagon or succumbing to the glittering generality or being dealt to by the card stacker?

There are very few hard and fast rules of speaking which apply to all speakers, all speeches, all audiences, and all occasions. One, however, always will apply: *Your purpose will indicate why, where, and how frequently you should use a speaking technique.* This rule is relevant especially to the use of transitions. The following specific suggestions, too, are pertinent.

(a) *Vary your word choice occasionally when relating one thought to another.* A synonym used in place of a frequently mentioned word can add variety and new meaning to a given thought. For instance, a "propaganda device" might at times be called a "tool" or "a technique" or "a trick." Consult your dictionary for synonyms, or better yet, a *thesaurus*, and get into the habit of enlivening your speaking with variety.

(b) *Be natural and unmechanical in the employment of transitions.* Usually there is a tendency for people to be rigid and mechanical when first trying something. It happens when one drives a friend's car or when one first handles a tennis racquet. In either case, the person feels a bit rigid or awkward because he is not familiar with the object. This is true, also, with the initial conscious use of transition. At first, you may feel restricted, awkward, or otherwise insecure, but with practice and the resulting familiarity, you will soon come to appreciate transitional aids. You will be able to use them gracefully and weave them into the total fabric of your oral effort.

Restatement

Another means for contending with the forces of confusion is restatement. This term, which is almost self-explanatory, refers specifically to repeating a thought once or a number of times, either in the same way as first expressed or with altered wording.

The values of restatement are apparent. If a listener's mind has gone astray, repeating an important idea may bring him back. If a listener is unimpressed with a vital point, restatement of it may cause him to recognize its worth. If a point is not clearly understood, repetition of it may create understanding. We see, then, that restatement can be used to clarify and impress a speaker's most meaningful thoughts. Probably the most commonly restated points in speeches are the main heads. This is not surprising, is it? After all, main heads are the chief pillars of thought in the body. Notice how restatements (italicized) strengthen the following main heads.

Franklin D. Roosevelt had an ability to relate an anecdote. *He had a special knack for telling a story.*

Smog limits visibility. *This haze occasionally prevents one from seeing clearly a hundred yards ahead. Yes, polluted air can be as restricting to the vision as fog.*

To get ahead in the world, you have to work. *You have to*

work to accomplish your goals. You have to work to make a name. You have to work to succeed.

Photography is enjoyable. *You can have the time of your life taking pictures. Whether you own a Brownie or a Leica, it can be fun.*

Definition

An all-too-frequent error in speaking is the assumption that one's chosen words will be understandable to all listeners. It is often hard for a person to realize that a certain word or phrase which he uses daily may not be meaningful to some listeners. We can appreciate this thought, certainly, when we consider ways in which we, as people, isolate our bodies and minds.

First of all, we set ourselves off in family units where we develop our usage of distinct terms, terms that may not be used at all by the family across the street or in another part of town. For instance, the members of one family may say "bumpershoot" and never umbrella, or "cornucopia" and never ice-cream cone. From your experience, can you think of such examples?

We also isolate ourselves geographically and learn to use words having meaning in the region in which we live. One student speaker in a college on the West Coast caused considerable consternation in his audience when, in a matter-of-fact manner, he mentioned "the dirty thirties" two or three times in a speech. Being from Kansas and often having heard Kansans refer to the terrible dust storms of the 1930s, the term was virtually a part of his life, but his West Coast listeners had not had his experience.

In this day of intense specialization, we isolate ourselves in our fields of primary interest. We adopt the language of our specialties and upon occasion find it difficult to communicate with people in other fields. We talk "electronics," "cost accounting," "education," "IBM stenography," "torque conversion," or "heatless cooking."

In order to be able to talk with people, it is first necessary to recognize your own areas of isolation and then to develop an awareness of the need for definition. Do not take it for granted that your audience is familiar with every word in your active vocabulary. Define your terms, especially the key terms and accompanying words. In addition to using mere synonyms, you can define in a number of ways.

1. CLASSIFICATION

Define by telling the class to which the word or phrase belongs.

A *hellgrammite,* much used as fish bait, is the larva of a certain insect, the dobson fly.

A *novel* is a long, fictional work of prose.

2. ETYMOLOGY

Define by telling the origin or derivation of the word or phrase.

Algebra comes from the Arabian word "al-jabr" which meant the reduction of parts to a whole or reunion of broken parts or bonesetting.

The *guillotine* was named after J. I. Guillotin, a French physician, who proposed that the instrument be used because other means of execution were inhumane.

3. EXAMPLE

Define by giving an example of what you mean.

I can define *juvenile delinquent* best by illustration. Let us say that Roy X is a sixteen-year-old boy who consistently finds himself in trouble with the law as a result of his treatment of others and his treatment of the property of others. Roy X goes beyond plain mischief and into the realm of the criminal—car theft, slashing tires, assault, wrecking school property. Roy X is a juvenile delinquent.

4. NEGATION

Define by telling what the term is not.

By *outlawing war*, I do not mean effecting merely a weak international agreement. I do not mean compromising to limit arms or deciding to annihilate only military installations. I mean . . .

The *heart of a business organization* is not the profit and loss statement, a battery of calculating machines, sales slogans, liberal expense accounts, or rich mahogany paneling. It is . . .

LET US SUMMARIZE

Strengthen your thoughts by using transitions to link them and to relate one to another. Further reinforce your talk by restating key ideas and by defining terms in the way that you want them to be taken. Such action on your part will help you to be clear and certain in meeting the ever-present forces of confusion.

FOR FURTHER STUDY

Gilman, Wilbur E., Aly, Bower, and Reid, Loren D., *Fundamentals of Speaking* (New York, The Macmillan Co., 1951), pp. 87-88.

McCall, Roy C., *Fundamentals of Speech* (New York, The Macmillan Co., 1949), Ch. 4, "The Process of Transition," and pp. 53-56.

Nichols, Ralph G., and Lewis, Thomas R., *Listening and Speaking* (Dubuque, Ia., Brown, 1954), p. 99.

White, Eugene E., and Henderlider, Clair R., *Practical Public Speaking* (New York, The Macmillan Co., 1954), pp. 136-141.

SAMPLE SPEECH OUTLINE 1
(In sentence form)

LOVE THYSELF IN ORDER TO LOVE THY NEIGHBOR

I. *Introduction*
   A. There are lots of unhappy people living in our time, a time that some call the "Age of Anxiety." (*Definition*)
   B. But there are many happy people, too.
   C. To get a firsthand view of the feelings of people, station yourself at some inconspicuous spot downtown and observe.
      1. Observe the behavior characteristics that indicate frustration, fear, insecurity, and general discontent.
      2. Observe the behavior characteristics that indicate confidence, security, satisfaction, and ability to cope with life. (*Example*)
   D. You may ask yourself what it is that makes one person happy and another person unhappy.
II. *Proposition:* May I offer two underlying qualities of the happy person?
III. *Body*
   A. His basic characteristic is that he likes himself.
      1. He respects himself and recognizes his own worth. (*Restatement*)
      2. His love of self is wholesome and balanced, not of the type referred to by George Elliot: "He was like a cock who thought the sun had risen to hear him crow." (*Definition*)
      3. His love of self comes from self-analysis both of his strengths and weaker areas.
      4. There is a vast difference between having true self-respect and being one's own worst enemy, as in the cases of Albert and Ernest. (*Example*)
   B. If he likes himself, the happy person will have a second feature; he will like other people.

1. By "like," I mean "get along with and accept." (*Definition*)
2. He will have a minimum of prejudice and hate. (*Example*)
3. He will be unafraid in his daily dealings with people.

IV. *Conclusion*

  A. The contented person has two prime qualities.
    1. He likes himself.
    2. He likes others.

  B. Knowledge is the real key to happiness.
    1. Learn to accept yourself by learning about yourself.
    2. Learn to accept people in general by studying the needs and motivations of people.
    3. Appreciate the wisdom of Alexander Pope who said, "The proper study of mankind is man." (*Quotation*)

SAMPLE SPEECH OUTLINE 2
(In topic form, except for main transitions)

THE GRAND WAGON

I. *Introduction*

  A. Different types of cars from which to choose
    1. Small foreign cars (*Example*)
    2. Moderately priced American cars (*Example*)
    3. The big automobile (*Example*)

  B. The ideal all-around car, the station wagon

II. *Proposition:* Let me suggest that you investigate the station wagon before you buy.

III. *Body*

  A. This versatile vehicle is just the thing for daily use.
    1. For shopping
    2. For transporting children
    3. For studying between classes with built-in desk (*Example*)

  B. Such a car is not restricted to serve merely as a shopping cart or mobile office; it can help you earn money.
    1. To help pay your way through school (*Restatement*)

    2. To distribute newspapers to a crew of paper boys (*Example*)

    3. To deliver mail during Christmas season (*Example*)

    4. To transport children in recreation department work (*Example*)

  C. If you do not need a station wagon to do daily chores and to earn money, you will surely want one for vacation use.

    1. The best way to travel to the mountains or the seashore (*Restatement*)

    2. Space for camping gear

    3. Easy to load and unload (*Example*)

IV. *Conclusion*

  A. Summary of benefits

    1. Daily benefits

    2. On your job

    3. On a vacation trip

  B. Thousands of happy station-wagon owners

  C. The grand wagon

SAMPLE SPEECH OUTLINE 3
(In sentence form)

BY THE GOLDEN GATE

I. *Introduction*

  A. I'd like to ask if you have ever ridden on a cable car, or gone over a bridge 8¼ miles long, or been in the largest Chinese settlement outside of China.

  B. If your answer is "No," then probably you have not experienced a singular American delight—San Francisco.

II. *Proposition:* Allow me to take you on a tour of four points of interest in San Francisco.

III. *Body*

  A. We shall start with a visit to Fisherman's Wharf.

    1. The atmosphere is authentic.

    2. The seafood is unequaled anywhere; today we shall lunch at Joe DiMaggio's. (*Example*)

  B. After eating, we will go to Golden Gate Park.

    1. Flowers and trees are in abundance.

2. The Oriental Tea Garden is a major attraction. (*Example*)

3. In the Steinhart Aquarium we will see thousands of fishes from many seas. (*Example*)

C. We have fed ourselves on fish, and we have seen the live variety; our next stop will be the downtown district.

1. Shops of all kinds compel our attention.

2. We see the pigeons and gulls in Union Square.

3. Our exciting cable-car ride up Powell Street will be remembered forever. (*Example*)

D. It has been quite a day of eating, riding, and viewing; let us indulge in the Oriental atmosphere once more and visit Chinatown.

1. Again the food lures us, and we decide to have dinner at the Yat Gan Low. (*Example*)

2. We might buy some gifts for the family at home. (*Example*)

3. We notice the customs of the people.

4. We listen to corner conversations in Chinese.

IV. *Conclusion*

A. As we prepare to leave, a map posted on the wall at the airport reminds us of where we have been today.

1. There on the map is Fisherman's Wharf.

2. Across town to the west is Golden Gate Park.

3. Between these two points is the downtown section.

4. Not far from the heart of the city is Chinatown.

B. Someday we shall surely go back to San Francisco to see what we have not been able to include in this tour, such places as Nob Hill, the Mark Hopkins Hotel, the Yacht Harbor, the Mission, and Fleishacker Zoo.

C. We shall surely go back to San Francisco. (*Restatement*)

BASIC ASSIGNMENT NO. 4

Prepare a speech and include in it all of the details required in Basic Assignment No. 3 (p. 48). Use transitions at the key points as discussed in this chapter. Restate thoughts and define terms which need clarification or emphasis.

Reminders:

1. Think of transitions, restatements, and definitions as natural helpers and not as mere mechanical devices.

2. The more demanding each new speech assignment becomes, the more it becomes necessary for you to prepare thoroughly. Compose carefully and rehearse sufficiently.

SUGGESTED EXERCISE A

Listen for transitions as used by speakers who earn their livelihood by talking (radio and television commentators and newsmen, teachers, lawyers, salesmen, and so forth). To report on the effectiveness of usage, quote three actual main transitional statements used, and tell specifically what each transition did to further the speaker's efforts.

SUGGESTED EXERCISE B

Be prepared for an oral class activity in which each class member will be asked to make a transition between the two headings below. Strive to make your wording different from that of the other speakers. Use your imagination.

1. History is the study of great men.
2. History is the study of great events.

SUGGESTED EXERCISE C

Copy the following partial speech outline, and write in transitions at major points. Just for the experience of it, word your last transition in such a way as to make main head "C" the most significant point. In effect you will be subordinating "A" and "B."

    II. *Proposition:* Perhaps you believe as Francis Bacon did that some books should be read differently from others.

   III. *Body*

      A. Some are to be tasted.

      B. Some are to be swallowed.

      C. Some are to be chewed and digested.

SUGGESTED EXERCISE D

Select a term from your field of major interest which might not be meaningful to everyone. Define the term in a one-minute talk. Use one or more of the definition types explained in this chapter.

SUGGESTED EXERCISE E

Make a brief announcement about some coming event (game, dance, cake sale, television program, musical program, visiting lecturer, and so forth). For clarity and emphasis restate all the key factors: What it is, what day, what time, and where. For further help, turn to Chapter 13.

SUGGESTED EXERCISE F

Shorten and make more concise one of the three sample outlines on pages 64-67. Rewrite it in the form of a speaking outline as specified by your instructor.

SUGGESTED EXERCISE G

To complement your instruction on "meeting the forces of confusion," you may want to refer now to Chapter 9, "Improving Listening Skills."

5

Developing Your Thoughts With Physical Materials

THE GENERAL AND THE SPECIFIC

Let us begin by defining two principal terms of the chapter title. By "your thoughts," we mean your main ideas, your primary headings and subheadings, those points which make up the bare skeleton of your speech. For instance, the following speech outline consists of thoughts:

    I.   *Introduction*
        A. Man has devised many ways to entertain himself.
        B. Golf is one such means of enjoyment.
        C. But considerable skill is required.
   II. *Proposition:* I'd like to discuss with you the four steps involved in hitting a golf ball.
  III. *Body*
        A. Grip the club.
           1. Method No. 1 is used by some golfers.
           2. Method No. 2 is used by others.
        B. Approach the ball.
           1. Your stance is important.
           2. Maintain the correct distance of foot to ball.

C. Swing the club.
   1. Keep leg movements to a minimum.
   2. Arm movements are made in this manner.
   3. Keep your eyes on the ball.
D. Follow through.

IV. *Conclusion*
   A. Now I shall summarize for you.
   B. There are golf links close by.
   C. Try golfing.

This is an outline of statements and partial statements, of rather general and unexplained headings, and when you read the outline, you get a *general* notion of the content as planned by the speaker. This is not the entire speech. It could take a speaker five minutes or perhaps a full half hour to deliver this speech, and yet you can read the outline aloud in thirty seconds. We can see that something is missing, and this leads us to another term in the title: Developing.

"To develop" means to unfold more completely and to give greater meaning. Therefore, when you develop your thoughts, you expand on them and heighten or enhance or magnify or explain. You *support* your thoughts by giving them the backing of elaboration.

The golf outline has not been developed. The points have not been supported. It is but a skeleton and lacks those specific details which it needs to give it meaning and life. Thus we see that there are two primary types of data to be found in any speech—the general and the specific. General data are the framework, while specific data are those concrete materials which make the generalizations real or believable.

MATERIALS

Specific data are either physical or verbal. Physical materials are those which can be seen and sometimes felt or sometimes tasted, smelled, or heard. They make strong appeals to the senses. The speaker who wants to explain how to hit a golf ball would use some physical materials, at least a club and ball. He would develop the thoughts in his outline by demonstrating how to hold the club, how to address the ball, how to swing, and how to follow through. Imagine how much more effective this demonstration would be than merely *telling* about how to do it. When you use physical materials, the listeners not only hear, but also *see*.

Verbal materials, which we shall discuss in the next chapter, are, as the name implies, made up of words. Even though they (examples, statistics, and quotations) are not physical, a good speaker can prompt an audience to see, feel, taste, or smell, at least in their minds. For instance, a speaker's vivid illustration of a sizzling steak can cause a listener's mouth to water. Verbal materials, like physical materials, can evoke sensory reactions and otherwise make a speaker's generalizations meaningful.

USEFULNESS OF PHYSICAL MATERIALS

Because they are concrete and appeal to the senses, physical materials are valuable to the speaker.

1. *In getting attention and interest.* People respond to visible movement. This has been known for a long time by persons whose responsibility it is to save human life. An American roadway with its variety and types of flashing lights, pendulumlike warning arms, and traffic signs is a pertinent example. Such stimuli arrest attention because they are strong and demanding. The speaker can captivate an audience by using materials which appeal directly to the senses.

2. *In clarifying.* Sometime you may want to try this experiment on two friends. Describe to one, with words only, how to go to a certain place. Take the same amount of time in giving your directions to the second person, but this time use a sketch or drawing to help communicate the information. Ask each to give the directions back to you, and you will find that

the second person probably will be more correct. Why? It will be obvious that the visual aid helped to clarify your ideas.

3. *In impressing and causing listeners to remember.* Besides merely getting attention and interest and making thoughts clear, you want your audience to retain ideas. When the people to whom you have spoken leave the speech setting and go their separate ways, you should hope that they will take something of the message with them. Physical support for your verbal expression can help you to etch your ideas on the listeners' minds.

4. *In reducing fears.* When asked why he used a pointer while presenting all his speeches, one man replied, "My pointer helps me feel relaxed. I have something to hold and move." While we do not advocate using a pointer when delivering all your speeches, we do think that the man has a point. Holding and manipulating an object does reduce tension for most speakers. Being active helps them to loosen up and be more natural and, therefore, better speakers.

VISUAL AIDS

Visual aids are all materials which can be seen, with the exception of those having a primary appeal to our hearing sense. Recall your own listening experiences, and make a mental list of the materials you have *seen* speakers use. On your list will be such items as charts, graphs, maps and globes, blackboard sketches, models, moving pictures, projected slides, and photographs. In addition, you may have remembered objects of different types which were used as special aids to support ideas in speeches. A list of such special aids would be at least as long as a list of speech topics. The biology teacher showing the underside of a leaf to explain certain cell structure is using an object, a special visual aid. The mechanic holding and describing his customer's worn-out fuel pump is employing such a special visual aid. In other words, physical materials can be all objects that an audience is able to see.

Suggestions for Use

1. *Use visual materials purposefully.* The only justification for including any item in a speech is that it will help you to further your purpose. A speaker does not sketch on the blackboard for his own enjoyment or because he has heard that some sketching may help him. He draws or writes on the blackboard because *he has a point to make,* and his purposeful sketching will help him make the point.

2. *Be certain that all of your audience can see and appreciate your aid.* When sketching, for example, move aside occasionally to allow everyone a clear view. Right-handed people frequently stand to the left of the sketch and left-handed people to the right of it. Too, it is often wise to change your sketching position from one side to the other during the speech. Draw or write with large and broad lines; keep the drawing simple and not too detailed. Do not let the speaking stand or any other object block the view.

An object, too, must be used in such a way as to allow easy viewing. It should be large enough for all to appreciate and held at a satisfactory viewing height for as long as its presence is necessary. Resist any inclination that you might have to show the aid in the manner of a flash card. If it is important enough to include in the speech, you ought to use it carefully and get the most out of it. Occasionally it is necessary to walk out to the audience and move along in front of them as you demonstrate or display your object.

3. *Maintain contact as you use your aid.* In most cases, you will need to have a running commentary accompanying your use of visual aids. Words help to explain key points, and in addition words help to maintain interest. At times, pauses are unavoidable and even beneficial, but frequently they offer excuses for an audience to become restless and even to engage in side conversations. Therefore, it is strongly suggested that you keep the thought flowing and interest growing by having enough to say as you present the visual phases of your speech.

Eye contact, too, should not suffer when you are employing a physical aid. There is a tendency when you are sketching or demonstrating to attend to your aid and neglect your listeners. Loss of such valuable contact can be prevented by careful advance planning and practice.

4. *Control the use of your aid.* Avoid the danger of dividing attention. When planning how and where to use a given supporting device, ask yourself if timing is important. It frequently is. By "timing" we mean having the materials handy and ready to use, introducing them at the proper place, and putting them aside after they have been used.

When you bring objects to a speaking situation, put them in some convenient location near the speaking area or keep them with you at your seat. They should be available and yet inconspicuous.

Introduce your sketch or object at the point in your speech where it will serve you best. Early "unveiling" may destroy some suspense value or be a distraction; late showing may provide nothing but a weak anticlimax. Again, the importance of rehearsal cannot be overemphasized.

Put the object aside (or, in the case of sketching, erase the board) when you have finished with it, unless you want to leave it on display for certain reasons. Only on rare occasions should you chance distracting the audience by passing an object among them during your speech.

If you wish to support your ideas with objects, the use of which requires more space than a room provides, it will be necessary to arrange for an outside speaking scene. Many speech teachers report that at least once during a semester a student will bring a visual aid of unusual proportions. In this category are such prodigious supporting materials as automobiles, fishing (casting) equipment, motorcycles, archery equipment, and even horses.

AUDIO AIDS

Under this heading we put those devices which produce sound. Chiefly, they are tape recorders, record players, and musical instruments. Possibly a speaker plans to discuss the changes in popular music over the last ten years. He could illustrate each major stage in the development of popular music by playing recorded fragments. Of course, such record fragments should not take up an undue portion of the speaking time.

A speaker, in telling how to play the ukelele, might play the instrument to enhance his verbal explanation. He might even give a musical summary in his conclusion by playing an entire selection which could draw together all that he had discussed in the body of his talk.

Rules for using an audio aid are essentially the same as those for using a visual aid. Employ the device to help you reach your goal, first of all. Plan your use of the aid, and sustain audience contact. Practice using it sufficiently to avoid wasteful pauses.

LET US SUMMARIZE

Skillful use of audio and visual aids comes after extended experience, from watching others, and from extended practice on your own. Make it a point to note the techniques employed by some of your instructors and by other good speakers you observe. Notice how the use of these aids helps to get attention and interest, to clarify, to impress, and to reduce fears.

Use audio and visual aids wisely.
1. Use your materials purposefully.
2. Be certain that all of your audience can see (or hear) and appreciate your aid.
3. Maintain contact as you use your aid.
4. Control the use of your aid.

FOR FURTHER STUDY

Baird, A. Craig, and Knower, Franklin H., *General Speech* (New

York, McGraw-Hill, 1957), Ch. 12, "Physical Activity and Visual Aids."

Brigance, William Norwood, *Speech Communication* (New York, Appleton-Century-Crofts, 1955), Ch. 9, "Handling Demonstration Equipment and Visual Aids."

Oliver, Robert T., Dickey, Dallas C., and Zelko, Harold P., *Communicative Speech* (New York, Holt-Dryden, 1955), Ch. 10, "Using Visual Aids."

SAMPLE SPEECH OUTLINE 1
(In sentence form)

A HOUSE AND A HOME

I. *Introduction*

    A. Home is an important place in our lives.

        1. "Be it ever so humble, there's no place like home." (*Quotation* from Payne)

        2. "Home is where the heart is." (*Quotation* from Pliny)

        3. "Home makes the man." (*Quotation* from Smiles)

    B. Yes, home does make the man and the women and children, too.

    C. One should build a home that will fit the needs of the whole family.

        1. It should meet the present requirements.

        2. It should be planned to meet future requirements.

II. *Proposition:* The home-development plan that I shall show you should fit all needs.

III. *Body*

    A. When first married, start with a one-bedroom house like this one. (*Sketch*)

        1. It is inexpensive.

        2. It is attractive.

        3. It is adaptable.

    B. Add another bedroom when a child arrives. (*Sketch*)

        1. It is relatively inexpensive.

        2. It is easy to construct.

    C. An additional increase in family size can be handled with the addition of a third bedroom. (*Sketch*)

       1. Once again, the cost is moderate.

       2. Possibly you can build it yourself.

IV. *Conclusion*

  A. Adopt a basic plan.

  B. Add on later.

  C. The development of a house is much like one's development in speaking.

       1. You handle one phase at a time.

       2. You progress step by step.

SAMPLE SPEECH OUTLINE 2
(In sentence form)

DO YOU AVOID DRIPS?

I. *Introduction*

  A. The constant dripping of a leaking faucet can ruin one's disposition.

       1. It makes my sister irritable. (*Example*)

       2. Lawbreakers in ancient times were punished by being made to endure the slow dripping of water. (*Example*)

  B. If people knew the causes of leaking faucets, perhaps they would realize how easily the difficulty could be corrected.

II. *Proposition:* Today I would like to show you the two common problem parts of a water faucet.

III. *Body*

  A. The most prevalent trouble maker is the worn-out washer.

       1. The valve washer is one type. (*Showing of object*)

          a. Excessive pressure will cause it to wear.

          b. It is easy and inexpensive to replace.

       2. The gasket washer is another type. (*Showing of object*)

          a. Its life is unusually long.

          b. If it is worn, water will come through the stem of the valve.

          c. Before replacing it, see if you can correct the condition by tightening it.

  B. However, faucet troubles do not stop with defective washers, for worn threads can provoke household woes, too.

1. Contrast the threads on this worn part with those of this new one. (*Showing of object*)
   a. The wearing is caused by excessive pressure being exerted, perhaps, by leaning with the body. (*Example*)
   b. It may happen if you have a strong man around the house. (*Example*)
2. Unless you have spare parts, you will need a new faucet.

IV. *Conclusion*
   A. Now you know what it is that causes that sleep-robbing drip, drip, drip.
      1. It may be the washer.
      2. It may be the faucet threads.
   B. If you have a leaky faucet in your house, you owe it to everyone who lives there to take your tools in hand and march to the sink.
   C. Oh, yes, to prevent a flood, such as my neighbor had, close the master control valve before you start. (*Example*)

BASIC ASSIGNMENT NO. 5A

Prepare a speech in which you develop each main head by use of an object or objects. Demonstrate, manipulate, or show the object as you discuss each main head. You may use a single object or a number of such aids. Projection or sound equipment may be considered as objects.

Use transitions at all major points. Restate, define, or sketch on the blackboard whenever you feel it will help you to communicate.

Reminders:

1. Remember that the sole reason for using visual aids is to support your ideas; therefore, think of ideas first and of objects to explain those ideas second.
2. Some of the best supporting objects are those we use or observe everyday. Look around you.

BASIC ASSIGNMENT NO. 5B

Prepare a speech in which you develop each main head by sketching on the blackboard. Do some sketching as you elaborate on each main head. You may use an independent sketch for each main head or add to a single sketch as the speech progresses.

Use transitions at all major points. Restate thoughts and define terms where it is necessary to do so.

Reminders:

1. If possible practice your speech in a room equipped with a blackboard.
2. Review the section of the chapter on suggestions for using a blackboard (pp. 74-75).

SUGGESTED EXERCISE A

In a one-minute chalk talk discuss one of the subjects listed below. This will be an opportunity for you to try out your sketching techniques.

1. How to Get to Some Interesting Place
2. Vacation Spots in the State
3. How to Head a Letter
4. Driving Rules
5. Types of Moustaches
6. A Well-planned Park
7. Hair Styles
8. What to Avoid in Making a Chalk Talk
9. Military Insignia
10. How to Write a Check

SUGGESTED EXERCISE B

Report on the effectiveness of any special blackboard technique you have observed. One such special technique was used once by a student who was discussing three different ways to throw a bowling ball. He drew a separate bowling lane and set of pins for each main head. At the end of the speech, he said, "It makes no difference what type of ball you throw if you accomplish this—," and with one sweep of the eraser he "leveled" the pins on all three lanes. It was unusually effective.

SUGGESTED EXERCISE C

In a one-minute talk point out the uses or characteristics or disadvantages, and so forth, of one of the available objects listed below. You may substitute any other object that might be handy. Attempt to observe all of the helpful techniques suggested in the chapter.

Wallet or purse	Watch
Comb	Eye glasses
Change or currency	Keys
Hat	Cosmetics
Pointer	Notebook
Pen or pencil	Desk or chair
Shoes	Speaking stand
Books	Flag
Wastebasket	Bottle of ink
Eraser	A willing class member

SUGGESTED EXERCISE D

Report on a speech you have heard recently which included some type of visual material. Use the following questions as topics for your explanations:

1. Was the material pertinent to the speaker's ideas?
2. Did he make certain that all could see it to satisfaction?
3. Did he avoid long pauses in the use of it?
4. Was it ready and accessible at the time it was needed?

SUGGESTED EXERCISE E

To complement your instruction on adapting ideas, read Chapter 8, "Refining Speech Delivery."

6

Developing Your Thoughts With Verbal Materials

TO CONTINUE . . .

In the last chapter, our primary concern was with the use of physical materials, those specific supporting materials which have form and substance. Their concrete and tangible nature allows them to serve as excellent developers of generalized statements; they help the speaker to anchor his thoughts to reality, to make his abstractions meaningful.

The topic for discussion in this chapter is very closely related to that covered in Chapter 5. This is merely a continuation and completion of our study of methods for developing ideas. (Consult Chapters 10 and 12 for specialized discussions on the use of supporting materials.) Our attention now will be turned to those specifics that we call verbal materials. *Verbal* is derived from the Latin word *verbalis* which means "consisting of words," and this is precisely what we shall discuss—developmental materials consisting of words. There are three main types: examples, statistics, and quotations.

USEFULNESS OF VERBAL MATERIALS

Word developers of thought, like their physical counter-
parts, help to add meaning and believability to assertions in a
basic speech outline. They help an audience to visualize the
idea, to get a feeling of seeing, touching, or perhaps tasting
and smelling. They help the listener to "get the picture," to
understand or be moved by what the speaker is saying. Like
physical aids they are useful in these ways:
1. In getting interest and attention.
2. In clarifying.
3. In impressing and causing listeners to remember.

EXAMPLES

In *Roget's Thesaurus* you will find, among others, the following synonyms for *example:* instance, exemplification, illustration, specimen, and sample. As indicated by these words,
an example is an instance or case in point used to illustrate
or to serve as a specimen or sample. For example:

General statement: The rooting section went wild.

Example: There was one elated man, for instance, who
despite his more than sixty years, tossed his felt hat into
the air with the abandon of a teenager. His team had
scored, and his reaction was no less controlled than that
of the freshmen and sophomores who surrounded him.

General statement: Fishing is usually good on the North Fork
of the Gorgona.

Example: I went up there last week end armed with
nothing but my father's old glass rod and an assortment
of homemade flys. Despite my late start (the road had
washed out at Willow Bend) the trip was successful. I
arrived back home at eight that night with five rain-
bows, none of which weighed less than one pound.

For our purposes, there are two basic forms which the example can assume: the long, rather complete form which we shall call the *illustration* and the short, undeveloped form which we shall call the *instance*.

The *illustration* is used when the speaker needs to include many details in order to allow his listeners to participate extensively in the thought he is developing. The skillful speaker knows that in order to bring the audience "into his speech" he must offer supporting material which is in someway related to the lives and experiences of his audience. A good illustration, with its specific details and richness of meaning, has a broad and immediate appeal. We all enjoy a well-told story, especially if it has some current relationship.

> *General statement:* Luck often smiles on the needy.
>
> > *Example* (Illustration): Once upon a time there lived in Inglewood, California, an earnest young man wallet-deep in difficulties. The young man had lost his $140-a-week welder's job, his wife had been ill, and he owed hospital bills. Mortgage payments were due on the $9300 house he had bought three months earlier, and the bank was prepared to foreclose. Then up popped the young man's fairy godmother in the bureaucratic guise of the California Division of Highways. Negotiators informed him that the San Diego Freeway was headed through his living room. Twenty days before the bank was to take the house, the State of California paid $10,999 for it. The young man saved his $600 equity and recovered the $700 he had spent on a patio. He satisfied his debts, found another house, landed a new job, and as far as the highways department is concerned lived happily ever after.[1]
>
> *General statement:* Strong points may be weak points.
>
> > *Example* (Illustration): Take an illustration from the old Edinburgh Castle. Only once in the history of Scotland was it ever captured. And this is how it happened. The

---

[1] *Time,* March 24, 1958, p. 26. Courtesy *Time;* copyright Time Inc. 1958.

castle had a weak spot. Defenders guarded the spot. But the defenders thought that on one side the steepness of the rock made the castle inaccessible and impregnable and so they did not post sentries there. In the gray mist of an early morning a little party crept up that strong, unguarded, precipitous slope, surprised the garrison, and forced its surrender. You see, the defenders guarded the weak spot of the castle and so where the castle was weak, there it was strong; but the approaches they knew were strong, these they just forgot about, neglected, and so as it turned out, where the castle was strong, there it was weak.[2]

These illustrations serve the purpose of giving strength and concreteness to assertions. They amplify and add color. One person has described such examples as the "wings which carry ideas into a listener's consciousness."

The *instance* is usually shorter than the illustration, includes less detail, and is frequently used as one of a series of brief examples. A chain of instances can give an idea more believability than that provided by a single short example; there is usually more force and power in numbers.

General statement: The English language is unphonetic.
Instance: The "e" sound may be spelled "ea" as in "tea."
Instance: "uay" as in "quay"
Instance: "ey" as in "key"
Instance: "ee" as in "tee"
Instance: "i" as in "machine"
Instance: "y" as in "yperite"
Instance: "ei" as in "receive"
Instance: "ie" as in "believe"

General statement: Will Rogers commented on the foibles and follies of people and things where he found them.

[2] Rev. Harold C. Phillips, "Religion—A Prop for the Weak?", *Representative American Speeches: 1950-1951,* ed. by A. Craig Baird, New York, Wilson, 1951, p. 165.

Instance: He flayed the anti-Jewish Ku Klux Klan back in the 1920s.

Instance: He spoke against an income tax because he felt that a "slick lawyer" could help a person avoid heavy payment.

Instance: Will Rogers was a thorn (humorous thorn) in the side of congressmen because he poked fun at the lawmakers' attempts to raise their own salaries, make political speeches, or "get something done."

Instance: He once kiddingly referred to the New York Stock Exchange as a "racket."

Instance: In 1934 he had occasion to discuss the Russians and came to the conclusion that they would never be as happy as we are. We have more things that provoke laughter in our country.

Instance: Will once wondered if nudism were a religion. He felt that if it were, a lot of nudists would become atheists in the winter.

Instance: After visiting the famous race horse Man O' War, Will commented that the animal, to his thinking was the most beautiful living thing that he had ever seen.

An *illustration* coupled with a group of *instances* often provides stronger support than when either is used without the other. A most effective sequence of thought development consists of stating the point, giving an illustration to support it, and bolstering the point further with a series of instances.

General statement: Great men are versatile men.

Illustration: Benjamin Franklin, that shrewd and witty self-educated American and citizen of the world, is a prime case in point. Name any area of human endeavor, and the chances are good that Ben Franklin delved there. What can we call him? Printer? Printer he was, but don't overlook his activities as economist and businessman, author (everyone remembers *Poor Richard's Almanac*) and editor, community leader and humanitarian, statesman and diplomat, scientist and inventor, philosopher, and *bon vivant*.

It took a broad and active man, indeed, to help establish America's first circulating library, the first fire and police departments, and a free hospital. He reformed the postal system, took part in setting up a college which became the University of Pennsylvania, and helped further the science of electricity. His home was cluttered with novel devices which he had contrived. Franklin was truly much more of a man than is represented by the kite and the key, or the Franklin stove, or the lightning rod.

Instance: Versatile, too, was the boisterous Italian, Benvenuto Cellini, who carried his life beyond goldsmithing and into the fields of sculpture, music, literature, and politics.

Instance: Later in the sixteenth century Francis Bacon came on the scene and didn't leave until he had made an indelible mark as lawyer, statesman, developer of a scientific method, philosopher, and essayist.

Instance: John Locke pursued a medical career, but we do not remember him as a physician. To us he stands as one of the world's deepest thinkers. His mind was challenged and, as a result, it was productive—in economics, education, politics, philosophy, and literary expression.

Instance: We think of Goethe, and "author" comes to mind. This most universally renowned of all Germans held political offices, was a philosopher, art critic, and scientist who did brilliant work in classifying organisms in addition to earning his unsurpassed reputation as a man of letters—novelist, playwright, and poet.

Such a battery of examples gives a point the benefit of

both specific detail and strength of numbers. What Bacon said of his own essays, we might say of ideas supported with an array of pertinent examples—they "come home to men's business and bosoms."

SPECIAL CHARACTERISTICS OF EXAMPLES

1. EXAMPLES TO COMPARE

When you compare two or more persons, agencies, ideas, or things, you point up their similarities, and the result is an analogy. If the two items are of the same class, your analogy is *literal;* if they are of different classes, your analogy is *figurative.*

> *General statement:* American society needs to be re-evaluated.
> *Literal analogy* (comparison of two items from the same class, periods in history):
>> There are those who say that America will go the way of the Roman Empire, that we are like the Romans in letting ourselves get soft, that our primary goal is to indulge ourselves and seek an undue amount of personal pleasure, that our society, too, shall decay.

> *General statement:* The system for electing our President must be changed because it is outdated.
> *Figurative analogy* (two unlike items compared):
>> The electoral college system is like an old Model T Ford. Oh yes, it "gets us there," usually; the people's will is expressed, usually. But *usually* is not satisfactory. Let's junk this obsolete, antiquated machine and put into use a smooth-running, precision instrument which will unfailingly convey the will of the voters.

Use caution in employing analogies. Be certain that the two elements are enough alike to justify the parallel. Moreover, you should recognize the fact that an analogy alone usually does not "prove" a point. It serves but to clarify or to act as a base for adding real proof.

2. EXAMPLES TO CONTRAST

Illustrative material of this type is formed of two or more elements which differ, which have basic dissimilarities. They are put side by side to make the relevant thought interesting, graphic, or otherwise meaningful.

General statement: The "good old days" were not so good.

> *Example:* Consider the mortality factor, for instance. In 1890 there were no wonder drugs to combat pneumonia, no Salk vaccine to prevent polio, no blood banks, no massage technique for stimulating a stopped heart, and no fast vehicle for getting a doctor to an injured child.

3. HYPOTHETICAL EXAMPLES

Hypothetical cases are not actual, nor does the speaker present them as being actual. He asks his audience to imagine a possibility and introduces the example with, "Let us imagine . . ." or "Suppose that . . ." or "We will assume. . . ." When used with discretion, the hypothetical example can add to the molding of ideas.

General statement: Don't use Highway 32 in bad weather.

> *Hypothetical example:* Let's imagine what could happen. You're driving on Route 32 through the mountains in February, and it is snowing. You come to a point where you can go no further; the road is blocked. You attempt to turn around, but the road is narrow. You get off on the shoulder, and your wheels sink down. You attempt to maneuver out, but it is no use. You are stuck. What would you do? Where would you go? Such experiences occur quite frequently on Highway 32 in the winter.

Whether they are comparisons or contrasts or hypothetical cases, illustrations or instances, apt examples are the stock in trade of the speaker. Draw them from your experiences; "cast down your bucket where you are." Attune yourself to notice and remember the many interesting people, places, incidents, and objects with which you come in contact. Develop an appreciation for this most often used type of supporting aid which can help you adapt your thoughts to the audience by:

(*a*)   Adding concreteness;
(*b*)   Referring to the familiar;
(*c*)   Adding color and variety;
(*d*)   Stirring curiosity;
(*e*)   Adding humor;
(*f*)   Appealing to personal needs and emotions.

STATISTICS

There seems to be some confusion in the minds of many people about "facts" and "statistics." A fact may be statistical, or it may not be. Statistics are numerical data; something factual may be expressed either in statistics or in the form of a statement or actual example. We use many statistics daily. When we talk about mileage and distances, how much something weighs, what yardage the football team made, how many days are left in the month, salaries, percentages, and so on, we use statistics.

Numbers give weight and authority to your generalizations. The following points would mean little to an audience without the supporting statistics.

General statement: The teen-age business market is big.
   Statistics: There are 17.2 million citizens between the ages of 12 and 20. They have over 9 billion dollars to spend a year and typically spend 150 million dollars a year for records and buy 2.5 billion gallons of gas.[3]

---

[3] *Quote Magazine*, September 22, 1957.

General statement: Franz Joseph Haydn was a prolific composer.

Statistics: Born in 1732, he wrote 104 symphonies, 16 overtures, 76 quartets, 68 trios, 54 sonatas, 31 concertos, 24 operas, 3 oratorios, and hundreds of sundry pieces.[4]

General statement: Beards are becoming popular.

Statistics: Barbers report that approximately 200,000 men in the United States are letting their whiskers grow.[5]

Suggestions for Handling Statistics

1. *Use round numbers when possible.* If it is not important that the exact number be given, simplify and lighten your listener's burden. For example, the circulation of a daily newspaper which averages 124,891 might be stated as "about 125,000."

2. *Use statistics sparingly.* A sure way to lose listeners is to overload a speech with numbers of pounds, dollars, and measurements.

3. *Give them meaning.* Dramatize your statistics or relate them to something familiar. Instead of leaving your audience with the rather meaningless piece of knowledge that 132,000,-000 feet of cable was used in constructing a certain bridge, tell them that this equals approximately 25,000 miles or enough cable to gird the earth. When stating the distance that one who hits a home run must travel, say that it is 360 feet, yes, but looking at it another way, say that it is 60 feet more than the length of a football field.

4. *Use statistics honestly.* Figures can lie or at least give false impressions. A town with an average per-capita income of $4500 would seem to be quite prosperous, but remember that an average is found by getting a total and then dividing by the number of units. To get a $4500 average, you may be

---

[4] *Quote Magazine,* March 10, 1957.
[5] *Quote Magazine,* March 31, 1957.

dealing with hundreds of incomes below $3000 or hundreds above $15,000.

5. *Use recent statistics.* If your point is to show the need for more recreational facilities in your town, your case probably would not be strengthened if you used 1950 census figures, nor would your conscience leave you alone if you employed outdated statistics to argue against recreational development.

6. *Cite the source of your statistics.* Did they come from an expert in the field, from some reliable agency, or from an unrecognized, questionable source? A man recently said that in 50 years the United States will suffer a major psychological breakdown. Would you not as a listener like to know who said it and how he should have knowledge of such an eventuality? Certainly you would. As good listeners we should demand to know if the author of the data uses a crystal ball or a more scientific measuring instrument.

QUOTATIONS

The words of others can lend either authority or insight to your speeches; they can give your thoughts weight and help you to express them more aptly.

> *General statement:* We cannot neglect education.
>> *Quotation:* Admiral Hyman Rickover, father of the atomic submarine, recently wrote, "I believe that education is the most important problem that faces us today. It is even more important than atomic power or the Navy because if our people aren't properly educated in accordance with the terrific requirements of this rapidly spiraling scientific and industrial civilization, we are bound to go down." [6]

> *General statement:* Let us define mental health.
>> *Quotation:* Dr. Karl Menninger of the world-famous Menninger clinic in Topeka, Kansas, offers this defini-

---

[6] *Quote Magazine,* March 10, 1957.

tion: "Let us define mental health as the adjustment of human beings to the world and to each other with a maximum of effectiveness and happiness, not just efficiency, or just contentment—or the grace of obeying the rules of the game cheerfully. It is all of them together. It is the ability to maintain an even tongue, and alert intelligence, socially considerate behavior, and a happy disposition." [7]

General statement: Look for the good before criticizing negatively.

Quotation: Thomas Carlyle once said: "We are firm believers in the maxim that, for all right judgment of any man or thing, it is useful, nay, essential, to see his good qualities before pronouncing on his bad."

General statement: Perfection is a myth.

Quotation: Alfred de Musset tells us, "Perfection does not exist. To understand it is the triumph of human intelligence; to desire to possess it is the most dangerous kind of madness."

Quotation: In his *Essay on Criticism,* Alexander Pope agrees, "Who ever thinks a faultless thing to see, Thinks what ne'er was, nor is, nor e'er shall be."

Quotation: Further support is offered by Bayard Taylor: "The maxims tell you to aim at perfection, which is well; but it's unattainable, all the same."

General statement: Beauty is many things.

Quotation: Keats wrote in his *Ode on a Grecian Urn,* "Beauty is truth, truth beauty."

Quotation: Charles Reade has said that "Beauty is power; a smile is its sword."

Quotation: Shakespeare, who had something to say about everything, gave his idea of beauty in *The Passionate Pilgrim:*

"Beauty is but a vain and doubtful good;
A shining gloss that fadeth suddenly;

[7] *Quote Magazine,* March 31, 1957.

A flower that dies when first
  it 'gins to bud;
A brittle glass that's broken presently;
A doubtful good, a gloss, a glass, a flower,
Lost, faded, broken, dead within an hour."

Suggestions for Handling Quotations

1. *Use the author's exact words when possible.* Often the changing of a single word can alter the meaning, so be fair to the one who first said it.

2. *Know the author's background.* If he is not commonly known, give the quotation extra vigor by telling your listener who he is and why he is worthy of being quoted.

3. *If you take the quoted words out of context, be careful not to destroy the author's original intent.* A humorous example, somewhat related, is the case of a man who used to sell newspapers on the corner of a large American city. He would cry loudly, "Clark Cable died! Clark Gable died!" and then in a soft voice add "his whiskers red." An unethical speaker might quote Abraham Lincoln as saying, "Force is all-conquering," but he would not be doing our sixteenth President justice unless he completed the quotation. The statement in full is "Force is all-conquering, but its victories are short-lived."

4. *Use variety in introducing and closing a quotation.* Be certain that your audience knows when your quotation begins and ends; however, the trite phrases, "Quote" and "unquote" or "I have a quote," should not be overused. Vocal quality can help you set off quoted words, too.

CRITERIA FOR SELECTING VERBAL MATERIALS

1. *Select material which will allow adequate development of the idea.* Above all, make sure that the material you use is

any case relates directly to the point you are developing. The only justification for using a supporting aid is that it backs up or explains a thought; therefore, it should be relevant to the thought.

Choose enough material to give you full support of the idea. Some speakers make the mistake of stopping short of satisfactory development. This is like getting off a ship before it docks. Others, though more rarely, belabor their ideas with too great a quantity of materials.

2. *Select material which will help you adapt your speech to the audience.* Beyond being meaningful and including the right quantity of detail, developmental materials should meet other standards.

Before settling on any example, statistic, or quotation, ask yourself these questions: Will it appeal to the interests and motives of my listeners? Will it be immediately understood by my listeners? Will it help them to understand or to accept the point? Is it reliable? Is it accurate? Is it unprejudiced?

3. *Select material which will meet the demands of the occasion.* Observe the purpose of the speech setting and follow along with the theme if there is one. In other words, be consistent with the tone or desired atmosphere established by those responsible for your speaking. This criterion will be especially important to remember should you ever be called upon to talk to a group who are meeting for an express purpose.

FINDING MATERIALS

Where does one find materials to use in his speeches? The main source, of course, is the reservoir of personal experience:. What one has heard, seen, read, and done, and has taken time to ponder and assimilate is almost a part of him. Bits of this background in the form of stories, vivid descriptions, and apt phrases can be used to develop the ideas that you wish to get across. Dip down into that reservoir, then, and continue to observe and store for the future.

Occasionally you may not have the exact wording of a quotation that supports a given idea, or you may need some fresh statistics. In such cases, you can go to a *common* reservoir—the library. To save time, you should be purposeful in your quest. Know what you are seeking, and enlist the librarian's aid if you cannot find it.

In addition to the standard books, magazines, and newspapers at your disposal, there are many specialized references such as encyclopedias of various kinds, books of important statistics, and books of quotations.

When you find your information, record it accurately on index cards. We all know how memories can fail, as Lewis Carroll so wisely reminds us:

> "The horror of that moment," the King went on, "I shall never, *never* forget!"
>
> "You will, though," the Queen said, "if you don't make a memorandum of it."

This quotation was found in *Bartlett's Familiar Quotations*, a volume that most libraries possess. (For a further discussion of using the library, see Chapter 10.)

LET US SUMMARIZE

You cannot expect an audience to accept your ideas, to be influenced by you, unless you justify the ideas with carefully chosen supporting data. Alert, thinking people ignore or challenge mere generalizations; they want specifics. When hearing a flat assertion, they mentally ask, "So what?" Therefore, it behooves you to augment your thoughts with an ample supply of rich, pertinent, and appropriate examples, statistics, and quotations.

FOR FURTHER STUDY

Barnes, Harry G., *Speech Handbook* (Englewood Cliffs, N. J., Prentice-Hall, 1941), pp. 36-44.

McBurney, James H., and Wrage, Ernest J., *Guide to Good Speech*, (Englewood Cliffs, N. J., Prentice-Hall, 1955), Ch. 14, "Developing Your Ideas."

McCall, Roy C., *Fundamentals of Speech* (New York, The Macmillan Co., 1949), Ch. 6, "Developmental Materials."

Soper, Paul L., *Basic Public Speaking* (New York, Oxford, 1956), Ch. 6, "Supporting Materials."

SAMPLE SPEECH OUTLINE 1
(In sentence form)

MAN AGAINST MAN

I. *Introduction*
   A. It is my belief that war symbolizes the prime weaknesses of man.
      1. George Bernard Shaw seemed to agree; in *Man and Superman* he wrote: "In the arts of life man invents nothing; but in the arts of death he outdoes Nature herself, and produces by chemistry and machinery all the slaughter of plague, pestilence, and famine." (*Quotation*)
      2. "War is hell," exclaimed W. T. Sherman. (*Quotation*)
   B. We have had wars since the beginning of society.
      1. Cain and Abel started it all. (*Instance*)
      2. The Medes and Persians warred. (*Instance*)
      3. England and Spain fought bitterly. (*Instance*)
      4. We remember our own Civil War of the 1860s. (*Instance*)
      5. World Wars I and II and the Korean war are more recent examples. (*Instance*)
   C. Many reasons are offered for the cause of war.
II. *Proposition:* I should like to discuss three causes of war.

III. *Body*

   A. Nationalism is one reason for aggressive hostility between countries.

      1. By nationalism I mean a nation's dynamic and aggressive policy of striving for status and independence. (*Definition*)

      2. Germany under Hitler was a case in point. (*Illustration*)

      3. Mussolini's attack on Ethiopia was another case. (*Instance*)

      4. Nasser's Egypt is nationalistic. (*Instance*)

   B. Warfare is provoked by "isms" other than the nationalism; imperialism is a second reason.

      1. This refers to the spirit and principle of empire. (*Definition*)

      2. Here we are talking about the creation and maintenance of colonies. (*Restatement*)

      3. Consider Soviet Russia and the Communist International. (*Illustration*)

      4. The old British Empire was imperialistic. (*Instance*)

      5. The Dutch were imperialists. (*Instance*)

      6. The French were imperialists. (*Instance*)

      7. The Spanish were imperialists. (*Instance*)

   C. Some fight to assert themselves, others to acquire, and others because of militarism.

      1. A country may be fearful and anxious.

      2. It may face real or imagined military challenges.

      3. It engages in an arms race.

         a. Let us look at Europe prior to World War I. (*Illustration*)

         b. Then there was Germany under Hitler. (*Instance*)

         c. The East-West cold war is another such example. (*Instance*)

         d. The Arab nations today typify such action. (*Instance*)

         e. Bismarck attempted to justify his actions: "I am

accustomed to pay men back in their own coin."
(*Quotation*)

IV. *Conclusion*

   A. Read today's headlines.

      1. Note the signs of nationalism.

      2. Note the signs of imperialism.

      3. Note the signs of militarism.

   B. We all have seen the waste of war.

      1. There have been 24 major wars in modern times. (*Statistic*)

      2. There were 15 million deaths (nearly equaling the population of New York, Chicago, and Los Angeles), in World War II. (*Statistic*)

   C. Now may be our last chance to do something about it.

      1. The noted author, Philip Wylie, remarked in the *Science Digest:* "It is obvious to any physicist worth his salt, that man is not at the end of his weaponeering capabilities, but, rather, at a fresh beginning." (*Quotation*)

      2. If this is the genesis of war's potential, it may well be man's exodus.

SAMPLE SPEECH OUTLINE 2

(In sentence form)

PIGSKIN FANS

I. *Introduction*

   A. Many of us cannot wait until football season comes.

      1. We yearn for the arrival of fall. (*Restatement*)

      2. Just picture a packed stadium, a roaring crowd, a dog on the field. (*Illustration*)

      3. Some large universities report annual attendance at games as high as 500,000. (*Statistic*)

   B. Perhaps you have given thought to the reasons why so many people battle traffic and endure cold weather to watch twenty-two athletes run up and down a field.

II. *Proposition:* Today I wish to give my reasons for football's popularity.

III. *Body*
- A. First of all, this rough sport is loved by many because of the thrills it provides.
    1. You remember the exciting second half in last year's final game. (*Illustration*)
    2. Then there was the game that decided the championship. (*Instance*)
    3. Our bowl game produced thrills in every quarter. (*Instance*)
- B. If you don't come for the excitement, you may find it a convenient place to visit.
    1. I refer to the women, mainly, who go to sit and chat or to see what Mary Jane is wearing. (*Definition*)
    2. For example, Thelma didn't know who was playing but thoroughly enjoyed herself with constant chatter and shouts to acquaintances. (*Illustration*)
    3. One person that I know is an aisle-hopper. (*Instance*)
    4. Jean likes to discuss what others are wearing. (*Instance*)
    5. A few people of this type will leave the game when their social needs are satisfied. (*Instance*)
    6. An usher at our stadium said, "About 25 percent of the people who come here just use football as an excuse to have a social outing." (*Quotation*)
- C. In addition to those who attend for emotional and social reasons, there are some who like the science of the game.
    1. This science involves diagnosing plays, plotting defense weaknesses, and calling the next play. (*Definition*)
    2. Here is the way a friend of mine, a true football scientist, comments on a typical play. (*Illustration*)
    3. A would-be coach is of this type. (*Instance*)
    4. My neighbor has developed special charts for diagramming plays. (*Instance*)

IV. *Conclusion*
- A. I am sure that you can offer other reasons for the popularity of football in addition to these.
    1. It is a thrilling game.

2. It provides an excuse for a social spree.

3. Grandstand quarterbacks enjoy "running the team."

B. It makes no real difference why we go to the games as long as we enjoy ourselves.

C. One person that I know likes the game for all three reasons that I have mentioned. (*Illustration*)

BASIC ASSIGNMENT NO. 6A

Prepare a speech in which you use an illustration and a series of instances (at least two) to support each main head. Be certain that your instances support the illustration. Employ the following aids:

1. Meaningful statistics
2. A quotation
3. Transitions at all major points

Use your own judgment about the use of restatement, definition, and visual aids.

Reminders:

1. This is probably the most demanding assignment you have had so far this semester; therefore, get an early start. Begin your planning now, and let your speech grow and become a part of you.

2. If during practice you consistently go overtime, it may be necessary to limit the subject or shorten the length of your materials.

BASIC ASSIGNMENT NO. 6B

Prepare a speech and include all the elements you have used in previous assignments: transitions, restatements, definitions, visual aids (sketches or objects), examples, statistics, and quotations. Use your own judgment to determine how many of each to use and where to place them.

Reminder:

Consider your purpose carefully, and employ your materials with an end toward achieving that purpose.

SUGGESTED EXERCISE A

The following examples might be used to support points of speeches. Consider the essential idea that each expresses to you, and write an appropriate heading for it.

SAMPLE 1

Roy Jackson called his 13-year-old son aside one afternoon.

"Jack," he said, pointing to a polished hardwood post standing in the back yard, "I want you to do just one thing for me. Each time you make a mistake, I want you to drive a nail into this post. And, when you have done a good deed or performed a charitable act, you may withdraw a nail."

Jack agreed. He didn't understand why his father was asking this of him, but it seemed an easy request to fulfill.

Like most young men, he occasionally found himself driving a nail into the post—however reluctantly he did so. He also found that when he was able to withdraw one of the nails, it was a moment of triumph. It was then that he discovered the wisdom of his father's request. Although each good act balanced a bad act, the nail holes could never be erased.

And so it is with all our lives.

SAMPLE 2

Ralph and Ed had advanced to the finals of the state debate tournament, and a victory here would mean the championship.

In the final round, all went well for the fellows until the opposition pinned them down on a vital issue. A great deal was at stake, and they were at a loss for a reply. They frantically thumbed through their files in search of evidence to use in refutation. Ed mumbled in dismay.

An opposing speaker finished his rebuttal and sat down. Ralph got up to speak. He had planned to ignore the challenge of the opposition, but as the minutes passed he had become more and more worried about the outcome of the debate. Ralph had visions of clutching that trophy which was to be awarded to the winning team at the banquet.

Now he started to speak. Much to Ed's astonishment, Ralph hit the point head on and supported his refutation with a quotation of Senator Arden from *Time*, April 15, 1950, page 21.

After it was all over, everyone wondered why Ralph and Ed hadn't won the debate. Ralph knew why. You see, the judge who cast the deciding ballot happened to have a copy of *Time* of April 15 before him. He also happened to have it open at page 21—a full-page liquor advertisement.

SAMPLE 3

Two Boston women were seeing the sights in California on a very warm afternoon. "My, it certainly is hotter in California than it is in Boston," said one.

"True," replied the other, "but bear in mind that here we are 3000 miles from the ocean."

SUGGESTED EXERCISE B

The following statistics and quotations might be used to support points of speeches. Consider the essential idea that each expresses to you, and write an appropriate heading for it.

1. Thirty percent of 12,154 top high-school students indicated recently that they had selected teaching as a career. Of this thirty percent, 455 were boys and 3199 were girls.
2. In 1850 half of the family income went for food. In 1900 it was one third, and today we spend but one fourth of our salaries for food.
3. It is estimated that industrial injuries amount to a loss of 193 million man-days annually. This is enough to produce 100 million refrigerators, 200 million men's suits, 1.5 billion pairs of men's shoes, 26,000 jet bombers, 1 million six-room homes, or 2 billion tons of coal.
4. "Education is a companion no misfortune can depress, no

crime destroy, no friend alienate, no despotism enslave; at home a friend, abroad an introduction, in solitude a solace, in society an ornament, in old age a comfort—without it, what is man?"   —AUTHOR UNKNOWN

5. "Our youth now love luxury; they have bad manners, contempt for authority; they show disrespect for elders and love chatter in the place of exercise. Children are now tyrants, not the servants of their households. They no longer rise when elders enter the room. They contradict their parents, chatter before company, gobble up their food, and tyrannize their teachers."   —SOCRATES, 5th century B.C.

6. "That man's a fool who tries by art and skill to stem the torrent of a woman's will: For if she will, she will; you may depend on't—And if she won't, she won't—and there's an end on't."   —AUTHOR UNKNOWN

SUGGESTED EXERCISE C

Find two items of verbal supporting material for each of the following points. Use the "Criteria for Selecting Materials" (pp. 94-95) to check the importance of each item. State the sources of your materials. (Your instructor may want you to present one of these as a one-point speech.)

1. College athletics are no longer amateur athletics.
2. People should spend more time in recreation.
3. The number of farms in America is decreasing.
4. The number of job opportunities for women is increasing.

SUGGESTED EXERCISE D

Study a speech which you find in a newspaper, magazine, or anthology of speeches. List each item of verbal material used, what point it develops, and tell how the material helped in developing the point.

SUGGESTED EXERCISE E

Develop one point in a one-minute talk. Use an example, a quotation, and statistics.

II

COMPLEMENTARY METHODS

7

Using Effective Language

THOUGHTS AND SYMBOLS

People do not always say just what they want to say. Imagine a grandmother's bewilderment upon reading the following telegram: TWINS ARRIVED TONIGHT. MORE BY MAIL

Then there was the foreign visitor who told a New York bus driver, "Vill you procrastinate me at ze baseball park?" "Huh?" questioned the driver. "Procrastinate me at ze baseball park! Here, I vill show you." He took out a pocket dictionary and pointed to "procrastinate" which was defined "to put off." Ten blocks later he was put off at Yankee Stadium.

Little children offer some of the best examples of language difficulty. There is the story of Bobby, a second-grader, who asked his teacher how many people stayed in the "back tier" during America's pioneering days. His teacher was confused until she became aware of Bobby's reasoning: he thought of "back tier" as the opposite of "frontier."

Language is a vehicle, a conveyance made up of words, sentences, and groups of sentences; our thoughts and feelings are the cargo which it attempts to convey from us to other people. Language is a means to an end, not the end itself, but a *means* to an end.

Words in themselves are valueless, for they are nothing, really, but symbols for our ideas. The word *tree* is not a growing thing with a trunk, branches, and leaves. The word *tree* is a symbol composed of four letters of the English alphabet and put together into a pattern which is intelligible to those of us who speak English.

While words have no intrinsic value, it is of the utmost importance that we choose the right words and organize them into suitable thought groups. Ideas, the truly valuable, become casualties when language is neglected, for even the most practical thought cannot be shared with others unless the speaker is able to call up the appropriate language of expression. Many people possess wisdom, but those accounted *wise* are able to communicate what they know.

In choosing language, you the speaker, must consider the four familiar elements of speaking: Yourself, your speech, your audience, and the occasion. When preparing and rehearsing your speeches, ask this question about your choice of language: "Is this word (or phrase or sentence) suitable for *me* to use in communicating *this thought* to *this audience* on *this occasion?*"

USE LANGUAGE WHICH CLARIFIES YOUR THOUGHTS

1.   USE SIMPLE LANGUAGE

Unless more complex wording is needed to get the message across, say it simply. Communication can often break down if the terminology is too technical, if "big words" for their own sake are included, if the language is involved and too many words are used, or if there is unnecessary ornateness.

Ralph Waldo Emerson tells us, "An orator or author is never successful until he has learned to make his words smaller than his ideas." Winston Churchill, a man who has experienced some of the most crucial moments of this century and whose ideas have been of world consequence, is a fitting example of one who can use simple, yet effective, language. He spoke these words to a British audience during World War II:

> Perhaps you may say, "Yes, but has not the enemy, too, been busy?" I have not the slightest doubt he has. I would be the last to underrate the strength [of the enemy] or determination to use that strength without scruple and without mercy if he thinks he can do so without getting his blows returned with interest. I grant that. But I say this too: the very completeness of his preparations has left him very little margin of strength still to call upon."[1]

The simplest language is usually the most profound and practical, while flowery, glib, and profuse expressions distract listeners. When an audience is concerned about *how* it is being said instead of *what* is being said, communication suffers.

It is usually better to say:	*Instead of:*
lie	prevarication
name	cognomen
home	domicile
He was a successful lawyer.	As a member of the legal profession, he became, what you might say, successful.
I am happy to be home.	By virtue of the fact that I am in my own house, I feel a great deal of joy.

By all means give your thoughts significance and meaning, but in so doing, be guided by the declaration of a wise man: "Clearness ornaments profound thoughts."

2. USE PRECISE LANGUAGE

We all recognize that the human organism is not a preci-

---

[1] Winston Churchill, *The Gathering Storm*, Boston, Houghton Mifflin, 1951, p. 584.

sion instrument. We make mistakes; we waste motion; we are often quite inefficient. Pencils would not have erasers if we were really precise. And yet, paradoxically, we have distinguished ourselves despite our limiting human condition. As examples of notable oral communication, you remember The Gettysburg Address, Patrick Henry's "Give me liberty or give me death," or even possibly the campaign speech of a candidate for student office.

Yes, it is truly remarkable that *human beings* using *human skills* are able to create mutual understanding. Actually, we are able to communicate at best only a fraction of any total thought or feeling. Since speech is used primarily to influence people, does it not seem logical that every speaker has an obligation to be as exact and precise as is humanly possible?

It is often better to say:	*Instead of:*
commendable, useful, beneficial, advantageous, choice, priceless, genuine, valuable, *etc.*	good
coupe, sedan, convertible, *or* Chevrolet, Chrysler, Ford, *etc.*	car
replied, stated, cried, commented, uttered	said
pretty, neat, grand, worthy, attractive, desirable, pleasant	fine
novel, text, anthology, pamphlet	book
river, creek, brook, millrace	stream

Especially plaguing are the vague words, *very, nice,* and *interesting.* To find more specific substitutes for these and other hazy terms, consult your dictionary or thesaurus. Mark Twain quite persuasively summed up the need for being exact: "The difference between the right word and the almost right word is the difference between lightning and the lightning bug."

USE LANGUAGE WHICH ENLIVENS YOUR THOUGHTS

1. USE SENSE-APPEALING LANGUAGE

Paint word pictures which convey impressions of form, texture, and color. Put life into your speaking and use words that help you achieve your purpose. In his memorable speech, The New South, Henry Grady at one point might have remarked: "The dejected Confederate soldier started home after the war."

But his purpose was to create a deeper and more sympathetic feeling in his audience than that sentence could evoke. Instead, he touched their hearts with this image:

> Let me picture to you the footsore Confederate soldier, as buttoning up in his faded gray jacket the parole which was to bear testimony to his children of his fidelity and faith, he turned his face southward from Appomattox in April, 1865. Think of him as ragged, half-starved, heavy-hearted, enfeebled by want and wounds; having fought to exhaustion, he surrenders his gun, wrings the hands of his comrades in silence, and, lifting his tear-stained and pallid face for the last time to the graves that dot the old Virginia hills, pulls his gray cap over his brow and begins the slow and painful journey.

There are not very many Henry Gradys and Winston Churchills; however, we are all communicators, and in our own realms have significant ideas to share.

It might be better to say:	*Instead of:*
A blue-eyed sprightly girl of four tossed her blond pigtails into the air as she skipped and bounced across the school-yard.	The girl played.
The S.S. *Artemus,* decaying after forty years of unfailing service between James	The old ship sank.

Island and the mainland, settled to the muddy bottom of the harbor quietly and peacefully.

2. USE FIGURATIVE LANGUAGE

A fitting figure of speech can animate an abstract idea and enable a speaker to attain fullness and richness of expression. Although there are many such gems of language, simile, metaphor, personification, and irony are especially useful.

A *simile* is a short comparison introduced with *like* or *as*.

It might be better to say:	*Instead of:*
The fullback burst through the line like a charging bull.	The fullback burst through the line.
Running down the road as if tormented by a hornet, Raymond outdistanced his sister.	Running down the road, Raymond out-distanced his sister.

A *metaphor* is an implied comparison in which something is spoken of as being something else. The words *like* and *as* are not used.

It might be better to say:	*Instead of:*
Good books are ladders upon which the earnest reader can climb after the fruit of knowledge.	You can learn from books.
He was a lion.	He was mean (or vicious, etc.).

Personification gives human qualities to nonhuman things.

It might be better to say:	*Instead of:*
The pines whispered.	The wind in the pines made soft noises.
Law is a spokesman for every man.	Law is for the protection of every man.

Irony is a figure of speech in which the intended meaning is opposite to that indicated by the words used. It is generally sarcastic.

It might be better to say:	*Instead of:*
You know how children hate watermelon.	Children love watermelon.
Oh no, we just twiddled our thumbs on the ranch last summer.	We worked very hard.

USE LANGUAGE WHICH IS NOT DISTRACTING

USE VARIED LANGUAGE

We like variety in our lives. William Cowper once observed, "Variety's the very spice of life, that gives it all its flavour." We vary the placement of our living-room furniture, our choice of current songs to sing, our wearing apparel, and our sources of entertainment. We should do more to vary our language in speaking.

How can the desired variety be achieved?

First of all, you can try varying the features of sentences. If you characteristically employ long and loosely constructed sentences, it would be well for you to break up the pattern with a short, emphatic sentence now and then. If your habit is to use an overabundance of simple sentences that usually begin with the subject, you can add variety by introducing an occasional periodic sentence—that is, one that withholds the important thought until the end. If your practice is to rely almost entirely upon declarative and imperative sentences, perhaps you should a put question into your discourse at times.

Occasionally, it might be better to say:	*Instead of:*
From now on we will lock our doors. (Periodic)	We will lock our doors from now on.

Since its formation in 1945, the United Nations has helped to promote world peace. (Periodic)	The United Nations has helped to promote world peace since its formation in 1945.
What standards should be set down?	These standards should be set down.
How long has it been since our salaries were raised?	You know how long it has been since our salaries were raised.

Vary your use of individual words and phrases, too. In informal speaking situations, it is appropriate for you to add variety by including contractions and other acceptable colloquialisms. Be wary, though, of the *unacceptable* expression. Unfortunately some clichés and slang expressions which seem to serve us well on some occasions create listening blocks on other occasions. Certain old sayings that once were colorful are worn out and useless now; others, especially some slang terms, are repulsive to many listeners.

From your own experience as a listener, can you think of terms that grate on you and cause you to be distracted? Such distractions can be costly, indeed, when the speaker is a salesman, a politician seeking votes, or a young man being interviewed for a job. A word or phrase is acceptable if it does not call attention to itself, if it helps to communicate the ideas. When in doubt, you should ask yourself this key question: "Will *this wording* help me to communicate *this idea* to *this audience* on *this occasion?*"

Usually it would be better to say:	*Instead of:*
girl, lady, or woman	a member of the fair sex
He is growing rapidly.	He is growing by leaps and bounds.
finally or last on the list	last but not least
terrible or distasteful, *etc.*	gosh awful

poor, dreadful, imperfect, shocking, destructive, *etc.*	lousy
truly, true, actual, honestly, *etc.*	for real

USE CORRECT LANGUAGE

In addition to being overused, some of the above words and phrases are considered incorrect. Our main concern at this point, though, is with correctness of pronunciation, word choice, and grammar. Beyond taking pride in the beauty of our language, we have a practical reason for using it correctly. Many listeners are distracted by errors in English usage; their minds are taken away from the message and focused upon the error. When the listener hears "We was . . . ," he is stimulated to judge, not the ideas, but the person delivering the ideas. As unfair as it seems, his judgment may be against both the speaker and his speech.

It is correct to say:	*Instead of:*
We accepted the invitation.	We excepted the invitation.
regardless	irregardless
this	this here
burst *or* break	bust
can't	can't hardly
man *or* boy	guy
rather *or* somewhat	kind of
He did it.	He done it.
I am going to lie down.	I am going to lay down.
It is very hot today.	It is real hot today.

USE YOUR LANGUAGE

Use clear, vivid, and undistracting language, yes, but use *your* language. Improve your use of English, yes, but start from the foundation you have been laying these past years. Take yourself where you are, and start your program of self-improvement. Think not in terms of a major overhaul but in terms of gradual and steady development toward ever-increasing skill in the use of language. Avoid attempting a radical change in style. Instead, occasionally substitute new words, improved phrasing, and more correct forms for weaker and less effective units of expression. Such action will enable you to present yourself as yourself and to obviate the fear that so many seem to have: "If I don't make some English errors, my friends will think I am a stuffed shirt; if I change my speaking habits, I won't be able to talk with some people." Growth and personal appeal need not be incompatible.

DO YOU WANT TO IMPROVE?

It is one thing to read about how to develop language skills, but do you *really* want to improve? This is a basic question. Without the desire, it cannot be done. Without your recognition of the need for lucid and rich expression, the job cannot be started. It is much like a fundamental premise held by psychologists: If the patient himself does not want to be helped, he cannot be helped.

LET US SUMMARIZE

Assuming that you do wish to help yourself, where do you start? First, take an accounting of your strengths and weaknesses. Learn to listen to yourself, and become conscious of your usage. Next, gradually replace less effective terminology with stronger terminology.

1. Use simple and precise language which clarifies your thoughts.
2. Use sense-appealing and figurative language which enlivens your thoughts.

3. Use varied and correct language which does not subordinate your thoughts.

4. Use *your* language.

Above all, remember that the *thought* is the important factor, and the thought is what you wish to communicate. Language is only a vehicle, a conveyance for communicating ideas, a vehicle which, nevertheless, should be kept in constant repair.

Let us close this chapter with one last case in point, a not so serious, but relevant, reminder about using effective language.

Dear William,

Are you still upset about last night? If I could I would like to clarify that it was really in jest when I told you I really didn't mean what I told you about changing my mind about not reconsidering my decision. These are my sincere feelings.

Yours always,

Marjorie Y.

All phases of communication demand that we keep the vehicle of language in constant repair.

LANGUAGE BOOKS

To a speaker or writer (and who is not?), there are three essential books: a good dictionary, an English handbook, and a book of synonyms and antonyms or thesaurus.

DICTIONARIES

The American College Dictionary (New York, Random House, 1958).

Webster's New Collegiate Dictionary, 6th ed. (Springfield, Mass., Merriam, 1956).

Webster's New World Dictionary of the American Language (Cleveland, World, 1959).

HANDBOOKS OF ENGLISH

Greever, Garland, and Jones, Easley S., *The Century Collegiate Handbook*, 3d ed. (New York, Appleton-Century-Crofts, 1950).

Kierzek, John M., *The Macmillan Handbook of English*, 3d ed. (New York, The Macmillan Co., 1954).

Roberts, Charles W., Harris, Jesse W., and Johnson, Walter G., *A Handbook of English* (New York, Oxford, 1944).

Woolley, Edwin C., Scott, Franklin W., and Bracher, Frederick, *College Handbook of Composition*, 6th ed. (Boston, Heath, 1958).

THESAURI

Fernald, James C., *Standard Handbook of Synonyms, Antonyms, and Prepositions*, rev. ed. (New York, Funk and Wagnalls, 1947).

Laird, Charlton, *Laird's Promptory* (New York, Holt, 1947).

Roget, Peter Mark, *Roget's International Thesaurus*, rev. ed. (New York, Crowell, 1946).

——, *Roget's Thesaurus: In Dictionary Form,* ed. by C. O. Sylvester Mawson (New York, Doubleday, 1947).

FOR FURTHER STUDY

Chase, Stuart, *The Tyranny of Words* (New York, Harcourt, Brace, 1938).

Lee, Irving J., *Language Habits in Human Affairs* (New York, Harper, 1941).

Smith, Raymond G., *Principles of Public Speaking* (New York, Ronald, 1958), Ch. 7, "Language for Gaining Response."

Sondel, Bess, *The Humanity of Words* (Cleveland, World, 1958).

White, Eugene E., and Henderlider, Clair R., *Practical Public Speaking* (New York, The Macmillan Co., 1954), Ch. 12, "Using Language in Delivering the Speech."

SUGGESTED EXERCISE A

Prepare a speech in which you include the basic elements of speaking and whatever materials that are needed to develop your ideas. Use at least once each of the four figures of speech discussed in this chapter. Write them into your outline.

During one practice session record your speech, and analyze your use of language by answering the following questions after you play it back:

1. Was the wording simple and precise? What wording was not?
2. Can the language be made more vivid? How?
3. Were there any overused words or phrases?
4. Was any inappropriate slang used?
5. Were there any pronunciation or usage errors?
6. Was the language natural and representative?

During your next practice session, revise the speech on the basis of your answers to the questions.

SUGGESTED EXERCISE B

Listen to a speech of a known public figure. Analyze it, using the six questions stated in Suggested Exercise A above.

SUGGESTED EXERCISE C

Read a printed speech from a source such as *Representative American Speeches* or *Vital Speeches,* and cite ten specific uses of language which helped the speaker express his thoughts vividly and clearly.

SUGGESTED EXERCISE D

Here is a list of sentences containing usage errors. Do you see any that you make? Correct the sentences, and submit them to your instructor.

I seen her.

It don't do it.

They was often wrong.

Beings you aren't going, I won't.

He don't mean no harm.

I couldn't do it nohow.

They might of done it.

My, they did good.

It sure was swell.

He had ought to see a doctor.

Oranges are healthy.

She laid down for twenty minutes.

A criteria is a standard.

Let's go somewheres.

SUGGESTED EXERCISE E

Make two lists, one headed *Overused Terms* and the other headed *Ambiguous* or *Meaningless Terms*. Develop the lists by recalling terms you have heard and by listening carefully to the speech of people with whom you come in contact.

Your instructor may want you to report on your project orally, or he may want to make a master list from written class reports of all the students.

SUGGESTED EXERCISE F

Compose four figures of speech, each one of a different type, and explain how each might be used to help express a thought.

SUGGESTED EXERCISE G

Using a thesaurus, make a list of all the synonyms for *nice* (meaning "pleasing"), *very*, and *thing*.

SUGGESTED EXERCISE H

Write, word for word, a short speech to be read instead of delivered extemporaneously. Include all the basic elements called for in preparing speeches and whatever developmental materials you need. Give special attention to the language factors discussed in this chapter:

1. Simplicity
2. Preciseness
3. Vividness
4. Variety
5. Correctness
6. Naturalness

8

Refining Speech Delivery

ADAPTING

"To adapt," according to *Webster's Collegiate Dictionary,* means "to make suitable; to fit, or suit; to adjust." A speaker is successful to the extent that he is able to adapt his ideas to his audience.

In the predelivery stages of speech work, one makes major steps toward adapting by planning and composing thoughtfully. One attempts to adjust his ideas or to make them suitable and fitting in the following ways:

1. By choosing a suitable subject.
2. By carefully wording a purpose.
3. By analyzing and arranging his thoughts.
4. By strengthening and supporting his thoughts.
5. By preparing to use effective language.

Finally, he must adapt his prepared thoughts to the audience directly; he must deliver them. A speaker is much like a house painter at this point. The speaker has composed a speech, and the painter has mixed his paint. Now each has the job of applying his "content." Will the painter make efforts to work his paint into the wood, to adapt his paint? Will the speaker make efforts to work his ideas into the minds and hearts of his listeners, to adapt his ideas? In each case, a conscientious worker would make such efforts. Whether he is a painter or speaker, the experienced craftsman knows that to be effective his material must be accepted, assimilated, and retained. Delivery, for the speaker, is primarily a matter of adapting ideas.

As a speaker, you have one instrument to use in delivering your thoughts and feelings, and that is *you.* As parts of the total, integrated *you,* however, there are four elements which offer themselves for study: Your personality, your body, your voice, and your processes of articulation. None of these elements is independent; each one is related to the others. To gain a better understanding of the complete delivery process, let us isolate and examine them one at a time.

PERSONALITY

Personality can be defined as the sum total of one's body, mind, and emotional characteristics; those patterns of behavior, interests, temperaments, attitudes, values, and motives that distinguish one person from another.

What are the specific features of *your* personality? What are *your* distinguishing characteristics of body, mind, and emotions? Do you know what they are? Are you an outgoing person who enters into many social activities, or does your temperament influence you to minimize your social life? Are you generally liberal or rather conservative? Are you ambitious or easygoing, optimistic or frequently more despairing? Whatever your personal qualities are, it is important for you to recognize them, to begin to know yourself. Self-improvement is based upon self-knowledge.

Along with knowing yourself, to be an effective speaker you must accept yourself. This is not to say that you should curtail your program of self-improvement, for every human being who desires to better his personality is to be commended. No one, however, should refuse to recognize and accept his basic and important personal assets. Too many people totally reject themselves. As a result of this preoccupation with the negative, they cut down their own efficiency in speaking—indeed, in any social situation. When a person is apologetic and otherwise gives the impression that what he has to say is not worthwhile, the audience might believe him. If this happens, the speaker loses and the audience loses. On this point, Joshua Loth Leibman wrote in *Peace of Mind:* "Self-understanding rather than self-condemnation is the way to inner peace and mature conscience." It is also a way to more effective speaking.

Free yourself, and let your best self and whole self come forward to help you deliver your ideas. People usually respect other people who are willing to accept themselves and release their thoughts and feelings. From such willingness it follows that their ideas, too, will stand a better chance of being respected. We really cannot separate a person from his ideas, and great thinkers from Aristotle to most contemporary speech experts have found that a speaker's strongest point is himself. Do not be afraid to be yourself. Will Rogers was a man who knew thousands of people and yet was able to say, "I never met a man I didn't like." There is no better place to start gaining true freedom of personal expression than in your speech class.

BODY

Your bodily actions are also agents of expression and here, once again, we find differences among people. From each individual personality come individual forms of physical activity. Some people are extremely active and seem to move constantly, while others display a minimum of action.

Which pattern is the right one for a speaker, the active or

inactive? Actually, neither is right and neither is wrong. The right pattern for you is the one which is a reflection of you. Express yourself with as much bodily action as is consistent with both your personality and the idea that you are communicating. If you use physical movement extensively and on a given occasion happen to be delivering a strong thought, you will probably use arm gestures and other movements automatically. On the other hand, it may be your nature to limit yourself to less extensive physical expression.

There is, then, no set formula for bodily action or use of gestures that can be applied to all people. If you have a deep desire to communicate, generally your body will respond naturally to help you communicate. Your nature, associated with the content of your speech, will dictate the forms of your physical response.

A degree of control, nonetheless, may be called for at times. No element of delivery should call attention to itself since delivery is important only in so far as it assists in communicating the content of a speech. Therefore, you should avoid wasteful pacing, shifting weight from one foot to another, uncomfortable stances, window gazing, "waltzing" with the speakers' stand, and slouchy posture.

Heavy reliance on notes is another obstacle to communication. Ample practice along with real concern for reaching your audience will help you to escape this pitfall. Avoid also such mechanical techniques as fixing your eyes at a point over the heads of your listeners. Genuine eye contact can be accomplished only when a speaker *wants* to consult his audience visually. If you desire to inform or persuade an audience and if you realize how much they can pass back to you (to tell you how you are doing), then you will appreciate the need for eye contact.

Give your body a chance to help you in speech delivery. Free yourself physically. Use your body naturally to reflect your personality and your ideas and, yet, control your movements to minimize distracting elements.

VOICE AND ARTICULATION

A general understanding of how speech is made should be established before we discuss voice and articulation, the third and fourth elements of delivery. There are five steps in the production of speech: the mental phase, breathing, phonation, resonation, and articulation. We shall call them *steps* in examining the process, but, actually, they are so closely interrelated that it is difficult to say where one step ends and another begins.

Producing Speech

Like most bodily functions, producing speech is a complicated act, so complex, in fact, that explanation of it necessitates oversimplification. Bear that in mind as you read on. The purpose of our digression at this point is to draft a rough sketch of the speaking process, reasonably accurate in its simplicity, in order to establish increased appreciation of the act. For a more complete explanation, consult one or more of the sources listed in the "For Further Study" section of this chapter (p. 136).

1. THE MENTAL STEP

You possess certain thoughts or emotions that you wish to communicate. Possibly you speak to answer a question, to scold, to ask a question, to comment on a pretty sight, to express fear, or to instruct. For some reason or other, you are moved to speak; therefore, the act of speaking starts as a mental process with its origin and control in the brain.

2. THE BREATHING STEP

Our need to get air into and out of the lungs is exploited by the speech function. Making speech is dependent upon this

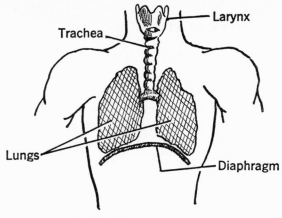

LOWER SPEECH ORGANS

flow of air since the outgoing breath is utilized as the power for producing sound.

When one inhales, nerve impulses from the brain cause the muscular partition that horizontally divides the body (the diaphragm) to be pulled down and pushed against the stomach organs. At the same time, the rib muscles contract to pull the ribs up and out. As a result, the chest cavity is given greater capacity, and a vacuum is created. Since nature abhors a vacuum, air immediately rushes in from the mouth or nose openings and down the trachea (windpipe) into the lungs.

Exhalation is characterized by a gradual relaxation of the parts that are active in inhalation. The diaphragm relaxes and is forced upward by the pressure of the crowded stomach organs. Rib muscles relax, too, and the ribs descend and draw in. The inward and downward force of the ribs and the upward force of the diaphragm cause air to be squeezed out of the lungs and up the trachea.

3.   THE PHONATION STEP

At the top of the trachea is the larynx or voice box. The larynx, the front part of which is frequently referred to as the Adam's apple, is the cartilage structure which houses the vocal

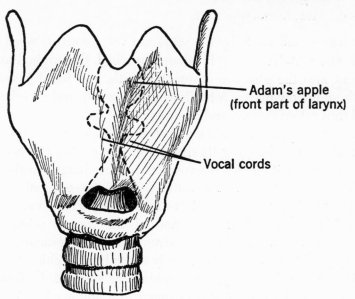

Adam's apple
(front part of larynx)

Vocal cords

THE LARYNX. The dotted lines give an x-ray
view of the vocal cords housed inside.

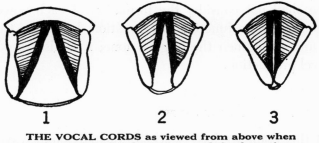

1   2   3

THE VOCAL CORDS as viewed from above when
(1) breathing, (2) whispering, and (3) phonating.

cords. These vocal cords are a pair of valvelike membranes
fixed in a horizontal position in the larynx. The vocal membranes are like two blunt, yet soft and pliable, ax edges whose
points face one another, and their length is less than one inch.

All air which is inhaled or exhaled must pass between
them. Air, forced up from the lungs, passes between the tight-
ened cords and vibrates them. This vibration produces sound
waves, the raw material of what is eventually to be speech.

4. THE RESONATION STEP

The sound made by the vibrating vocal cords is weak and lacks richness. To be amplified and enriched, the original sound is sent into the pharynx (throat), mouth, and nasal passages. In these hollow places, it is allowed to resonate and reverberate and thus attain volume and beauty.

One resonator, the mouth, has another very important obligation. By changing its shape and size during the production of speech it creates the vowels. Just as changes in the size and shape of automobile mufflers alter the original sound, changes in the mouth alter the sound of a person's voice. The movement of facial muscles and of the tongue within the mouth create variations in the structure of the resonator. For instance, the *ee* in *see* is commonly made by stretching the lips to form a small opening and arching the tongue. In forming the *o* of *go*, the resonator is changed to a hollowed shape; the lips are rounded, and extra enlargement is given to the cavity by a drawing back of the tongue.

We shall not consider the formation of each vowel, but remember that the function of resonation does more than enhance and strengthen the original tone; it is also responsible for vowel production.

5. THE ARTICULATION STEP

At this point we have voice—resonated sound waves—but we do not have speech. The last phase, which we call articulation, has to do with forming consonants, and joining or blending them with vowels and other consonants. Principally involved in this process are the tongue, lips, teeth, and palate. These articulators perform their highly important tasks mainly by channeling and altering the passage of breath through the mouth and nose. Such is the nature of articulation, the final step in the production of speech, and as we shall see (pp. 131 ff), the source of the most common speaking disorder.

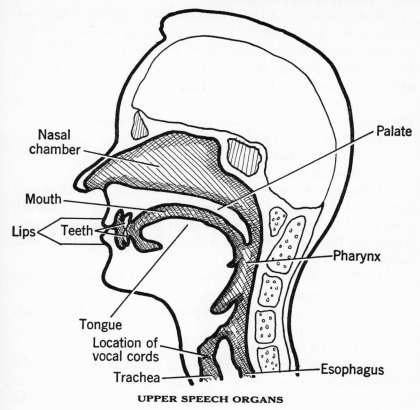

Nasal chamber

Palate

Mouth

Lips

Teeth

Pharynx

Tongue

Location of vocal cords

Trachea

Esophagus

UPPER SPEECH ORGANS

The Voice

Voice production is concerned with the steps of breathing, phonation, and resonation, and it is during these phases that distinguishing vocal characteristics of pitch, volume, duration, and quality are developed.

Pitch or frequency, as it is sometimes called, is the characteristic of a sound as it relates to the musical scale, the frequency with which the sound-producing object vibrates. The greater the number of vibrations, the higher is the pitch.

Each person's voice has a certain pitch level that may be considered high, low, or medium. The level depends upon the *tension, length,* and *weight* of the vocal cords. It is because of differences in these three features that women's voices are unlike men's, for example. Female cords are shorter. On the average, women's vocal cords are a half inch in length, while those of men average three-fourths of an inch. Then, too, female cords are stretched more tightly and weigh less.

Basically, there are three pitch conditions which can call attention to one's speaking and cause communication to suffer:

1. When it is too high;
2. When it is too low;
3. When it lacks variety (monotonous).

Volume or loudness is another factor that characterizes a voice. It is dependent upon the amount of a person's *breath power* and the degree of *amplification given by the resonators*. There are three conditions of volume that give speakers difficulty:

1. When it is too great (not adjusted to the room size, for example);
2. When it is too weak (especially at the ends of words or thoughts);
3. When it lacks variety.

Duration is the length of time a sound lasts, mainly the vowel sounds. An extending or prolonging of the vowels results in a drawn out characteristic commonly called a drawl. An omitting or cropping of the vowels results in a rapid or possibly staccato speech pattern. The two chief problems, then, are:

1. Overlengthening of the vowels;
2. Eliminating or shortening of the vowels.

Quality is difficult to explain in a few words, but perhaps we can be helped by a statement of Roy C. McCall. He explains quality as "that element of voice which makes one voice recognizably different from another or which makes it possible for us upon hearing a voice to say to whom it belongs."[1] Quality is that vocal characteristic most like a fingerprint; no two people have identical voice quality.

Quality is determined by the nature of the sound waves

---

[1] Roy C. McCall, *Fundamentals of Speech*, New York, The Macmillan Co., 1949.

you produce. Some sound waves have more noise elements, and some have more harmonious or musical elements. The greater the degree of harmony, the better the quality. Five common faults are:

1. Nasality (too much resonance in the nasal passages)
2. Denasality (too little nasal resonance, for example, when you have a cold)
3. Harshness
4. Hoarseness
5. Breathiness

Should a study of your voice indicate certain faults, what should you do then? First of all, consult your speech teacher for advice. It may be that what you consider to be faults really do not interfere with your communication. On the other hand, if your problem is a serious one, perhaps a program of correction can be set up for you, or you can take a special course in vocal improvement. Should you seek appropriate guidance and follow it earnestly, you can be assured that your chances for betterment are great.

Articulation

Articulation, you remember, is that phase of speech production during which the consonants are formed and joined with vowels. In a way, the articulators have a function similar to that of a football quarterback. It is up to him to decide upon the manner of advancing the ball, and it is up to the articulators to call the signals for advancing (emitting) the breath stream. If a "t" is to be uttered, the tongue tip is placed against the upper teeth or gum ridge; for an "m," the lips are placed together momentarily. The main inconsistency in our football analogy is that the articulators "call more plays" in a minute of speaking than a quarterback calls during an entire game. The average college student delivering a speech utters about 150 words per minute, and the average word is made up of four or five sounds. Therefore, the speech mechanism must handle at least 600 sound units a minute. Knowing the complexities of the articulatory process makes it easier for us to understand why it may break down under fatigue or emotional stress. It is no wonder that the articulators fumble a sound occasionally.

What is the difference between misarticulation and mispronunciation? In our treatment of speech delivery, we shall attempt to make little distinction; for the most part, they will be considered as a single problem of oral communication. However, Paul L. Soper offers an unusually clear explanation that we might keep in mind: "Pronunciation . . . refers to standards of correctness and to regional differences. Articulation refers to distinctness of pronunciation. We mispronounce words when we do not know how to pronounce them; we misarticulate words when we know how to pronounce them correctly but do not." [2] Therefore, if you say "mis-CHEE-ve-us" for *mischievous* you are mispronouncing a word. If you say *"nystays"* for United States you are guilty of misarticulation.

The most common reasons for poor articulation and faulty pronunciation are habit, carelessness, and occasionally indifference. People become accustomed to certain patterns and forms, frequently without an awareness of error. In childhood, one learns to speak by listening to others. By adopting the characteristics of those around him and by fusing them with his own personality, he develops a pattern of expression. It may be a pattern which has a minimum of articulation faults, or it may be sprinkled with many errors.

Together, indistinctness and incorrectness constitute the most common speech disorder, and since it is so prevalent, there is a possibility that you have difficulty with certain sounds or words. What are your problem spots? Let us ask some specific questions.

1. Do you ever incorrectly *substitute* one sound for another?

d *for* th—   dat *for* that, da *for* the, dis *for* this
d *for* t—   liddle *for* little, starded *for* started

---

[2] Paul L. Sopher, *Basic Public Speaking*, New York, Oxford, 1956, p. 163.

er *for* uh— idear *for* idea, amoeber *for* amoeba
u *for* aw— yur *for* your, fur *for* for
uh *for* oo— tuhday *for* today, ought tuh *for* ought to,
  yuh *for* you
uh *for* o— winduh *for* window, yelluh *for* yellow
ih *for* ee— crik *for* creek
ih *for* uh— jist *for* just
ih *for* eh— git *for* get

2. Do you ever *insert* extra sounds?

ath-*uh*-lete—athlete   umb*e*r-ella—umbrella
Ap-*e*r-il—April   acros*t*—across
fil-*u*m—film   e*k*scape—escape
sin-*y*ew—sinew

3. Do you ever *omit* important sounds?

em—them   er—her
hep—help   kep—kept
slep—slept   libary—library
at—that   lenth—length
diffrent—different   guvment—government
probly—probably   thurly—thoroughly
runnin—running   singin—singing
pitcher—picture   actshly—actually

4. Do you ever misplace an accent?

The-A-ter—THE-a-ter
im-PIE-ous—IM-pi-ous
AD-dult—a-DULT
pre-FER-a-ble—PREF-er-a-ble
FY-nance—fi-NANCE
AD-dress—a-DDRESS
HO-tel—ho-TEL

Indistinctness and incorrectness are even more apparent

when observed in continuous discourse. You have heard utterances similar to the following:

"Jeet?"—Did you eat?
"Wutchadoonigh?"—What are you doing tonight?
"Ahm gonna cuz uh hafta."—I'm going to because I have to.
"On Hallaween we sawr a hunderd punkins."—On Halloween we saw a hundred pumpkins.

Improving Your Expression

Force of habit, indifference, and carelessness cause people to give a poor representation of themselves. Faulty expression may not be a detriment to communication in the early years of one's life when his guiding standard is that of the "gang" or the neighborhood. Nevertheless, most people, and certainly those acquiring an advanced education, want to achieve success in their chosen fields. In the majority of occupations, advancement depends considerably upon skill in communication. At a certain rung on the ladder of success, a person begins to realize that he must speak correctly and clearly. It may happen when he receives a promotion or when he is selected to represent his company.

What do you want for yourself? How far do you want to go? You may be able to go further than you presently realize, and it is time to make preparations for the future. In addition to preparing yourself in accounting, engineering, social work, sales, or music, and so forth, attend to your speech habits—your voice, pronunciation, and articulation. Become conscious of any vocal problems and of the sounds you omit, substitute, insert, or accent improperly. Torture yourself a bit by consciously reminding yourself of the need to put the *ern* syllable in *government* or an *ng* in *running*. Strive for more vocal variety and expressiveness. You may feel awkward and self-conscious at first, but with willingness and work you can make clear, distinct speech a part of you.

GOOD DELIVERY

As we have seen, delivering ideas involves a speaker's total self and especially his personality, his outward bodily movements, his voice, his articulation, and his pronunciation. Consequently, what a speaker is and what a speaker does determine whether he will be effective in delivering his message. What should *you* be and what should *you* do in order to be successful?

1. *Have the welfare of your audience at heart.* We cannot separate character and intent from speaking, nor can we say that one who seeks to delude or deceive is a good speaker. It is true that charlatans and swindlers seem to be quite effective for a time, but eventually people are able to see through the false front and, as a result, reject their ideas. As the man, so is his speech. Honesty, sincerity, and respect for others are constituents of good delivery. As one criterion, we have the provocative point of view held by Quintilian and other renowned speech scholars that *the good speaker is the good man speaking well.*

2. *Have something that you want to say.* Ideas coupled with a desire to convey the ideas are prerequisites to good delivery. Your subject matter and how you feel about it should influence the manner in which you express it. Good delivery, then, should be a natural response to a yearning to communicate your ideas.

3. *Make a personal investment.* Assuming that you have chosen content that you want to deliver, you should release yourself and deliver it. Let your personality, body, and voice speak out for you. Let yourself go. You may be amazed at how effective you can be when you are able to free your real self. One who gives little, gets little in return, and a willingness to invest yourself in the speaking situation will bring you truly satisfying rewards.

4. *Try to remove distracting elements when practicing.* A sincere speaker who is concentrating upon delivering his ideas

to his audience is doing about all that can be asked of him at the moment. Before the speech, however, during practice sessions and in daily life, he can do much to prevent the inclusion of negative elements. He can sharpen his articulation, practice pitch variation, and otherwise be alert to correcting faults. Prior to giving your speech, when rehearsing you should attempt to exclude from your style any characteristic which competes with your ideas for the attention of listeners. When actually giving the speech, though, your concentration ought to be on your ideas and not on yourself.

LET US SUMMARIZE

When one makes a speech, one's personality, body, and voice should work naturally and harmoniously together. Only during rehearsal should one be concerned with improving his techniques of delivery. As he gives the speech, his concern should be with ideas. Good delivery places four basic demands upon you:

1. You should have the welfare of your audience at heart.
2. You should have something that you want to say.
3. You should make a personal investment.
4. You should do nothing that calls attention to itself.

A passage from the writings of Thomas Carlyle provides an excellent final thought for our discussion of delivery.

> Let each become all that he was created capable of being; expand if possible, to his full growth; resisting all impediments, casting off all foreign, especially all noxious adhesions; and show himself at length in his own shape and stature, be these what they may.

FOR FURTHER STUDY

Anderson, Virgil A., *Training the Speaking Voice* (New York, Oxford, 1942).

Eisensen, Jon, *The Improvement of Voice and Diction* (New York, The Macmillan Co., 1958).

Fairbanks, Grant, *Voice and Articulation Drillbook* (New York, Harper, 1940).

Hahn, Elise, Lomas, Charles, W., Hargis, Donald, and Vandraegen, Daniel, *Basic Voice Training for Speech* (New York, McGraw-Hill, 1952).

McCall, Roy C., *Fundamentals of Speech* (New York, The Macmillan Co., 1949), Ch. VIII, "The Visible Aspects of Speech." This is highly recommended.

Redding, W. Charles, "Presentation of the Debate Speech," in *Argumentation and Debate*, ed. by David Potter (New York, Holt-Dryden, 1954), pp. 229-239. This is highly recommended for all speakers.

SUGGESTED EXERCISE A

Analyze your delivery characteristics. Do you have speaking habits (other than those which require specialized attention such as stuttering) which call attention to themselves? Enlist the services of your friends, the instructor, your family, or a tape recorder to help you in the analysis.

Make specific suggestions for improvement under three headings: Voice, Body, and Articulation-Pronunciation.

SAMPLE

Voice

1. Needs more variety; should bring out the full color of my ideas.
2. In too much of a hurry; should take time to express the meaning.

Body

1. Constantly shift my weight from one foot to the other. This takes the listener's mind off my speech.
2. I twist the ring on my finger. Probably half the class could describe my ring

Articulation—Pronunciation

1. *Substitutions:* git (get), jist (just), fur (for), yur (your), becuz (because)
2. *Additions:* Aperil (April), filum (film), acrost (across)
3. *Omissions:* gover-ment (government), singin (singing), walkin (walking), lenth (length), kep (kept), probly (probably)
4. *Misplaced accents:* luh-MENT-uh-ble (LAM-en-tuh-ble), dih-CIP-lin (DIS-uh-plin)

SUGGESTED EXERCISE B

Make a list of sentences which include examples of your pronunciation and articulation faults. Practice by saying each sentence twice; first, incorrectly and then, correctly. Do this until the appropriate expression comes easily.

SUGGESTED EXERCISE C

Listen to a speaker, someone outside the class, and analyze his vocal, body-movement, pronunciation, and articulation characteristics. List the features which seem to call attention to themselves.

SUGGESTED EXERCISE D

Practice reading one of the speech excerpts below. Put yourself into the reading in order to bring out the full meaning; invest yourself—your personality, your voice, and your body. Sound the words clearly and accurately. Add other selections of your own choice when you have perfected these.

Practice many times until you are convinced that you are adequately expressing the content. A tape recording will help you to determine how successful you are.

> With malice toward none; with charity for all; with firmness in the right, as God gives us to see the right, let us strive on to finish the work we are in; to bind up the nation's wounds; to care for him who shall have borne the battle, and for his widow, and his orphan—to do all which may achieve and

cherish a just and lasting peace among ourselves, and with all nations.

—ABRAHAM LINCOLN, *Second Inaugural Address,* 1865

The unity of government which constitutes you one people is also now dear to you. It is justly so, for it is a main pillar in the edifice of your real independence, the support of your tranquility at home, your peace abroad, of your safety, of your prosperity, of that very liberty which you so highly prize. But as it is easy to foresee that from different causes and from different quarters much pains will be taken, many artifices employed to weaken in your minds the conviction of this truth, as this is the point in your political fortress against which the batteries of internal and external enemies will be most constantly and actively (though often covertly and insidiously) directed, it is of infinite moment that you should properly estimate the immense value of your national union to your collective and individual happiness; that you should cherish a cordial, habitual, and immovable attachment to it; accustoming yourselves to think and speak of it as the palladium of your political safety and prosperity; watching for its preservation with jealous anxiety; discountenancing whatever may suggest even a suspicion that it can in any event be abandoned, and indignantly frowning upon the first dawning of every attempt to alienate any portion of our country from the rest or to enfeeble the sacred ties which now link together the various parts.

—GEORGE WASHINGTON, *Farewell Address,* 1796

My urgent advice to you would be, not only aways to think first of America, but always, also, to think first of humanity. You do not love humanity if you seek to divide humanity into jealous camps. Humanity can be welded together only by love, by sympathy, by justice, not by jealousy and hatred. I am sorry for the man who seeks to make personal capital out of the passions of his fellow-men. He has lost the touch and ideal of America, for America was created to unite mankind by those passions which lift and not by the passions which separate and debase. We came to America, either ourselves or in the persons of our ancestors, to better the ideals of men, to make them see finer things than they had seen before, to get rid of the things that divide and to make sure of the things that unite. It was but an historical accident no doubt that this great country was called the "United States"; yet I am very thankful that it has the word "United" in its title, and the man who seeks to divide man from man, group from group, interest from interest in this great Union is striking at its very heart.

—WOODROW WILSON, *Address to Foreign-born Citizens*, 1915

In the future days, which we seek to make secure, we look forward to a world founded upon four essential human freedoms.

The first is freedom of speech and expression—everywhere in the world.

The second is freedom of every person to worship God in his own way—everywhere in the world.

The third is freedom from want—which, translated into world terms, means economic understanding which will secure to every nation a healthy peacetime life for its inhabitants—everywhere in the world.

The fourth is freedom from fear—which, translated into world terms, means a world-wide reduction of armaments to such point and in such a thorough fashion that no nation will be in a position to commit an act of physical aggression against any neighbor—anywhere in the world.

That is no vision of a distant millennium. It is a definite basis for a kind of world attainable in our own time and generation.

—FRANKLIN D. ROOSEVELT, *Message to Congress*,
January 6, 1941

A ship lost at sea for many days suddenly sighted a friendly vessel. From the mast of the unfortunate vessel was seen a signal, "Water, water; we die of thirst!" The answer from the friendly vessel at once came back, "Cast down your bucket where you are." And a third and fourth signal for water was answered, "Cast down your bucket where you are." The captain of the distressed vessel, at last heeding the injunction, cast down his bucket and it came up full of fresh, sparkling water from the mouth of the Amazon River. To those of my race who depend upon bettering their condition in a foreign land or who underestimate the importance of cultivating friendly relations with the Southern white man, who is their next-door neighbor, I would say: "Cast down your bucket where you are"—cast it down in making friends in every manly way of the people of all races by whom we are surrounded.

—BOOKER T. WASHINGTON, *Atlanta Exposition Address*, 1895

SUGGESTED EXERCISE E

How many of the words listed below with approximate phonetic spellings are troublesome to you? Do you sound them distinctly and accurately? Can you add some to the list? Write an anecdote in which you include those most difficult for you. Spell them phonetically. Review the exercise daily, and be ready to read it when the instructor calls on you.

acquiesce	AK-we-ess
adversary	AD-ver-sair-y
agile	AD-jul
alacrity	uh-LAC-ruh-ty
arduous	AR-dyoo-us
armistice	AR-mis-tus
bade	bad
barbarous	BAR-buh-rus
cello	CHEL-o
cement	sih-MENT
chasm	KAZ-um
chaste	chased
comparable	KAHM-puh-ruh-bl
copious	KO-pee-us
corps	cor

dearth	durth
decadent	dih-KAY-dunt
defense	dih-FENCE
detail	dih-TAIL
discretion	dis-KRESH-uhn
docile	DAHS-uhl
efficacy	EF-uh-kuh-sy
emaciate	ih-MAY-shee-ayt
epitome	ih-PIT-uh-me
exquisite	EX-kwih-zit
gala	GAY-luh
genuine	JEN-yoo-in
gesture	JES-tyer
grievous	GREE-vuhs
gross	grohs
hearth	harth
height	hite
hiccough	HIK-up
human	HYOO-mun
infamous	IN-fuh-mus
inference	IN-fuh-ruhns
insurance	in-SHOOR-uhns
Italian	ih-TAL-yun
integral	IN-tuh-gruhl
irrevocable	ih-REV-uh-kuh-bl
library	LY-brer-y
maintenance	MAIN-tuh-nuhns
municipal	mew-NIS-uh-pl
naive	nah-EEV
novice	NAHV-ihs
orgy	OR-jy
propitious	pruh-PISH-us
recess	rih-SESS
rendezvous	RAHN-duh-voo
respite	REHS-piht
saga	SAHG-uh
salmon	SAM-uhn

schizophrenia	skiz-uh-FREEN-nih-uh
scion	SY-uhn
servile	SER-vl
solace	SOL-ihs
subtle	SUHT-uhl
suite	sweet
superfluous	soo-PUHR-flew-uhs
tyrannical	tih-RAN-uh-kl
vehement	VEE-uh-munt
wane	wayn
zoology	zo-AHL-uh-jy

9

Improving Listening Skills

HOW IMPORTANT IS LISTENING?

An ancient proverb tells us, "He who speaks, sows; who listens, reaps." Now while we might argue that he who speaks also reaps and gains great satisfaction from his speaking, we cannot overlook the other vital aspect of oral communication—listening.

Where does a good listener do his "reaping"? He may do it, of course, whenever he listens, which is more frequently than most people realize. Paul Rankin at The Ohio State University found that adults spend about 70 percent of their daytime hours engaging in communication activities. They devote 9 percent of this time to writing, 16 percent to reading, 30 percent to speaking, and *45 percent to listening*. The study indicates that about a third of our lives is spent in listening.

In the classroom and in one's everyday life, effective listening helps one to get along and to learn. Wilson Mizner expresses it humorously: "A good listener is not only popular everywhere, but after awhile he knows something." Getting the most out of our hours of leisure requires adequate listening habits. Enough of our time is spent these days in front of the television set and watching plays and movies that getting the maximum benefits from such experiences becomes important. Then, too, rearing a family, carrying out civic obligations, and being successful on the job demand proper listening. "Nobody ever listened himself out of a job," remarked Calvin Coolidge. The benefits of good listening cannot be overrated wherever we find a message worthy of our attention.

WHAT IS LISTENING?

To listen is to do more than to hear. Hearing is a physiological function and involves *receiving* a message; listening is a mental function which involves *perceiving* a message. After a sound or series of sounds is picked up by the auditory mechanism and transmitted to the higher nerve centers—after it is heard—it must be interpreted and given meaning. Once the message is received, skill in listening is dependent upon how well the message is translated and understood.

We are dealing then, with a mental process. Actually, there are two mental processes to be considered. Listening is part of a two-way act between the one who originates the message and the one for whom the message is intended. Each agency in this transaction should have a purpose. A speaker's goal will be to entertain, to inform, or to persuade, but what is the listener's goal? Since he and the speaker are "in it together," it is logical to assume that his purpose is determined by that of the speaker, and the listener must adjust himself accordingly. Though speakers and, therefore, listeners have multiple and overlapping general goals, let us discuss three main ones.

1. TO ENJOY

We listen to stories, after-dinner speeches, poetry reading, or dramatic programs mainly to be entertained. The usual attitude that we assume in such a situation might be called one of attentive relaxation. Our listening behavior is guided by our tastes, by what we as individuals appreciate.

2. TO UNDERSTAND

This is a basic listening goal. To understand does not mean to accept but merely to know what the speaker means. We listen to understand sermons, class lectures, newscasts, debates, and conversations. We may want to remember a speaker's ideas, to apply or reject them, but, first, we must understand what he is saying.

3. TO EVALUATE

Critical listening places heavy demands upon the listener, a burden that we who live in a free country must carry. We are guaranteed freedom of speech which means that a person can say nearly anything he wishes. Yet, we do not have to condone every speaker or to accept all of his ideas. In fact, one of our prime democratic responsibilities is to develop an ability to judge, to learn how to think critically. Thoughtful critics help to maintain in American society a wholesome spirit of checks and balances. Listening to evaluate, critical listening, is everybody's daily business.

HOW DOES LISTENING BREAK DOWN?

Many studies have been made in recent years to find out how well people listen. The results indicate that there is much room for improvement of listening skills; people do not listen as well as they should. Tests show that, at best, the average person retains only 60 to 70 percent of what he has heard, and after a lapse of time the percentage scores drop markedly. From a study of many cases, Ralph G. Nichols and Thomas R.

Lewis, leaders in speech education and listening research, draw this conclusion about the problem of listening deficiency:

> It would seem that after a lapse of two months or more, learning through listening seldom operates at more than a 25-percent level of efficiency. In the bulk of these studies the materials orally presented were usually ten or fifteen minutes in duration.[1]

There are several critical factors to be analyzed in the study of listening. The difficulty may be traced back to the speaker, to the physical environment, to the listener, or to a combination of these elements. If the speaker does not do his part, he cannot expect the audience to listen to him. When there are extraneous noises and other environmental conditions which compete with the listener and speaker, there is a definite possibility of breakdown in the listening process. Finally, the fault can rest with the listener himself. If communication is to occur, he must do more than occupy a seat. He must be willing to accept an active role.

HOW CAN LISTENING BE IMPROVED?

Let us look on the positive side of the problem and consider the three elements of the communicative process mentioned above as they apply to you.

The Speaker

The speaker, of course, must assume his share of the responsibility for establishing communication. You are aware of the specific criteria that you follow in preparing and delivering a talk, and we need not review those now. In general, though, you have three basic obligations:

[1] Ralph G. Nichols and Thomas R. Lewis, *Listening and Speaking*, Dubuque, Iowa, Brown, 1954. p. 4.

1. To choose your ideas wisely;
2. To use proven methods of composition;
3. To adapt your speech to the audience.

The Environment

The physical environment should be conducive to good listening. We all know how important it is to have a fitting atmosphere accompanying any activity. Somehow, a steak eaten in a restaurant by candlelight and with soft music playing in the background tastes better than it would if it were eaten in a brightly illuminated and noisy setting. It is the atmosphere that makes the difference. When you are a chairman or otherwise responsible for a speaker-listener situation, it is your obligation to set up and maintain an atmosphere appropriate for the occasion:

1. By controlling distracting noises;
2. By providing ample ventilation;
3. By controlling the temperature of the room;
4. By providing comfortable and properly arranged seating;
5. By making the environment attractive.

The Listener

The listener, as a partner in the communication enterprise, should hold up his end of the unwritten compact that he has with the speaker. Attentiveness is dictated by simple courtesy, if not also by the possible benefits of knowledge and enjoyment that can be gained from a speaker. In fairness to the speaker, to the audience as a whole, and to yourself as a listener you have the following responsibilities. Let us call them Guides to Good Listening.

1. *Come with a desire to participate.* Be ready and willing to be a listener. The speaker needs you, and it is very

likely that he will have something to offer in return for your participation.

2. *Choose an appropriate seat.* Find a spot which will allow you to see and hear comfortably. If you are one of the 4-6 percent who have serious hearing losses, you will want to seat yourself close to the speaker.

3. *Handle distractions.* Some distractions are unavoidable while others can be eliminated. If the construction gang down the corridor cannot be asked to desist, you must do your best to "listen louder than they are pounding." Whisperers, however, can be given courteous suggestions to be quiet; doors and windows can be opened or closed depending on the need, and lights can be turned on. It should be each listener's duty to help curtail distracting physical elements and to ignore those which cannot be eliminated.

Distractions that are emotional in nature may be even more bothersome. A listener brings with him a complex of feelings. On Monday he may be confident and secure, but on Wednesday he may come plagued with certain anxieties and extensive self-concern (even though he does not have to speak that day). How can he put aside his personal disturbances and attend the speaker? The answer is not a simple one, nor do we presume that you will solve the problem by reading a chapter on listening. Nonetheless, there are some possible starting points. First of all, some people find that they can side-step their own feelings by plunging themselves wholeheartedly into a speaker's speech, by giving their keen attention to the speech, and eventually by forgetting about themselves. Others get success by self-analysis. They attempt to determine why they feel as they do, why their personal problems are more stimulating than the speaker's ideas. A listener's competing feelings constitute one of the major obstacles to communication.

There is another type of distraction which stems from one's reactions to the speaker. Have you ever considered someone a bit strange until you got to know him? Sometimes speakers have individual characteristics that tempt a listener to be distracted. It may be a speaker's unusual mannerism, his voice, the style of his clothes, or the way he walks. In a large American city there is a man so skilled in speaking that hundreds come to hear him. The fact that he has a decided lisp does not deter his listeners. Because he has something to say and the ability to say it and because his audiences are unwilling to be distracted, all participants profit. Listen for ideas, and ignore the minor, seemingly peculiar characteristics that you may notice.

4. *Give the speaker a fair chance to reach you.* Give the speaker the courtesy of a hearing; go along with him as far as you can go. Look at him, and acknowledge his comments; let him know that you are with him. Repress your prejudices and preconceived ideas. Try to be patient, and avoid drawing conclusions too hastily. After you hear him out and understand his ideas, then you can decide upon what ideas to accept and what ideas to reject.

5. *Analyze.* Make an over-all running analysis during the speech. Be alert and grasp the speaker's purpose, first of all. Remember that it may be stated directly or merely implied.

When you have perceived his purpose, work along with the speaker by mentally outlining the points and subpoints he sets down in developing the purpose. To help reconstruct the broad structure of his speech, you should observe little cues which indicate his movement from thought to thought. Such transitional aids are usually verbal, but very often they are enhanced by vocal inflection or body movements. Since seeing is a part of listening, facial expressions and gestures can assist you in following the flow of ideas.

Immediately after the speech, analyze further. Think back to the speaker, the reasoning he used, and the conclusions he drew. Ask yourself some key questions. Was his appeal basically emotional or did he reinforce his talk with logic? Did he have enough evidence to support his generalizations? Did he have an ax to grind? Is he a man of character? Can you believe in him? All speeches should be subjected to this type of postanalysis but especially those that are intended to change our beliefs and influence our actions.

LET US SUMMARIZE

Perhaps the only activity which takes up more of our time than listening is sleeping. Since listening is such a frequent and vital function and *can be improved*, it is indeed a waste of human resources when neglected. How much have you missed in your life because of your listening habits? How many times have you responded to the persuasive efforts of speakers only to be sorry later that you had been so gullible? Realistically, it is impossible for us to measure what we have wasted by our mistakes and perhaps foolish to do so anyway. The truly hopeful prospect is that it is not too late. You can strengthen your ability to enjoy oral presentations, to understand, and to evaluate. To do so, you should

1. Do your part in setting up and in maintaining pleasant surroundings;
2. Come with a view toward listening;
3. Choose an appropriate seat;
4. Handle distractions;
5. Give the speaker a fair chance to reach you;
6. Analyze during and after the speech.

FOR FURTHER STUDY

Brigance, W. Norwood, *Speech Communication*, 2d ed. (New York, Appleton-Century-Crofts, 1955), Ch. 12, "Listening Efficiently."

Gilman, Wilbur E., Aly, Bower, and Reid, Loren D., *The Fundamentals of Speaking* (New York, The Macmillan Co., 1954), Ch. 22, "Listening to Speeches."

Nichols, Ralph G., and Lewis, Thomas R., *Listening and Speaking* (Dubuque, Ia., Brown, 1954).

—— and Stevens, Leonard A., *Are You Listening?* (New York, McGraw-Hill, 1957).

Oliver, Robert T., Dickey, Dallas C., and Zelko, Harold P., *Com-*

municative Speech, rev. ed. (New York, Holt-Dryden, 1955), Ch. 4, "Effective Listening."

Weaver, Andrew T., and Ness, Ordean G., *The Fundamentals and Forms of Speech* (New York, Odyssey, 1957), Ch. 5, "How to Listen Effectively."

SUGGESTED EXERCISE A

Make an honest and objective analysis of your own listening characteristics. As you analyze, keep in mind typical speaker-audience situations in which you might find yourself. Include in the report answers to the following questions:

1. On what basis do you choose your seat?
2. What factors might cause any lack of desire to listen or closed-mind attitude on your part?
3. What methods have you devised for handling your own distracting emotions?
4. In what situations might you deny speakers your full participation?
5. Are you usually able to grasp a speaker's purpose and main ideas?
6. Usually are you able to determine when a speaker is employing a transitional aid?
7. What are some characteristics of delivery and language usage that you have allowed to distract you recently?
8. What is your usual practice in analyzing a speaker's reasoning, judgments, character, and personal interests?

SUGGESTED EXERCISE B

Toward the end of the hour on a day of student speaking, your instructor may test your listening by asking you to answer key questions about the speeches. Be ready!

SAMPLE

1. *May's speech:* What was the proposition?
2. *John's speech:* What were the main heads?
3. *Roger's speech:* Where did he neglect to employ a needed transition?

4. *Marjorie's speech:* What samples of sound reasoning did you note?

5. *Sam's speech:* Which supporting materials seemed especially effective?

SUGGESTED EXERCISE C

Observe an off-campus audience and list the weaker listening habits as you see them. You may be asked to use your list as the basis of a short speech or discussion.

SUGGESTED EXERCISE D

Your instructor will read to the class an article containing controversial ideas. Attempt to follow faithfully the thoughts during the presentation.

1. After the reading, *interpret* what the author wrote by listing his main ideas.

2. Next, *evaluate* each idea by telling why you agree or disagree with it. Show fairness in interpretation and intelligence in evaluation.

3. Is there a difference between your interpretation and your evaluation?

SUGGESTED EXERCISE E

On radio or television listen to a controversial news analyst. After you have heard him, repeat the directions in Suggested Exercise D.

SUGGESTED EXERCISE F

Analyze the environment of a speaker-audience situation you have been in recently.

1. Was the ventilation adequate? If not, how might it have been improved?

2. Were there distracting noises? If so, how might they have been handled?

3. Was the room temperature satisfactory? Too hot? Too cold?

4. Were the seats reasonably comfortable and well arranged? If not, what improvements would you have made?
5. Were the speaker's needs met? If necessary, did he have a properly functioning microphone and a speaking stand? Was he placed in a satisfactory location from which to address the audience?

SUPPLEMENTARY
METHODS

10

Participating in Group Discussion

EXCHANGING IDEAS

> Where there is no mastery of the medium for exchanging ideas, ideas cease to play a part in human life.
> —MORTIMER J. ADLER [1]

This chapter is about discussion, exchanging ideas with others in a group. This we do quite frequently and in all sorts of settings. An interesting discussion took place recently in a student council meeting:

HANK: Well, I got the word just a few minutes ago. They aren't coming!

EARL: Who isn't coming?

HANK: The quintet for our show on the 20th.

PATTY: Not coming? Why, they can't do that! We've had this arranged for a month.

HANK: I know, I know, but what can you say when the booking agent tells you, "Sorry, but Mr. Raine's group will be playing at the University of Washington on February 20th"?

---

[1] Mortimer J. Adler, *How to Read a Book*, New York, Simon and Schuster, 1940, p. 365.

EARL: And just ten days to go! We've got a problem!

HANK: That's life, one problem after another!

Even though we sympathize with Hank, that *is* life—one problem after another. Some problems are easy; some are difficult, but we all have them.

Of course we should attempt to answer most of life's perplexing questions ourselves by using past experiences and our powers of reasoning and investigation. To a large degree, a person's growth and maturity are dependent upon his learning to handle his own affairs, for a mature person cannot expect someone else to solve all of his problems. Nevertheless, there are times when *group action* is necessary. The problem-solving process is often more democratic and more effective that way. One student cannot be given the sole responsibility for allocating student-body funds, for example. The job is too big and, besides, others deserve to have a voice in the matter. Many points of view must be represented and expressed. "How much money should be spent on athletics?" "What can we cut in order to balance the budget?" "Should we grant the band an extra $200?" If you have ever been a part of such an important group, you know the problems involved. Hours of discussion must be spent in deliberation if fair and intelligent decisions are to be made.

Group discussion is necessary in all phases of life—social, political, economic, educational, and religious. The family assembles to talk things over. A senator calls his committee together. The schoolboard convenes. Church leaders hold a meeting. Or a group of friends sit down to work out a solution to a mutual problem informally; several heads are better than one. It behooves everyone to understand this frequently used and effective democratic process.

THE DISCUSSION PROCESS

Before going on, let us make a distinction. The main oral assignments for this unit of work will call for participation in forms of public discussion (panel, symposium, lecture panel), those presented before audiences. Even though the majority of one's discussion experiences are informal or not public, training in public discussion helps to prepare one for less formal situations such as committee meetings or family conferences.

Now, a discussion designed to determine a plan or reach a solution is more than aimless talk. As with other forms of speech with which you are familiar, there should be a purpose for speaking. The discussion method of oral communication is but another type of speech making, a type set up as a problem-solving or information-getting venture. When a number of people discuss a question in a group, they build a speech together. Each member contributes his part to the total group effort. The speakers are guided by a leader who helps them move along in an organized manner toward the desired goal. They have a reason for deliberating, and they know that success depends upon their use of a proven method. Just as in making an individual speech, there are techniques to follow in making a "collective speech." There are fitting ways to start a discussion, to develop the body of it, and to conclude. All purposeful speech calls for a planned procedure.

CHOOSING THE SUBJECT

After a group has been formed, the first step in preparing for a discussion is to decide upon a subject, if a certain subject is not the cause for discussion in the first place. How is a subject chosen? You should, of course, choose a subject that is appropriate for you (your group), the audience, and the occasion. Let us be more specific.

1. *Your subject should be meaningful and interesting to all parties.* Avoid selecting an insignificant subject. Choose an area that touches upon the lives of the discussion members and the audience. What of importance is happening in the school, community, state, nation, or world at this time? Is there a question on the scene today that is worthy of investi-

gation and consideration? What are the present problems facing the student council or the city? Assemblies? Recreation? Elections? Juvenile delinquency? Is there a national matter of special significance to you? Draft laws? The vote for eighteen-year-olds? Narcotics laws?

2. *Your subject should be one with which you can increase your familiarity.* Can you learn more about it? To insure a worthwhile discussion, it is necessary to investigate, to find new information; therefore, it is necessary also to know if new information is available. You should survey possible sources of material before settling upon your subject.

3. *Your subject should be appropriate for the occasion.* In class, the setting usually remains the same unless a hypothetical situation is set up. If you plan a discussion for presentation elsewhere, you will be expected to adhere to the demands of the occasion.

NARROWING THE SUBJECT

Take a close look at your subject, and decide if it is too broad to be treated in the allotted time. If so, select a portion or division of it as your area for consideration. A group could talk endlessly on the subject of Lumbering without getting anywhere; whereas, a discussion on Improving Lumbering Practices might be quite profitable.

WORDING THE QUESTION

The specific question or proposition is worded to indicate the scope of the discussion. Like all propositions, it should contain one idea, be worded clearly and briefly. Unlike many propositions, it is frequently stated in the form of a question. A question suggests that the matter is *up for discussion* and unsolved at the present; it is open for consideration.

State the question fairly without bias or prejudice for a

particular point of view. An unfair question suggests that the group already agrees on the answer or solution. With such a question, the members cannot talk impartially, for they are prejudiced from the beginning. This violates the basic characteristic of group discussion: *an honest search for the solution to an important problem.* The inclusion of the italicized words in the following question makes it unworthy:

How can our *wayward* teenagers spend their time profitably?

Could a group in your class carry on an impartial search for a solution to this problem? It is not likely. The question makes a biased assumption, and a full hour could be spent in debate over the one word. These questions, also, are not worded fairly:

Should the *useless* system of giving final examinations be abolished?
What can be done to improve our *backward* school system?

Then, too, you should word the question in a way that will avoid setting up sides. If a discussion results in one side upholding the "con" and another side the "pro," you do not have a discussion; you have a debate; and the fault often lies in the wording of the question. Notice how these sentences suggest debate rather than cooperative problem solving:

Should all U. S. citizens be encouraged to live abroad for a year?
Should capital punishment be abolished?
Should speech be a required course?

Instead of discarding them let us restate each in a way which should encourage cooperative discussion:

What can we do to improve world understanding?
How should we punish those who commit the most serious crimes?
What can we do to provide training in oral communication for all students?

In summary, these are the marks of a good discussion question:

1. It contains one idea.
2. It is brief.
3. It is worded clearly.
4. It is frequently worded in the form of a question.
5. It is worded fairly.
6. It is designed to encourage discussion.

ORGANIZING THE DISCUSSION

How do you start? What steps are followed? Since discussion is based upon sound reasoning, it follows that the steps in the process should be related to the process of thinking. Most systems for organizing a discussion are offsprings of John Dewey's pattern for reflective thinking which we can interpret as follows:

1. Recognition of a problem condition;
2. Analysis (definition, limitation, causes and effects of the problem);
3. Consideration of possible solutions;
4. Selection of a satisfactory solution;
5. Implementation of the solution.

You can apply this same pattern in organizing a discussion. The outline below is an extension and adaptation of Dewey's steps in reflective thinking to the familiar speaking formula.

I. *Introduction* (presented by the leader)
   A. The area of difficulty
   B. General background
II. *Proposition* (statement of the problem as presently visualized)
III. *Body*
   A. Analysis of the problem

      1. Determining the extent of the problem; limiting and defining
      2. Citing causes and effects
    B. Consideration of possible solutions
      1. Strengths
      2. Weaknesses
IV. *Conclusion*
    A. Selection of a satisfactory solution
    B. Determining a course of action to put the solution into effect.

DETERMINING THE FORM

There are various forms which a discussion may take. Some are quite formal; others are more informal. Some demand more of the leader; others give the members a greater burden. Some call for a "guest expert"; others depend solely upon the original group. The one you use should be one which will provide the best framework for you to achieve your goals.

As we mentioned earlier, informal forms are used frequently by the leaders of businesses, churches, and clubs to solve the internal problems of their organizations. These are not public discussions because the officers or executives deliberate among themselves without the presence of an audience. Different names are often attached to such forms. Some may call them conferences. Others may refer to them as round tables, committee meetings, councils or merely meetings.

Three very useful forms for public discussion are the panel, the symposium, and the lecture panel.

The Panel

The *panel* is probably what most people have in mind when they think of group discussion. The participants assemble themselves before an audience in positions which will allow visual and oral contact with the audience and among the group. This may be accomplished by arranging the chairs in a semicircle or by placing the chairs around a table. The leader seats himself in a central position in view of the audience and panel members.

The panel is usually composed of four to seven persons, who, under the guidance of a leader, set about to resolve a difficulty in an orderly fashion. There are no "set" speeches. Each person taking part has studied the question carefully, and he may make contributions freely, based on his thorough preparation. This is not to say that he may talk of anything at any time. For the benefit of everyone concerned, all remarks should be pertinent to what is being discussed at a given moment. To help the group avoid straying from the point, the leader keeps an outline before him as a constant reminder of their over-all plan.

Take note of one word of caution regarding use of the outline. It should be an "assistant," not a "dictator." Use it; let it help you, but do not allow it to handcuff you. You know how it is in individual speaking. Occasionally you change some bit of your speech as you are speaking. You omit a certain example or add one. You think of a good statistic on the spur of the moment and decide to include it. You make adjustments because the situation seems to demand changes. Fresh thinking increases effectiveness. Maintain the basic structure of your discussion, but permit worthwhile alterations.

To illustrate a panel in action, let us examine a hypothetical case. We shall assume that Donna, Ron, Ruth, Vickie, and George have selected Improving School Dances as the subject for their panel and that George was chosen to lead it. They held two preliminary planning meetings, and each person, including the leader, studied the problem thoroughly. In one column below you see the general outline and beside it a summary of the discussion as it developed.

OUTLINE	ACTUAL DEVELOPMENT
I. *Introduction*	George introduced the panel members and explained why the
A. The area of difficulty	topic was up for discussion. He said that there had been some dis-
B. General background	satisfaction among the student body with the school dances and that such an essential part of school life should not be neglected.
II. *Proposition*	Let us consider the matter of improving school dances.
III. *Body*	George asked Donna if she felt that conditions were serious. Donna
A. Analysis of the problem	gave statistics to show that attendance had dropped 50 percent in the past two years. Ron cited
1. Extent of: limiting and defining	two examples of poorly attended dances. Ruth and Vickie agreed that the problem was serious and widespread, but all agreed that they should discuss student-body-sponsored dances only.
2. Citing causes and effects	"What are the causes?" asked George. Vickie presented the results of a poll she had taken of the student body which brought out two reasons for the disinterest: (1) too many juke box dances and (2) week-night scheduling. Ruth and Ron added two more causes: (1) competition with other community events and (2) lack of pub-

licity. Donna disagreed with the charge that there was insufficient publicity. She worked on the *Red and White* and has personally written several articles publicizing the dances. Ron said that other means of publicity had not been used.

George asked if there were any more possible causes, and Ruth stated that the gymnasium floor was poor for dancing.

B. Consideration of possible solutions

Donna spoke for having more dances with live music. Ron brought out the factor of cost. He cited figures to show why the student body could not afford it. Ruth got off the subject, and George reminded her of the present topic. Vickie agreed with Ron about the cost being great.

1. First solution: strengths and weaknesses.

2. Second solution: strengths and weaknesses.

"Why not hold the dances on Friday nights?" Ruth volunteered. Ron mentioned possible conflicts with athletic events. Donna said that games were not scheduled for every Friday night. "We could schedule our dances on other Friday nights," she added. Vickie agreed and pointed up the need to work out a schedule early in the year. Ron went back to the subject of live music for a moment but showed how it applied to the present topic.

George, who had been asking occasional questions and otherwise helping them along, summarized the two proposed solutions.

3. Third solution: strengths and weaknesses.

"What else can be done?" George asked.

Vickie told of the need to avoid conflicts with other local events. Ron stated that careful scheduling could prevent such difficulties, and Donna referred to what they had said about that matter earlier in the discussion.

4. Fourth solution: strengths and weaknesses.

Ron felt that more publicity would help. Vickie did not think that it was so vital in this case. George noticed that Ruth had been silent for a long time and spoke to her. "Ruth, we would like to hear your views on this idea." Ruth agreed with Vickie and expressed the necessity for wise scheduling.

IV. *Conclusion*

A. Selection of a satisfactory solution

Before summarizing, George made certain that no one had any more important contributions. "What is our best solution?" questioned George. The group weighed and evaluated each proposal they had made. They ruled out expensive orchestras and finally decided upon a combination of the second and third solutions: dances to be held on carefully selected Friday nights.

B. Determining a course of action

George restated the solution and announced, "All right, we have a solution, but what are we going to do with it? How can we put it into effect?" All agreed that the only way was to present their idea to the student council.

That afternoon George arranged for a hearing before the student council.

This is only a summary of a hypothetical panel discussion. Just the highlights were presented, and you can fill in the details mentally. We did not repeat all the examples, statistics, quotations, and visual aids that might have been used. We did not go into the finer points of leadership which George might have employed.

Nor did we suggest how much time elapsed during the discussion. Timing depends upon the peculiarities of the problem. For some questions it may take the majority of your allotted minutes developing the problem. Others require a longer consideration of solutions. Assuming that the preceding discussion lasted thirty minutes, the following is a *possible* distribution of time:

Area of difficulty and general background	3 minutes
Analysis of the problem	8 minutes
Consideration of possible solutions	11 minutes
Selecting a satisfactory solution	5 minutes
Determining a course of action	3 minutes

The Symposium

The *symposium* follows the same pattern of organization as the panel but differs in other ways. The panel is characterized by free exchange of ideas within the pattern; whereas the symposium is composed mainly of prepared speeches on phases or subtopics of the total problem. With the exception of the conclusion, a symposium is made up of a series of speeches similar to the ones you presented in the early part of this course. The conclusion in a symposium may be the same as in a panel discussion.

If we assigned George, Ron, Ruth, Vickie, and Donna to a thirty-minute symposium, their parts might be distributed as follows:

Area of difficulty and general background	George: 3 minutes
Analysis of the problem	Vickie: prepared speech, 6 minutes
First solution	Donna: prepared speech, 4 minutes
Second solution	Ruth: prepared speech, 4 minutes
Third solution	Ron: prepared speech, 4 minutes
Selecting a satisfactory solution and a course of action	Entire membership: panel discussion, 9 minutes

In addition to introducing the general area for discussion and guiding the concluding discussion, George has the responsibility of tying each speech together with effective transitions. For example, following Vickie's speech, he would summarize the problem briefly and introduce Donna who would offer the first solution.

The Lecture Panel

The *lecture panel* is a third discussion form. This variation calls for a resource speaker, someone who has a close acquaintanceship with the question, to deliver a prepared speech.

After the leader introduces the problem area and the speaker, the speaker analyzes the nature of the problem and presents possible solutions. A panel discussion follows at which time the members may ask questions of the resource speaker, make comments of their own, and discuss any aspect of the matter among themselves. They may accept, reject, or modify any of the offered solutions. Finally, with a solution in mind, the members may work out a plan for putting the solution into practice.

The nature of the problem will dictate your selection of a resource speaker. He may be from outside the class, or he may be one of your class members who is well versed on the subject. Outside resource people often invited are police department members, recreation department personnel, radio and television authorities, athletic coaches, teachers, lawyers, businessmen, agriculturists, and newspaper personnel.

If an outside person is not available, do not despair. Someone in your class can be encouraged to come to your rescue. He may have to make a careful study of the subject, but, of course, you will too. Here is a sample thirty-minute lecture-panel time distribution plan for a thirty-minute lecture panel.

Area of difficulty, general background and introduction of the speaker	Leader, 3 minutes
Analysis of the problem and possible solutions	Resource speaker, 15 minutes
Questions, comments, and selection of a satisfactory solution and course of action	Panel members, 12 minutes

Audience Participation

In our explanation of discussion forms, the audience should not be forgotten. The listeners are participants, also, in that they actively follow the course of the discussion. They, too, have an interest in the problem and, therefore, must be alert in their efforts to understand, consider, and evaluate.

Public discussion forms provide for oral audience participation after the group has concluded. This part of the program is called a *forum*. A forum in Rome was the market place, a large public square where public or private affairs were discussed, speeches delivered, and court held. Today we use the word to indicate an occasion at which everyone has a right to express his ideas. Actually, when the audience is allowed to speak following a discussion, the entire program is called a forum. Thus we have the panel forum, the symposium forum, and the lecture-panel forum.

Audience members may ask questions of specific discussion speakers or of the group as a whole. They may refer to some phase of the subject and make statements of their own. A question from the audience is directed to the leader who, in turn, submits it to the group or to a certain member for response.

GATHERING MATERIALS

A critic once defined discussion as "pooled ignorance." Possibly this definition would apply to some situations, but certainly not to a well-informed, alert group. You can become informed on your subject by collecting pertinent data. Where should you look for your materials?

1. *Check your own experiences first.* Perhaps you have had some contact with the subject area. A summer job might have introduced you to labor-management relations. Baby-sitting could have provided you with knowledge about raising children. What have you read about the subject? What have you seen that pertains to it? What have you heard well-informed people say about it?

2. *Visit the scene of action related to your subject.* One of the best ways to become well informed is to make firsthand observations. If you will be discussing Community Recreation, visit the playgrounds, the pools, and other facilities. Make the field trip a worthwhile one by planning carefully in advance and by keeping your purpose uppermost in your mind.

Arrange an interview with an authority. The head of the recreation department, for example, would be glad to help you. Make an appointment; be prompt; and prepare your questions in advance.

3. *Use the library services.* Here is a source of materials on almost any subject. The library is valuable not only be-

cause so much information is deposited there but, also, because the librarian can be of great assistance in helping you to find it.

Become familiar with and use the research aids found in the library:

(*a*) The *card catalog*, contained in a filing cabinet, lists alphabetically every book in the library. You can find the information card for a certain book by title, author, or subject; each work is listed in these three ways.

(*b*) The *Reader's Guide to Periodical Literature* is an index of articles published in many magazines. The listings in this aid, too, are by author, subject, and title. If you are not acquainted with the *Reader's Guide*, learn how it can work for you.

(*c*) Many students find the library pamphlet file to be extremely helpful in preparing for a discussion. Ask your librarian about it.

(*d*) Newspapers, encyclopedias, dictionaries, yearbooks (including almanacs), or biographical dictionaries may be of use to you. Browse around the reference section and notice the varied volumes on the shelves. In addition to the standard encyclopedias and dictionaries, you will find special aids which treat specific areas of knowledge. There is an encyclopedia of music and one of social science, for example.

(*e*) The United States Government Printing Office publishes thousands of pamphlets and books on a great variety of subjects. Ask the librarian for a catalog pertaining to your subject.

Assuming that you are now ready to gather information from your personal experiences, from field trips, and from the library, how will you record your data? You will need to proceed systematically. A method is necessary in order to make the fruits of your research usable at the time of discussion.

The best plan calls for recording your materials on 3 × 5 or 4 × 6 cards. Observe the following suggestions:

1. Use a different card for each new subtopic.
2. Include a topic heading.
3. Record the material accurately.

4. Enclose quoted material with quotation marks.
5. Include the author, source, and date.

SAMPLE CARDS

Need for Recreation Facilities in Our Town

"Our present recreation facilities are too meager to serve our growing town. The population has nearly doubled in twenty years, yet we have not increased our services.
"Something must be done soon to correct this difficulty."

Anderson, Howard F., head of the Johnstown Recreation Department, in an interview on March 5.

How to Interest the Public in Recreation Needs

"A well-organized student speaker's bureau helped a community in the state of Washington to wake up to the importance of having an active, wholesome recreation program."

Braydon, Samuel A., Spending Leisure Hours, New York, Riordan Press, 1959, p. 39.

Benefits of a Good Recreation Program

Towns have already observed decreases in juvenile delinquency rates after instituting good programs.
Springfield—down 10% after 5 years
Clayton—down 12% after 4 years
Newton—down 21% after 6 years

The Johnstown Daily Herald, editorial, March 11.

CHECKING THE MATERIALS

You will recall from previous speech activities that you were asked to test the value of your materials. This same sort of checking is needed to evaluate discussion materials. Ask these questions:

1. Do I have enough to make my share of contributions in the discussion?
2. Have I gathered an ample amount of data from all sides of the question?
3. Are the data related to probable subtopics of the discussion?
4. Are the statistics accurate?
5. Are my quotations authoritative?
6. Are any of my sources prejudiced or biased?
7. Are my materials not likely to arouse needless debate?

BEING A GOOD MEMBER

If you appreciate the purpose of discussion and understand the basic methods, you are almost ready to participate. Before starting, study the following standards of membership, and keep them in mind as you take part in group discussion.

1. *A good member is cooperative.* Recognize the need for a cooperative spirit in achieving a successful discussion. You may not always agree with the ideas of others, but be tolerant and willing to try to understand all points of view.

Acknowledge your prejudices. Anyone may have a prejudice, but not everyone has that special kind of courage it takes to admit it to himself. A good member examines his own opinions and attempts to cull out those that are based on mere prejudice.

Too, the effective participant is alert and enthusiastic. Such a member is a willing, active, responsible participant who knows that his contributions are important.

2. *A good member is prepared.* When you have analyzed the problem, organized your thoughts, and gathered substantive materials, you are ready to contribute whenever your remarks will help the development of the group effort.

3. *A good member avoids needless debate.* This is not to say that a person should refrain from supporting his convictions. It merely means that the good discussion speaker knows that extended debate can incur strong feeling and perhaps cause the discussion to bog down. Persistent debating forces people to take sides and rules out open-mindedness and objectivity. Know when to stop, when to yield for the sake of the discussion as a whole.

4. *A good member contributes his share.* The occasion is not one for long, time-consuming speeches. His contributions should be short, clear, and relevant. Regardless of how wise and fluent a member may be, if he is considerate he will avoid taking up an unreasonable share of time. Discussion is a *group* effort.

Then too, the good member avoids the opposite extreme, that of too little participation. You must realize that any solution reached cannot be yours if you have had no part in finding it. Some people underestimate their own value as much as others seem to overestimate theirs. In addition to the right to speak, you have an obligation to speak.

5. *A good member is tactful.* Discuss *ideas* and avoid personal ridicule. Use tact, and do not injure the feelings of others. A good member guards against making remarks, unintentional or otherwise, which will antagonize or offend. In other words, social propriety is the guiding standard.

6. *A good member accepts the guidance of the leader.* Remember the importance of the orderly progression of thought for which the leader is responsible. Respect the leader's actions, and refrain from getting ahead of the discussion. For example, you should not insist on discussing solutions when the group is still developing the problem.

7. *A good member uses appropriate language.* Commu-

nication among the members is based on concrete and accurate speaking. Vague and abstract thoughts usually mean very little to others. The good member adapts his ideas to the lives and experiences of his listeners.

8. *A good member is a capable listener.* He is conscientious in following the flow of discussion and attempts to understand and interpret comments before referring to them. The effective speaker ignores emotional and physical distractions and listens intelligently.

When in doubt about what to do in a discussion, ask yourself this question: "What can I do for the good of the discussion?" If you are undecided about expressing a given thought, ask yourself: "Will it help or hinder the progress of the discussion?" In all cases, be guided by a desire to make the *group* efforts successful.

BEING A GOOD LEADER

As mentioned earlier in this chapter, a discussion is a collective speech. It is the task of each member to make contributions to the development of the discussion. You can see quite readily that another agent is needed in the process. In order to make the activity a purposeful one, someone must act as a guide. This person is, of course, the leader. His job begins in the planning period at which time he leads the group in selecting and narrowing the subject, wording the question, determining the form, and preparing an outline of the main points to be discussed.

What are the standards of leadership?

1. *A good leader is cooperative.* As a leader, you must have deep respect for the discussion process, an awareness of the "working together" nature of discussion. Be honest, tactful, friendly, and impartial. Avoid being an overlord, and yet be firm when necessary. Use your intelligence and your sense of humor. Have an attitude which will enable the group to have

confidence in you. Remember that you are the leader and not a member; as such, you offer leadership but not your views on the topic.

2. *A good leader is prepared.* You should have substantial over-all knowledge of the subject. After all, you are responsible for the development of the discussion. A captain must know the whole ship in order to coordinate the work of the various officers.

3. *A good leader provides an appropriate beginning.* Open the program in much the same way as you would commence any speech. An example might be used or possibly a quotation or a statistic. Work in an explanation of the subject's importance along with background information. Introduce the individual participants, and announce the procedure which will be followed.

4. *A good leader gives guidance.* This is your main job. It is your duty to insure orderly progress toward the final goal. You may clarify or ask for definitions and restatements. You should summarize whenever the group needs to be reminded of what it has accomplished. Occasionally ask questions to keep the discussion moving or to bring out key points. Recognize the key points presented, and see that they get sufficient emphasis.

Be sure to encourage all members to participate. Help the quiet member by asking for his ideas. He has something to share, too. On the other hand, be ready to deal with the over-talkative member. Be gentle and tactful, and maintain a balanced discussion.

5. *A good leader provides an appropriate ending.* Include a summary of what has been accomplished along with other remarks designed to round out the discussion. If the audience is to take part, remind them that they may ask questions of individual discussion speakers, or the group as a body, and that they may make comments of their own. Guide the forum period, and bring the program to a smooth conclusion.

LET US SUMMARIZE

Discussion, the medium for exchanging ideas and solving problems, is part of all phases of life. Whenever group action is called for, this method can be utilized to implement the proceedings. Discussion can be a trusted form of communication if it is respected and used wisely, if—

1. The spirit of discussion is appreciated.
2. The subject is acceptable.
3. The question is well stated.
4. The organization is sound.
5. The form is suitable.
6. The supporting materials are worthwhile.
7. The members are effective.
8. The leader is capable.

Thomas Macaulay once said: "Men are never so likely to settle a question rightly, as when they discuss it freely."

SUGGESTED QUESTIONS FOR DISCUSSION

How should we deal with academic dishonesty?

How can automobile accidents be reduced?

What can be done to improve our cafeteria service?

How should an individual plan to meet his medical needs?

How can more students be provided with a college education?

What can be done to make more part-time jobs available?

What should a family do to help a boy and/or girl with personal problems?

What standards should guide a person in choosing his lifework?

What should be the minimum voting age?

What can be done to achieve harmony among nations?

How can the teacher shortage be alleviated?

How can divorces be prevented?

What should be the parents' policy regarding the reading of comic books by their children?

What should be the age limit for compulsory education?

What should be school policy regarding teaching about sex?

SUGGESTED TOPICS FOR DISCUSSION

Labor-management Relations

Sportsmanship

The School Paper

Air Travel

Advertising Methods

Extracurricular Activities

Natural Resources

Overcoming Emotional Problems

European Unification

Slum Clearance

Outlawing War

Military Service

Homemaking

Women in Industry

Providing for the Future

Crowded Highways

Air Pollution

Using Personal Talents

Keeping the Campus Clean

Parking Problems

Buying a Car

Tolerance among People

Modern Fashions

Popular Music

Student Government

City Planning

Going Steady

Increased Population

College Entrance
    Requirements

Propaganda

Taxation

The United Nations

Rearing Children

Spending Leisure Time

Choosing a Major

Problems of Alcoholism

Dating

Teaching Methods

Preparing for Examinations

Raising Money for a Club

Choosing a Play

FOR FURTHER STUDY

Behl, William A., *Discussion and Debate* (New York, Ronald, 1953).

Ewbank, Henry L., and Auer, J. J., *Discussion and Debate*, 2d ed. (New York, Appleton-Century-Crofts, 1951).

Howell, William S., and Smith, Donald K., *Discussion* (New York, The Macmillan Co., 1956).

Keltner, John W., *Group Discussion Processes* (New York, Longmans, Green, 1957).

Sattler, William M., and Miller, N. Edd., *Discussion and Conference* (Englewood Cliffs, N. J., Prentice-Hall, 1955).

Wagner, Russell H., and Arnold, Carroll C., *Handbook of Group Discussion* (Boston, Houghton Mifflin, 1950).

SUGGESTED EXERCISE A

Organize your class into groups of five or six, and select a qualified leader for each. The leader will guide the group in choosing the subject, narrowing the subject, wording the question, determining the form, and preparing an outline of the points to be discussed. Allow time for a forum period if you plan to have audience participation.

Before starting to do research, review the sections of this chapter on gathering and evaluating materials. Prior to the time for which your discussion is scheduled, review the sections on being a member and being a leader.

SUGGESTED EXERCISE B

Analyze your efforts as a participant in the group discussion by commenting upon these questions:

1. Did you have a discussion attitude? (Were you cooperative, willing, and responsible?)
2. Were you prepared? (Did you do enough thinking and investigating?)
3. Did you contribute your share of ideas? (Did you present enough ideas? Did you do more than you should have?)
4. Were you tactful? (Did you respect the feelings of others?)
5. Did you use appropriate language? (Did you avoid ambiguous words and phrases?)
6. Were you a good listener? (Did you understand and interpret correctly the thoughts of others? Were you able to ignore distractions?)

7. If you were a leader, did you guide the discussion adequately?

   a. Did you provide an appropriate beginning and ending?

   b. Did you introduce the question and the participants?

   c. Did you clarify, summarize, and ask questions when necessary?

   d. Did you recognize key points when they were presented?

   e. Did you encourage participation?

   f. Did you guide the forum period successfully?

SUGGESTED EXERCISE C

As a discussion observer, analyze the efforts of a group presenting a discussion in your class. Comment constructively and fully.

1. Was the subject well chosen?
2. Was the spirit of discussion appreciated?
3. Was the question clearly stated?
4. Were the form and organization suitable?
5. Were the materials well chosen?
6. Were the members effective?
7. Was the leader capable?
8. Were the goals realized?

SUGGESTED EXERCISE D

Participate in an informal class discussion of how you may use group discussion in the future: In business; in family affairs; in civic affairs; in your lodge or club; or in your church.

11

Applying Parliamentary Law

A GUIDING STANDARD

Centuries of human experience have shown that the affairs of men must be governed by law. We have learned, and sometimes at great cost, that the absence of law results not only in anarchy and chaos but also in tyranny and widespread violence. Laws protect men and serve as standards of guidance; a code of just laws is the foundation of a free state. "Where there is no law, but every man does what is right in his own eyes, there is the least of real liberty." [1]

The guiding law for the operation of deliberative bodies, whether they be special-interest clubs, social fraternities, professional associations, or the United States Senate, is called parliamentary law. Originally developed by the British Parliament, it has been modified considerably over the years. The rules of order that you observe in your club are those that fit your needs. Those adhered to by the United States Senate are necessarily more complex and detailed. Regardless of the group's purpose or size, people who deliberate in organized

---

[1] Henry M. Robert, *Robert's Rules of Order*, rev. ed., Chicago, Scott, Foresman, 1951, pp. 13-14.

groups need a governing system. It is the purpose of this chapter to explain the main elements of the system. If you think of parliamentary procedure as something too complicated and mysterious to master, we ask that you put aside this preconceived notion and seriously attempt to learn the fundamental rules. Regard the rules not as devices for making a pretentious show or for confusing people, but as valuable tools which, when used simply and conscientiously, work for the welfare of your group.

Specifically, there are three basic services which parliamentary law has to offer:

1. *It provides means for orderly deliberation* by demanding that elements of business be handled one at a time and according to priority.
2. *It encourages courtesy and dignified action* by demanding civility and use of reason.
3. *It implements democratic principles* by demanding recognition of majority rule and respect for minority rights.

BEING A GOOD CHAIRMAN

The presiding officer of any association, whether he be called chairman, president, or by some other title, should be a responsible and intelligent person in whom the membership can have confidence. In large measure the success or failure of the organization depends upon him. We shall make repeated references to the role of chairman in this chapter, but at the outset let us set down four standards of chairmanship.

1. *A good chairman keeps himself informed.* He knows the history and traditions of his organization as well as the current operational procedure. A workable knowledge of parliamentary law is, of course, indispensable to him.

2. *A good chairman conducts business in the proper order.* He follows a sequence prescribed by his organization. The following is a typical order of business plan:

Call to order
[Roll]
Reading of minutes
Committee reports
Unfinished business
New business
Announcements
Adjournment

3. *A good chairman is effective in guiding the delibera-tions of his group.* He opens meetings promptly. In maintain-ing order, he is fair and tactful, yet firm and sure. He refers to himself as "the chair." For example, he may say, "The chair stands corrected," or "The chair recognizes Jim Albright." Keeping discussion on the question at hand, clarifying, and giving all members a chance to speak are other obligations of the presiding officer. The chairman does not participate in the actual discussion except when he steps down and allows the vice president or another member to occupy the chair tempo-rarily.

4. *A good chairman is effective in handling the voting.* He restates a motion before putting it to a vote and allows ample discussion on debatable questions. The chairman him-self does not vote except in the case of a tie or when voting is by ballot. Immediately after the voting, he announces the result.

BEING A GOOD MEMBER

Standards of good membership, although not as stringen as those to be met by the presiding officer, are important fo us to consider. Associations are not formed merely to elec officers and to have an occasional meeting. They are forme for a greater purpose, and a good member will do all that h can to further that purpose.

1. *A good member keeps himself informed.* Like th

chairman, he must know the nature of his organization's business and be able to use parliamentary procedure efficiently.

2. *A good member knows how to obtain the floor when he wants to speak.* He should stand or raise his hand, and when recognized by the chairman, he should say, "Mr. Chairman" or "Mr. President." A good member is patient and waits his turn; nonetheless, he should not allow himself to be frightened out of making a helpful contribution merely because he has difficulty in obtaining the floor.

3. *A good member knows how to share his ideas.* First of all, he is willing to participate and share. A member should address all remarks to the chair and not engage in side conversations. Of course, he should confine all discussions to the question before the house. The correct wording for him to use in making motions is, "I move that . . ." or "I move to . . . ," and never, "I make a motion. . . ."

MOTIONS

In a group governed by parliamentary procedure, business is presented in the form of a motion. A motion is a proposition or proposal that is offered to the membership for consideration. Being similar to a speech proposition, it is simply worded and contains only one item of business. This is the order followed in presenting and disposing of most simple motions:

1. After a member obtains the floor, he states his motion.
2. Another member must second it.
3. The chairman announces, "It has been moved and seconded that . . . ," (the full and exact wording of the motion).
4. The chairman asks, "Is there any discussion?"
5. After allowing ample discussion time, the chairman puts the question to a vote. "All those in favor, say 'aye.' All those opposed, say 'No.'"
6. The chairman announces the result.

Main motions or ordinary motions are the most common.

Having the lowest priority status, a main motion can be made only when no other motion is before the house. "I move that we donate five dollars to the Community Chest" and "I move that we send our president to the annual convention" are main motions.

Subsidiary motions relate to other motions being considered by the group. They are used to handle or dispose of other motions. Below are seven of the most important subsidiary motions, listed according to rank. Sample motions and rules governing their usage follow the titles.

1st *To lay on the table* (To set the question aside)

> SAMPLE: "Mr. Chairman, I move that the motion to raise dues be laid on the table [*or* tabled]."
>
> RULES: Seconded; Not debatable; Not amendable; Majority vote.

2d *Previous question* (To call for a vote on the pending question. Sometimes this is called "To close debate." If this motion carries, the pending motion is voted on immediately.)

> SAMPLE: "Mr. Chairman, I move the previous question" *or* "I move that we close debate and vote immediately on the pending question."
>
> RULES: Seconded; Not debatable; Not amendable; Two-thirds vote.

3d *To limit debate* (To restrict discussion time)

> SAMPLES: "Mr. Chairman, I move to limit debate on this question to one half hour." "Mr. Chairman, I move to limit the time of each speaker on this question to two minutes."
>
> RULES: Seconded; Not debatable; Amendable; Two-thirds vote.

4th *To postpone to a certain time* (To delay action on the question temporarily)

SAMPLE: "Mr. Chairman, I move to postpone further consideration of this motion until our next regular meeting."

RULES: Seconded; Debatable; Amendable; Majority vote.

5th *To refer to committee* (To allow further study of the question)

SAMPLE: "Mr. Chairman, I move that the chair appoint a committee of three to investigate this matter and report at our next regular meeting."

RULES: Seconded; Debatable; Amendable; Majority vote.

6th *To amend* (To modify the motion)

MAIN MOTION: I move that we invite the principal officers of the Sociology Club to attend our forum.

SAMPLE AMENDMENTS:
(1) "Mr. Chairman, I move to amend the motion by striking out 'principal.'"
(2) "I move to amend the motion by adding 'to be held in November.'"
(3) "I move to amend by substituting 'entire membership' for 'principal officers.'"

RULES: Seconded; Debatable; Amendable; Majority vote.

7th *To postpone indefinitely* (To put an end to a main motion)

SAMPLE: "Mr. Chairman, I move that the matter of changing our club name be postponed indefinitely."

RULES: Seconded; Debatable; Not amendable; Majority vote.

A subsidiary motion takes precedence over the motion to which it refers, and, therefore, must be voted on before action can be taken on the main motion. In keeping with the rules of precedence or rank, when a given subsidiary motion is before the house the only additional subsidiary motion that can be made is one of higher rank. For example, when the motion to lay on the table is pending, no other subsidiary motions can be attached to the main motion. The motion to lay on the table has the highest ranking among the subsidiary motions.

To illustrate further, let us imagine that someone on the student council has moved "that the student body buy a color television set for the lounge." The motion is seconded. During the discussion of this main motion, an economy-minded member obtains the floor and says, "I move to amend by striking out 'color.'" After being seconded, the motion to amend is discussed.

Perhaps it is felt by some that the council is acting too hastily. One member states, "I move to postpone further action on this question until our next council meeting." Since the motion to postpone is of higher rank than the pending motion to amend, the president allows it to be introduced. It is seconded. At this time any of the three subsidiary motions of higher rank than the motion to postpone would be in order. They are: to lay on the table, the previous question, and to limit debate.

Assuming that no other motions are presented, the group disposes of its three pending motions in this manner:

1. Ample time is allowed for the motion of highest rank (the last one made) to be discussed; then, it is voted on. It is, of course, the question on postponement. If it loses, the motion next highest in rank is brought up for consideration. If the postponement question carries, the other pending motions are automatically disposed of along with it for the term of the postponement.

2. Assuming that the postponement motion loses, the pending motion (to amend) is put before the house. The chairman allows time for further debate, and puts it to a vote. If it carries, the question before the house is the main motion as amended. If it does not carry, the question to be discussed and voted on is the original motion

Before leaving subsidiary motions, let us add a word regarding motions to amend. Only two motions to amend may be pending at any given time: the first motion to amend and another to amend the amendment. For example:

MAIN MOTION: "I move that we take funds from the treasury to send President Rogers to the convention in Dallas."

AMENDMENT: "I move to amend by inserting 'to the amount of $100' after the word 'funds.'"

AMENDMENT TO THE AMENDMENT: "I move to amend the amendment by substituting '$125' for '$100.'"

Neither amendment should alter the intent of the motion to which it refers. They are disposed of in the reverse order of presentation; the motion to amend the amendment is taken up first.

Incidental motions also relate to pending motions or to matters of procedure. They may interrupt other business, and they have precedence over the motions to which they relate. The following incidental motions are frequently used.

To withdraw a motion (To cancel a motion you have made)

SAMPLE: "Mr. Chairman, I wish to withdraw my motion."

RULES: If there is no objection, the request is handled informally. If there is objection, a formal motion must be made.
No second; Not debatable; Not amendable; Majority vote.

To suspend a rule temporarily (To deviate from following an accepted rule. It must not be in conflict with the constitution or by-laws.)

SAMPLE: "Mr. Chairman, I move that we suspend our order of business rules and hear the nominating

committee's report after we discuss unfinished
business."

RULES: Seconded; Not debatable; Not amendable; Two-
thirds vote.

Point of order (To question use of parliamentary law,
order of business, etc.)

SAMPLE: "Mr. Chairman, I rise to a point of order." The
chairman responds, "State your point of order,"
and after it has been stated, he rules on it.

RULES: No second; Not debatable; Not amendable;
Chair rules.

To appeal from a decision of the chair (To question a decision of the chairman)

SAMPLE: "Mr. Chairman, I appeal from the decision of the
chair." The chairman responds after the second,
"Shall the decision of the chair be upheld?"

RULES: Seconded; Debatable; Not amendable; Majority
vote.

Privileged motions, unlike subsidiary and incidental motions are not related to other motions being considered by the
group. They are important enough to be allowed at any time.
The only restriction is that such a proposal cannot be made
when another privileged motion of higher rank is before the
house. These are the most common privileged motions:

1st   *To fix the time of the next meeting*

SAMPLE: "Mr. Chairman, I move that we set the time of
our next meeting at seven o'clock p.m., January 28."

RULES: Seconded; Debatable (if no business is pending); Amendable; Majority vote.

2d   *To adjourn*

SAMPLE: "Mr. Chairman, I move that we adjourn."

Rules: Seconded; Not debatable; Not amendable; Majority vote.

3d *Questions of privilege* (To close the windows, bring in more chairs, to raise the volume of the public address system, and so forth.)

Sample: "Mr. Chairman, I rise to a question of privilege." The chair responds, "State your question."

Rules: Not seconded; Not debatable; Not amendable; Chair rules.

4th *To call for the orders of the day* (To remind the chairman of an item of business that he has omitted. He may have neglected to call for a reading of the minutes or perhaps he failed to ask for a scheduled committee report.)

Sample: "Mr. Chairman, I call for the orders of the day."

Rules: Not seconded; Not debatable; Not amendable; Not voted on.

The *unclassified motions* listed below are used to bring matters back to the floor which have been tabled or otherwise dispensed with. They may be made whenever another motion is not pending.

To take from the table (To bring back a tabled motion for deliberation)

Sample: "Mr. Chairman, I move to take from the table the motion to paint the club house."

Rules: Seconded; Not debatable; Not amendable; Majority vote.

To reconsider (To discuss and vote on a question previously decided)

Sample: "Mr. Chairman, I move to reconsider the decision to raise membership dues."

Rules: Can be made only by someone who originally voted with the majority.

Seconded; Debatable (if the motion to which it refers is debatable); Not amendable; Majority vote.

To rescind (To reverse a decision previously made)

SAMPLE: "Mr. Chairman, I move to rescind the action taken at our meeting of March 1st regarding membership regulations."

RULES: Seconded; Debatable; Not amendable; Majority vote (if previous notice has been given; otherwise a two-thirds vote is needed).

VOTING

Most motions are passed by a simple majority vote, that is, more than half of the votes cast. Others require a two-thirds majority, and some are decided by the chairman.

There are good reasons for requiring a two-thirds majority to pass certain motions. The motions presented in this chapter to which the two-thirds majority rule applies are to limit debate, the previous question, to suspend a rule, and to rescind. Motions to limit debate and stop debate (the previous question) curtail speaking time and would be undemocratic actions if a great majority did not agree to the measures. Motions to suspend rules and to rescind are made to repeal some decision, and no deliberative body should be allowed to alter its decisions because of whim or fancy. There must be certainty that the action is desired by the larger majority.

LET US SUMMARIZE

For handy reference you can consult this chart which lists motions and the main rules governing their use.

As you apply parliamentary procedures in class exercises

CHART OF PARLIAMENTARY MOTIONS

Types of Motions	Rank	Seconded	Debatable	Amendable	Vote
MAIN	12	Yes	Yes	Yes	M
SUBSIDIARY					
To postpone indefinitely	11	Yes	Yes	No	M
To amend	10	Yes	Yes	Yes	M
To refer to committee	9	Yes	Yes	Yes	M
To postpone to a certain time	8	Yes	Yes	Yes	M
To limit debate	7	Yes	No	Yes	2/3
Previous question	6	Yes	No	No	2/3
To lay on the table	5	Yes	No	No	M
INCIDENTAL—Have precedence over motions to which they refer					
Withdraw a motion		No	No	No	M
To suspend a rule temporarily		Yes	No	No	2/3
Point of order		No	No	No	Chair
Appeal from a decision of the chair		Yes	Yes	No	M
PRIVILEGED					
To call for the orders of the day	4	No	No	No	None
Questions of privilege	3	No	No	No	Chair
To adjourn	2	Yes	No	No	M
To fix time of next meeting	1	Yes	Yes, if no business pending	Yes	M
UNCLASSIFIED—May be made when another motion is not pending					
To take from the table		Yes	No	No	M
To reconsider		Yes	Yes, if motion it refers to is debatable	No	M
To rescind		Yes	Yes	No	2/3 (M if previous notice given)

and in your clubs and associations, keep in mind the purpose of the rules. Make them work for the general welfare and never against it. Wise usage of parliamentary law by the leaders and members of any organization will ensure orderly handling of business, and courteous, dignified, and democratic operation.

BOOKS ON PARLIAMENTARY LAW

Card, Marjory W., and Wines, Emma M., *Come to Order!*, rev. ed. (New York, Odyssey, 1941).

O'Brien, Joseph F., *Parliamentary Law for the Layman* (New York, Harper, 1952).

Robert, Henry M., *Robert's Rules of Order* (Chicago, Scott, Foresman, 1956).

Sturgis, Alice F., *Learning Parliamentary Procedure* (New York, McGraw-Hill, 1953).

Wagner, Joseph A., *Successful Leadership in Groups and Organizations* (San Francisco, Chandler, 1959).

SAMPLE CLUB CONSTITUTION AND BY-LAWS

ARTICLE I. NAME

The name of this organization shall be the Quintilian Club.

ARTICLE II. PURPOSE

The purpose of the club shall be to increase the speaking proficiency of its members and to create a campus-wide appreciation of the values of oral communication.

ARTICLE III. MEMBERSHIP

Membership shall be extended to all student body card holders.

ARTICLE IV. OFFICERS

Section 1. The officers of this club shall be a president, a vice president, a secretary, a treasurer, and an historian.

Section 2. Officers shall be elected at the second meeting of each new semester.

Section 3. Vacancies in office shall be filled by a special election.

ARTICLE V. MEETINGS

Section 1. The club shall have biweekly meetings during the regular school year.

Section 2. Special meetings may be called by the president or by a majority vote at a regular meeting.

ARTICLE VI. AMENDMENTS

Section 1. This constitution may be amended at any regular meeting of the club by a two-thirds vote of the members, the amendments having been submitted in writing and read at a previous regular meeting.

Section 2. The by-laws may be amended at any regular meeting by a majority vote.

BY-LAWS

ARTICLE I. DUES

The dues of the club shall be one dollar a semester, payable at the second meeting of the semester.

ARTICLE II. OFFICERS

Section 1. A nominating committee of three members shall be elected to nominate one or more candidates for each office.

Section 2. The duties of the officers shall be those which are implied by their titles.

ARTICLE III. COMMITTEES

Section 1. The president shall appoint standing committees.

Section 2. The membership committee is responsible for acquiring new members.

Section 3. The program committee is responsible for planning, and presenting the club activities during the semester.

ARTICLE IV. PARLIAMENTARY AUTHORITY

Robert's *Rules of Order* shall be the final parliamentary authority of this club.

ARTICLE V. QUORUM

One third of the active membership of this club shall constitute a quorum.

SUGGESTED EXERCISE A

Set up a hypothetical club or legislative assembly in your class. Your instructor will lead while you nominate and elect a presiding officer. Under the leadership of your elected chairman, conduct a business meeting in which you make and dispose of main motions and various types of subsidiary motions only. When half the period has expired, nominate and elect a new chairman and continue. During this second "meeting," include an occasional privileged motion.

SUGGESTED EXERCISE B

Have each member of the hypothetical club compose a club constitution. Elect a committee to study those submitted, and select one to present to the "club" for adoption.

SUGGESTED EXERCISE C

Define these parliamentary terms:

before the house	rank
debate	second

deliberation
motion
obtaining the floor
pending
precedence
previous question

simple majority
the chair
the floor
the question
to dispose of

SUGGESTED EXERCISE D

What motions would you present to meet the following conditions?

1. To improve some part of a main motion.
2. To dispose of a motion for an indefinite time.
3. To cancel a motion you have made.
4. To ask the chairman to allow discussion before a certain subsidiary motion has been seconded.
5. To propose that a smaller group investigate a question.
6. To postpone a decision on a proposal until the next meeting.
7. To correct the chairman when he rules incorrectly on a point of order.
8. To restrict the time for discussing a measure.
9. To put the ventilating system in operation.
10. To reverse a decision of the group on a proposal.
11. To consider a tabled motion.
12. To bring a motion (on which you voted with the prevailing side) previously disposed of back for deliberation.
13. To stop discussion and take a vote.
14. To require the chairman to follow the prescribed order of business.

12

Speaking To Persuade

LET US FACE IT

How many times in the past two or three days have you heard a persuasive argument? How many times have people attempted to influence your outlook or behavior? Unless you are reading this chapter in isolation, possibly in a remote mountain cabin without even a radio, you have been the target of numerous persuaders this very day. In their quest to reach us, persuaders use radio, television, billboards, the newspaper, moving pictures, books, magazines, the telephone, the public platform, and direct personal contact. What are they trying to do? What do they want? They are trying to win us over, of course, and effect a change in our thinking or actions. They want us to trade in the old car or give to the Community Chest or go to church or believe in reciprocal trade or join the Navy or realize the need for raising taxes or make a five-dollar loan or arrange a date with Nancy Doe or buy a ticket to the ice show.

Is persuasion bad? Is it wrong for salesmen, politicians, ministers, teachers, or our friends and neighbors to do their best to influence us? Is it wrong for us to use persuasion? No, persuasion is not bad. It is merely an instrument or means and as such might be regarded as a neutral agent in our society. Nor is it wrong to employ the instrument.

Some persons rely upon unethical means to sway others, but instead of offering an excuse for condemning persuasion, cases of unethical behavior should offer a challenge to responsible citizens. Ethical persuasion is never needed more than when unethical persuasion is being used. Do not blame the instrument of persuasion when you hear a speaker insincerely play upon the sorrows of mothers whose children are on crutches. Blame the one who is using the instrument, and do your part to prevent his being effective.

The purpose of this chapter is to explain the rudiments of persuasive speaking. Since everyone is affected by it and is a persuader himself, he must understand persuasion in order to recognize it when listening and use it skillfully and responsibly when speaking.

THE AUDIENCE

Every speaker should attempt to analyze the audience he will be facing. An understanding of the people to whom you are speaking is important in all oral communication and is essential in persuasion. It is true that some success can come from adapting to the general nature of people or to the "average man," but without an earnest effort to clothe your ideas in terms of what the immediate audience requires, you may not gain your end. Be guided by the following suggestions in analyzing your prospective audience:

1. *Learn their backgrounds.* What is the predominant age level and sex? Your approach to a group of teen-agers would vary greatly from your approach to people in middle age, and what might be pertinent at a men's club meeting perhaps would not stir an assembly of women.

For additional assistance in planning your talk you should

try to learn their family status as well as their educational, economic, political, social, and religious backgrounds. You can sympathize with the speaker who found out later that his lecture on "Go to church on Sunday" had been presented to a gathering at least half of whom celebrate their sabbath on Saturday. He did not know his audience.

2. *Learn how much they know about the subject.* Determine the extent of their familiarity with the subject and whether the acquaintanceship is from formal study or direct experience. If the audience knows something of electronics, is it based on classroom training, practical experience, or both? Such an analysis will help you to come into the lives of your listeners at the proper point, the point to which their learning has advanced.

3. *Learn about their attitudes toward the subject.* An audience which might become uneasy at the slightest mention of certain subjects can make the speaker's task formidable. You should know what emotional involvements the audience has in your subject area and if they are likely to be favorably or unfavorably disposed or indifferent.

4. *Learn about their attitudes toward you.* Learn how much they are likely to know about you and what their opinion is of you. This information will tell you how much time should be spent in getting acquainted and in establishing good will. Listeners who respect a speaker tend to respect his ideas.

THE SPEECH

With some knowledge of the audience in mind, you will begin to prepare your speech. Since persuasion is used to alter belief or behavior, it is necessary to plan ways of accomplishing your desired end. There are three elements to be taken into consideration in your planning: the logical, the psychological, and the personal. We shall discuss the first two of these at this time.

LOGICAL ELEMENTS

The logical elements are those involved with the processes of reasoning. One cannot expect to move a thinking audience unless he reasons with them and makes his ideas logically acceptable.

In Chapters 5 and 6 we discussed the four main types of developmental materials: audio-visual aids, examples, statistics, and quotations. In persuasion these developmental aids are called evidence, that which supports what you say. It is not sufficient in persuasion, however, to state a point and cite evidence to support the point; you must *reason* with your evidence in an effort to draw valid and acceptable conclusions. In other words, you use logic to show your listeners the meaning or inescapable conclusions to be drawn from your accumulation of evidence.

Induction

Inductive reasoning is the process of deriving a general premise from a consideration of specific data, evidence. This example illustrates a form of induction called *generalization*.

> Jones, a successful salesman, has had training in persuasive speaking.
> Smith, a successful salesman, has had training in persuasive speaking.
> Brown, a successful salesman, has had training in persuasive speaking.
> Therefore, training in persuasive speaking probably helps one to be a successful salesman.

Is this reasoning sound? To check the validity of a generalization reached inductively, you should ask yourself three questions:

1. Do I have a sufficient number of instances?
2. Are my instances typical or representative?
3. Can contradictory instances, if any exist, be explained?

Causal reasoning, a form of induction, is commonly used in speeches to persuade. Here are some types and samples:

1. Reasoning from cause to effect:

    Those oily rags (*cause*) piled in the closet may start a fire (*effect*).

2. Reasoning from effect to cause:

    The bridge collapsed (*effect*) because its main span was too long (*cause*).

3. Reasoning from effect to effect:

    The fact that Peterson's Department Store is crowded (*effect of a sale*) indicates that by three o'clock the merchandise will be well picked over (*second effect*).

To check the accuracy of a conclusion reached by causal reasoning, you should ask yourself the following questions:

1. Is there more than a chance relationship between cause and effect?
2. Was the cause sufficient to produce the effect?
3. Have I considered other possible causes?

Reasoning by analogy is another form of induction, one with which the speaker attempts to make a point by comparing two phenomena. If you reason that the honor system which has worked at Stanford University should be instituted at your school, you develop the point by analogy. To make your argument acceptable you must show that conditions at the two institutions are similar enough to warrant your conclusion. Because of all the varying and intangible factors, reasoning by analogy is risky business. When extreme care is taken to choose closely related phenomena it can be helpful especially in clarifying.

Test the validity of an analogy with these questions:

1. Are the cases similar in all vital aspects?
2. Can dissimilarities be explained?

Deduction

Deduction is the process of reasoning by which a general premise is applied to a specific case in order to reach a conclusion. In formal logic, a sample of deductive reasoning is called a *syllogism*. Study the following types of syllogisms and accompanying samples:

1. *Categorical*

MAJOR PREMISE:	All automobiles are subject to mechanical failure.
MINOR PREMISE:	The Rolls Royce is an automobile.
CONCLUSION:	Therefore, the Rolls Royce is subject to mechanical failure.

2. *Hypothetical*

MAJOR PREMISE:	If the carload of grain has arrived, we must work overtime.
MINOR PREMISE:	The carload of grain has arrived.
CONCLUSION:	Therefore, we must work overtime.

3. *Disjunctive*

MAJOR PREMISE:	Jenkins was asked to restore the money or go to prison.
MINOR PREMISE:	Jenkins went to prison.
CONCLUSION:	Therefore, Jenkins did not restore the money.

Typically, formal, three-part syllogisms are not presented as such in speeches; however, they can serve as skeletal plans to be expanded upon in developing ideas and as tests to check the validity of your reasoning.

Verifying the accuracy of syllogisms depends upon the type of syllogism, and we shall not discuss the technical details here. There are two questions, nonetheless, that you can ask, questions which apply to all deductive reasoning:

1. Is the generalization true? In a speech, the generalization is a proposition, main head, or subhead; in the syllogism, it is the major premise.

2. Is the specific case relevant to the generalization? The "specific case" refers to the evidence of the speech or the minor premise in a syllogism.

3. From the premises offered, does the conclusion logically follow?

Fallacies in reasoning should be avoided, and you should be able to detect those made by others. There are many errors of reasoning; here are the most common types:

1. Hasty generalization (jumping to conclusions):

> I saw a drunk on Main Street and another on Front Street. This town is full of drunks.

2. Coincidence of events ("after this, therefore, because of this"):

> State scored on us because Johnny Stone had gone out of the game.

3. No relationship (a connection of "unconnectable" phenomena):

> The new courthouse in the next county is beautiful. They must have an efficient system of government.

4. Insufficient relationship (false analogy):

> Since New York and Seattle are cities with important harbors, they have similar bus transportation problems.

5. Either-or (offering only two solutions when others are possible):

> Either we levy a sales tax or endure our present financial struggle.

6. Begging the question (false assumption):

> Now we all know that war is inevitable [Do we?] so let's reason from there and plan. . . .

7. Personalizing (referring to irrelevant personal characteristics):

I wouldn't vote for Greta Hammond. You can't trust a woman who smokes cigarettes.

8. Arguing in a circle (using a point to "prove" the point):

Dr. Carson, who has lectured far and wide on animal husbandry, is well known in the field because he talks to many groups, large and small.

PSYCHOLOGICAL ELEMENTS

The psychological elements of persuasive speaking, in contrast to the logical, are those employed to appeal to the emotions of listeners. It must be remembered that the logical and psychological factors never can be completely separated. They do not exist in isolation. Nevertheless, motivating an audience and causing it to be favorably disposed toward your proposition usually require more than rational thought development. People have emotions, and more frequently than not their responses to a speaker's proposal are dictated by their personal needs and feelings.

Listeners want to know how a given proposal will affect them before they decide to accept it or act upon it. "Will his suggested plan to change the company's hiring policy endanger my security?" the personnel manager asks himself. "Can you really make me beautiful with Dazzle Cream?" a girl silently asks the television announcer. "Will a correspondence course in accounting help me get ahead down at the plant?" questions the employee as he reads the brochure.

Human Motives

The human motives to be taken into account in persuasion depend, in large measure, upon the people to whom you are speaking. The analysis of your prospective audience will give you guidance in the selection of effective appeals.

Where are appeals to be placed in the speech? In your introductory remarks and throughout the entire talk you should augment the development of your thoughts with appeals to motives. Consider them in your choice of language, and weave them into the fabric of your ideas as you elaborate.

Some cautions and suggestion are in order. It is strongly suggested that you vary your approach by using a variety of appeals. Then, too, you should avoid being obvious when you use persuasive methods. A wise man once said that the best artist is the one who conceals his artistry. Be sincere, and never be guilty of misrepresentation. Listed below are some of the motives manifested by most people.

1. To protect one's self (health, avoidance of danger, physical security):

> We need a revival of sound and safe American Government. We have left that far afield. We need to regain safe moorings. . . .
>
> —ALBERT C. RITCHIE, 1935

2. To acquire material goods (pleasant house, labor-saving devices, automobiles, gracious living conditions):

> On this Labor Day, the American worker stands head and shoulders above the workers of any other land. His wages and working conditions are better. He and his family have better homes to live in, better food to eat and better clothing.
>
> —GEORGE MEANY, 1953

3. To maintain self-respect (self-realization, feelings of adequacy, unbothered conscience):

> But *you* are young. You are hard. Your fires are not dampened by luxury. God knows you have had no chance

for luxury. Your muscles are not filled with the fat of having things come too easily."

—BRUCE BARTON, 1938

4. To be competent socially (have friends, approval, be attractive to opposite sex):

Would you like to be the life of the party? The center of attraction? To be known as a "good Joe"? Come on down to Danny's Dancing School. Why, in no time we can teach you to. . . .

5. To acquire power (urge to compete, success in work, hurdling obstacles, handle situations):

Stop and think, now. Aren't you just as good as the next man and maybe just a little bit better? Surely the new job would mean added responsibilities, but it's a big step up the ladder. I urge you to accept it.

6. To see justice done (fair practice, sportsmanship, consideration of others):

That is why the oppressive shackles which communism places on people will be—must be—ultimately thrown off. Liberty—not communism—is the most contagious force in the world.

—CHIEF JUSTICE EARL WARREN, 1954

Consider, briefly, two opposing views regarding the use of emotional appeals in persuasive speaking. The first might be stated in this way: "People are gullible, easy to fool or flatter. If you find their weak spots, you can lead them around by the nose." This cynical outlook reflects a rather dismal picture of mankind in general. In contrast, we have the second point of view: "People can be moved when they are offered satisfaction of their needs and desires; they can be led to better their opinions and improve their ways of doing."

What is the essential difference between these two views? Both agree that motivational persuasion is *effective*, but the second statement suggests that it can and should be *responsible* also. Persuasive speaking is responsible if the listener is respected as a dignified human being. Conversely, persuasive speaking is irresponsible if the listener is shown the disrespect of being subjected to heartless, crude, or unprincipled appeals.

Whether he wants it or not, whether he is willing to accept it or not, everyone has an obligation to be a responsible communicator.

Holding Attention

Methods of holding attention and building interest should be reviewed within the context of persuasive speaking. Successful persuaders adhere to these admonitions when composing their speeches:

1. *Be concrete and specific.* Instead of saying, "Join the Army!", ask the audience to "become a vital part of your country's proud infantry, tough tank corps, or big-gunned field artillery—each one an alert fighting force—all a part of the United States Army." Include particulars in your illustrative material.

2. *Refer to the familiar.* Far away places with strange-sounding names may appeal to some audiences, but the well-known things of life are more meaningful and give us a greater feeling of security.

3. *Introduce color and variety.* Be lively. Paint full word pictures, and vary your technique. People respond to richness and movement.

4. *Stir the curiosity.* Build up suspense. On some speech occasion try leaving one of your minor ideas at least partially veiled; notice the listeners' reactions. Too, you might say at the outset of a given talk that you will make a prediction or important announcement later on in the speech. Do not let the audience down!

5. *Use humor.* Relieve your listeners' tensions and put them in a receptive mood by bringing in an occasional short

funny story or quip that seems relevant at the time. Though you may have an intense and serious desire to persuade, you should realize that a little lightness may help you reach the goal.

ORGANIZATION

In the organization of ideas in persuasive speaking, you should take into account both logic and psychology. You need to develop your thoughts in a sequence which is, on the one hand, logically sound and, on the other hand, psychologically advantageous. It is folly to stand and aimlessly cast ideas in all directions; you must proceed in an orderly manner with a well-conceived plan.

A *deductive plan* for organizing speeches was discussed in Chapter 3; it is the Introduction-Proposition-Body-Conclusion formula with which you are so familiar. The essential characteristic of the deductive plan (based on deductive reasoning) is that it involves a movement from the general to the specific in thought development. General points are presented before specific supporting details are offered.

It is a practical plan, certainly logical and easy to handle; however, care should be taken to make it work for you in persuasion. The proposition and main heads must be worded with a particular audience in mind. To illustrate: "I will convince you that Harry Haskell is the man to elect to the City Council" in many speech situations would be a poorly worded purpose sentence. It is a challenge and could bring forth a wave of hostility. Instead, one might say, "Let us consider the qualifications of Candidate Haskell" or "I would like to discuss what Mr. Haskell will do for our city—for you and me." Most audiences cannot be forced to accept a proposal, but they can be encouraged to give it a hearing.

Persuasive speeches set up according to this deductive plan frequently include only two main heads: Problem and Solution. One popular variation is a five-part pattern based upon John Dewey's problem-solving formula (see Chapter 10). The primary value of the five-part pattern is that it impels the listener to move along with the speaker from one step to the next. If he agrees with the speaker during presentation of parts one and two, he will more than likely go along with him as he introduces the next logical step. This is the five-part plan:

I.   *Attention*
    A. Stimulation of interest
    B. Recognition of a problem condition
II. *Problem*
    A. The extent of the problem
        1. Limitation
        2. Definition
    B. Causes and effects
III. *Possible Solutions*
    A. Strengths
    B. Weaknesses
IV. *The Most Satisfactory Solution*
    A. Interpretation
    B. Values
V.   *Action*
    A. An appeal for overt action to put the solution into effect or—
    B. An appeal for change in belief.

Before going on to another system of idea arrangement, let us offer one other suggestion about the use of the five-part plan: Have a thorough knowledge of your problem. Many persuasive speeches break down because the speaker really does not understand the problem that he is attempting to treat. Be sure that you know the history, extent, causes, and effects of the problem.

The *inductive plan* is considered by some authorities to be psychologically more effective than the deductive. This is the "upside-down" system of arrangement in which the proposition is placed near the end of the speech along with the conclusion. The speaker presents a brief opening, develops the main heads, and finally unveils his proposition. Development of the individual main heads may be done deductively, the way most familiar to you, or it may be done inductively. If accomplished inductively, the speaker gives all of his supporting material for a given main head before he states the main head. The main head comes as a "conclusion" to the gathered evidence.

The inductive approach, which allows the speaker to withhold the statement of his objective until "the last minute" has two main values: (1) It minimizes the development of negative feelings against the proposal and (2) it adds suspense to the speech. The following outline is one that a friend of Harry Haskell might use to support his candidacy for the City Council:

1. You will make a major decision next Tuesday.
2. This is the most important city election to be held in many years.
   a. The man we elect will handle 13,000,000 taxpayers' dollars annually. (*Statistics*)
   b. He will vote on several new traffic safety measures. (*Example*)
   c. He will be charged with helping to set policies for the police and fire departments. (*Example*)

Main head A. Therefore, the man we elect must be *responsible*.

1. Our new city councilman will help decide on a plan to rezone certain areas for light industry. (*Example*)
2. The next five years will see this city remain at a standstill or progress like such cities as Northborough and Sexton. (*Example*)
3. Judge Waite always said, "The progress of a city depends upon the vision of her leaders." (*Quotation*)

Main head B. Therefore, the man we elect must be *forward-looking*.

Proposition-Conclusion: The candidate who is both responsible and forward-looking is (Need I
tell you?) Harry Haskell—the man
that our city needs!

THE PERSONAL ELEMENT

The most conclusive proof possessed by a speaker to make
his ideas acceptable and telling is *himself.* Conversely, his
most damaging factor can be himself. One's reputation, appearance, personality, and character affect an audience and influence their analysis of his ideas. If the audience is favorably
impressed by the speaker, they will be moved to give him and
his ideas a fair hearing; if they suspect or fear the speaker, he
has the necessary chore before him of creating an attitude of
confidence and friendliness. When an audience is kindly disposed toward the speaker, it will be kindly disposed toward
his speech.

How does a speaker develop this element of persuasion
known as personal proof? We have four suggestions, none of
which is an easily applied, magic key to success. Refining the
many components that make up personal proof may be a life-
time project.

1. *Continue to build a good reputation.* What people
think of you affects the reception of everything you say. A
known and respected person has fewer obstacles of audience
indifference or negativeness to surmount than others who are
not as fortunate. A good name is important for effective public
speaking.

2. *Attend to your physical appearance.* We need not expand upon how important neatness and grooming are to the
speaker who desires to persuade. You should be pleasant in
appearance and appropriately dressed. Do be careful, though,
of fashion extremes. Clothing that is too dapper or too chic
may cause some audiences to be suspicious and unwilling to
put their trust in you. If this seems unfair to you, then you

will sympathize with those whose occupations involve the handling of other people's money. Bankers and investment brokers, you know, are expected to dress quite conservatively.

3. *Give evidence of your personal merits.* Modestly and humbly work into your discourse an occasional remark referring to your worth as a person speaking on the chosen subject. Along with other commendable characteristics, you might show that you have a sense of humor, self-confidence, sound character, and knowledge of your material. Here are some excerpts from actual speeches which show the use of personal proof.

> I am little accustomed, gentlemen, to the part which I am now attempting to perform.
>
> I hope I have too much regard for justice, and too much respect for my own character, to attempt . . .
>
> Though I could well have wished to shun this occasion, I have not felt at liberty to withhold my professional assistance . . .
>
> —DANIEL WEBSTER, prosecution of the Knapp-White murder case

> And I should like to say to my friends of the press and radio that I regret that I have no manuscript and have therefore been unable to give them an advance on what I shall say. What I shall say, therefore, shall be spoken from the heart and not from a piece of paper.
>
> Four years ago, when I had the honor to be the temporary chairman of the Democratic convention in Philadelphia and to deliver the keynote address . . .
>
> —VICE PRESIDENT ALBEN BARKLEY, 1952

4. *Show respect for your audience.* If you have studied the audience beforehand, you can avoid such poor practices as speaking down to them or over their heads. Show respect for your listeners by accepting them as partners in the communication enterprise. As you speak for your proposition, be tactful, keep your audience's welfare uppermost in your mind, and manifest a feeling of goodwill toward them.

LET US SUMMARIZE

Persuasion is the highest form of oral expression and demands the best in intelligence and character that the speaker has to offer. It is an art and a skill which no one can afford to ignore or blanketly condemn as being improper for use by members of polite society. Persuasion is used to further all causes, good and bad; consequently, if the supporters of a bad cause are effective, more than likely their success is due to lack of support for a good cause.

To be successful in influencing the thinking and acting of others, you should:

1. Know your audience.
2. Use strong logical and psychological proof.
3. Organize purposefully.
4. Be a personal example of the worth of your message.

William C. Hazlitt offers a fitting, and in itself persuasive, final word: "Honesty is one part of eloquence. We persuade others by being in earnest ourselves."

TOPICS FOR PERSUASIVE SPEECHES

Television is not meeting the public needs.

Our government is moving toward socialism.

As an American, you should not tip.

Donate to the March of Dimes.

Join the Speech Club on our campus.

Religious instruction has no place in the public schools.

The Post Office should be operated as a private business.

Everyone should subscribe to the *Saturday Review of Literature.*

Organized labor is becoming too powerful.

Join a fraternity (or sorority).

Attend religious services regularly.

Buy a small automobile.

Improve your study habits.

All women should take courses in home economics.

Resist the fashion trends.

Poor mental health is our most serious problem.

Participation in athletics builds citizenship.

Take a course in geology.

The jury system should be abolished.

This political party (Democratic or Republican) will win at the next election.

Go fishing during your next vacation.

A liberal education is rewarding.

The proper study of mankind is man.

Enlist in the Marine Corps.

Drive safely.

Learn to play bridge.

A man should be a dog's best friend.

Be a responsible speaker.

The greatest virtue is prudence.

Know thyself.

Give every man equal opportunities.

In speaking, practice must be preceded by theory.

Start to build a record collection.

Avoid overeating.

The good businessman is ethical in his actions.

Learn to detect fallacies in reasoning.

The meek shall inherit the earth.

Learn to appreciate good music.

A student should go away to college.

Lou Gehrig was the greatest baseball player of all time.

Take an active part in politics.

Recognize the extent of Aristotle's teachings.

All young men should have some military training.

Poetry is the highest form of literary art.

Improve your listening.

Take a vacation in Oregon.

Buy more life insurance.

Study a foreign language.

Procrastination is a thief of time.

FOR FURTHER STUDY

Baird, A. Craig, and Knower, Franklin H., *General Speech* (New York, McGraw-Hill, 1957), Ch. 17, "Persuasive Speaking."

Braden, Waldo W., and Brandenburg, Earnest S., *Oral Decision-making* (New York, Harper, 1955), Ch. 23, "The Means of Persuasion."

Brembeck, Winston L., and Howell, William S., *Persuasion* (Englewood Cliffs, N. J., Prentice-Hall, 1952).

Chase, Stuart, *Guides to Straight Thinking*, (New York, Harper, 1956).

Hummel, William C., and Huntress, Keith G., *The Analysis of Propaganda* (New York, Holt-Dryden, 1949), Ch. 3, "Logic," and Ch. 4, "Propaganda in Action."

McCall, Roy C., *Fundamentals of Speech* (New York, The Macmillan Co., 1949), Ch. 6, "Patterns of Organization."

Oliver, Robert T., *The Psychology of Persuasive Speech*, 2d ed. New York, Longman's Green, 1957).

Wagner, Joseph A., *Successful Leadership in Groups and Organizations* (San Francisco, Chandler, 1959).

SAMPLE SPEECH OUTLINE 1
(The five-part plan in sentence form)

A HELPING HAND

I. *Attention*
   A. We Americans enjoy our way of life.
      1. Our supermarkets are laden.
      2. Our homes are comfortable. (*Example*)
      3. Our schools are outstanding.
   B. Some people of other countries, especially children, have never known how it feels to have their stomachs filled or their minds properly trained.
II. *Problem*
   A. Many are homeless.
      1. There are thousands of homeless orphans in Korea. (*Example*)
      2. India has a similar problem. (*Example*)

   B. Many are hungry.
1. Natural disasters frequently cut off the food supply in the Orient. (*Example*)
2. Poor farming methods impede agricultural output.
3. There are merely too many mouths to feed in some countries. (*Examples*)
   C. Many are uneducated.
1. There is too little money for schools. (*Statistics*)
2. Pagan beliefs hold back educational progress in parts of Africa. (*Examples*)
3. Many youth, such as Francisco Santillan of the Philippines, must forego school in order to earn a living. (*Example*)

III. *Possible Solutions*
   A. We could relax our immigration restrictions.
   B. We could send more experts abroad to offer assistance.
   C. We could make personal contributions.

IV. *The Most Satisfactory Solution*
   A. The problem must be met immediately.
   B. I would like to suggest that we consider the possibility of making personal contributions through the Children's Aid Plan.
1. One may "adopt" (support) a boy or girl in an orphanage in one of twenty-eight different countries.
2. His benefactor receives the child's history and may correspond with him.
3. The plan is nonpolitical and nonsectarian.
4. The support is nonobligatory, i.e., it may be withdrawn at any time.
5. The cost for one month is $15.00.

V. *Action*
   A. From an individual or from a group, this is not much money.
1. Less than $3.75 a week will help to provide a young and innocent victim of circumstance with nutritious food, adequate shelter, and proper schooling.
2. The average American wastes this much each week. (*Statistics*)

B. As an individual or member of a group, you can make your contribution with very little inconvenience.
   1. Just write to Children's Aid, New York 12, N. Y.
   2. Jean de la Bruyere said "Liberality consists less in giving a great deal than in gifts well timed." (*Quotation*)
   3. Now is the time to help our world's hungry children—before they become hungry men.

SAMPLE SPEECH OUTLINE 2
(The five-part plan in topic form)

OUR NOT-SO-FAIR CITY

I. *Attention*
  A. The Willow Avenue neighborhood
    1. Trim and comfortable houses
    2. Happy, healthy families have fun
    3. Spacious playgrounds and modern schools
  B. The Front Street district
    1. Shacks and decaying apartment dwellings
    2. Filth and disease
    3. Junk-littered lots and bleak school buildings

II. *Problem*
  A. An economic problem
    1. Inadequate housing accommodations
      a. Only 13 new houses since 1949 (*Statistics*)
      b. Bath facilities for but 50 percent of the families (*Statistics*)
      c. A family of ten in a three-room shack (*Example*)
    2. Other squalid features
      a. Cheap, rundown business places (*Examples*)
      b. Two elementary schools with average class size of 42 (*Statistics*)
      c. Narrow streets and filthy alleys
  B. A social problem
    1. Juvenile delinquency
      a. 25 percent incidence (*Statistics*)
      b. The case of Tom C. (*Example*)
    2. Drunkenness

        a. 120 beer and wine licensees (*Statistics*)

        b. 200 drunks arrested weekly (*Statistics*)

        c. Liquor causing break-up of homes (*Examples*)

    3. Crime

        a. Five stabbings, 41 burglaries, and 11 brawls in December (*Statistics*)

        b. Tuesday night's barroom gun fight (*Example*)

III. *Possible Solutions*

  A. Education

  B. More social work

  C. Removal of the slums

IV. *The Most Satisfactory Solution*

  A. More than one approach needed

  B. A combined attack

    1. A program of enlightenment as carried on in other cities (*Examples*)

    2. Along with more attention from the Social Welfare Department

    3. Plus gradual replacement of substandard buildings (*Hypothetical Example*)

V. *Action*

  A. Must be initiated by you, the responsible citizen

    1. By talking to city council members and others of influence

    2. By writing letters to the newspaper

    3. By voting for improvement measures and persuading others to do so

  B. Benefits to you, the responsible citizen

    1. Pride in your city

    2. Financial gain from our increased wealth

    3. Security when your children are out at night

SAMPLE SPEECH OUTLINE 3

(The inductive plan in sentence form)

LEISURE AND LEARNING

1. At the end of the spring semester, thousands of people will flock to the lakes, rivers, and seashore.

2. In winter, the mountain slopes are crawling with skiers. (*Statistics*)

3. Some fortunate souls, like Ralph Simpson, take trips to Europe. (*Example*)

4. There are those like my father who have fun puttering around the yard. (*Example*)

Main head A. One thing is certain then, people desire pleasure.

1. In a different vein, consider the case of Mr. Nellis, my neighbor, who attends school three nights a week. (*Example*)

2. In this city 200 people meet in various study groups each week. (*Statistics*)

3. The Community Forum was attended by over 600 people last week. (*Statistics*)

4. The enrollment of our college has doubled in the past ten years. (*Statistics*)

5. Only last Wednesday, Professor Hunter said, "Never before have I seen such a clamor at the school gates." (*Quotation*)

Main head B. This activity indicates that people desire an education.

Proposition-Conclusion: Like Ralph Simpson and Mr. Nellis you can help to satisfy further your yearnings for pleasure and learning by joining a Great Books Discussion Group.

1. The enjoyment and knowledge that is gained by people in groups all over the country can be yours, too.

2. Complete information is here in this brochure, and I have copies for each of you. (*Visual aid*)

3. You are invited to attend an introductory meeting in the library tomorrow night at eight.

4. As Sophocles, one of our Great Book's authors observed, "Though a man be wise, it is no shame for him to live and learn." (*Quotation*)

5. I shall be looking for you tomorrow night.

SAMPLE SPEECH OUTLINE 4

(The inductive plan in sentence form)

1. Wilma was unsuccessful in talking herself out of fearing high places. (*Example*)
2. Marvin failed in using reason to fight his serious emotional problem. (*Example*)
3. Other resolutions to "get better" are often broken. (*Examples*)

Main head A. Therefore, will power does not cure serious mental disturbances.

1. Well-meaning family members may worsen conditions. (*Hypothetical example*)
2. A friend tried to help someone but gave up in disgust. (*Example*)
3. Thomas à Kempis: "Be not angry that you cannot make others as you wish them to be, since you cannot make yourself as you wish to be." (*Quotation*)

Main head B. The advice of associates does little to allay deep-seated emotional problems.

1. There are meaningless generalizations in some popular do-it-yourself psychology publications. (*Quotations*)
2. Ed was not helped even after reading 17 books (3927 pages) on popular psychology. (*Example* and *statistics*)

Main head C. To those severely plagued, articles and books offer little therapy.

Proposition-Conclusion

1. You have seen the ineffectiveness of an exercise of will, the counsel of friends, and the use of written materials; the answer to the emotionally afflicted lies in psychotherapy.
   a. Consult a psychologist, psychiatrist, or psychoanalyst. (*Definitions*)
   b. There are many cases of successful therapy. (*Examples*)
   c. Fees may not be exorbitant. (*Statistics*)
2. Get names of qualified therapists:
   a. Call the local university;

    b. Call the Family Service Agency;

    c. Call the Health Department;

    d. Call medical or psychology associations.

SUGGESTED EXERCISE A

Prepare a speech designed to alter beliefs or to move your audience to act. To be effective in adapting it, you must analyze the audience. Follow the four suggestions given in the chapter.

Include logical, psychological, and personal proofs, and use a deductive pattern of organization, either the four-part or five-part.

SUGGESTED EXERCISE B

Select another proposal and repeat Suggested Exercise A using the inductive pattern of organization.

SUGGESTED EXERCISE C

Reword the following statements to make them propositions of deductive persuasive speeches which would be acceptable to your class as an audience.

1. You are duty-bound to attend all of your basketball games.
2. Fraternities and sororities should be banned from all college campuses.
3. Teaching by television will replace "live teaching."
4. The ideas of the ancient Greeks are too impractical for the twentieth century.
5. Every instructor should require his students to write a 2500-word term paper.
6. If America is to survive, you must spend less time in leisure and more in work.

SUGGESTED EXERCISE D

Find a provocative newspaper or magazine editorial. Subject the writer's arguments to critical analysis, and present your reactions to the class in the form of a short oral critique. Support your views.

SUGGESTED EXERCISE E

Hear a speaker, on or off the campus, whose end is to persuade. Analyze his reasoning and psychological appeals. What did he do to hold attention and build interest? What other techniques were particularly effective?

SUGGESTED EXERCISE F

Study a written speech from *Vital Speeches, Representative American Speeches,* or other speech anthologies. Discover examples of deductive and inductive reasoning used by the speaker.

SUGGESTED EXERCISE G

View and/or listen to three television or radio commercials. List the human motives to which the messages appealed. With what type of audience would each commercial have been effective?

SUGGESTED EXERCISE H

Let us assume that you are planning a speech to be given at a high school assembly. You want to convince your audience that the automobile is the greatest invention of all time. What points would you include? If your audience were composed of retired men and women, what points would you include?

SUGGESTED EXERCISE I

What speaker currently on the scene stands out in your mind as one who manifests strong personal worth? What specific qualities give him this enviable asset?

SUGGESTED EXERCISE J

What persuasive speaking practices that you have noticed do you consider unethical? Submit the list to your instructor. He may wish to discuss the topic in class.

SUGGESTED EXERCISE K

What fallacy is being committed in each of the following examples?
1. I've seen a lot of cheating around this campus; all students cheat.

2. Have you noticed the new football uniforms? We'll have a great team.
3. He has had a siege of bad luck as a result of walking under a painter's ladder last spring.
4. The little man doesn't have a chance these days. He must play ball with the big operators or perish.
5. It's his name that bothers me. Do you want a president named Ziggleton?
6. Our economic situation here in Kansas is just like the one they had on San Cristobal Island in 1915.
7. We all understand, of course, that engineering is the most important profession, but it is an underpaid profession also.
8. Arthur, who reads Einstein's works, must be very intelligent because he has read nearly all of the great man's writings.

13

Preparing for Various Occasions

YOU MAY BE CALLED UPON

The nature of any speech that you plan to make will be determined by your assessment of the entire situation. In effect, you must ask yourself, "What kind of speech should I make to this audience on this occasion?" Fundamentally, all types of original speeches are similar. All require thoughtful consideration of the subject, formulation of a definite purpose, sound organization, adequate development of ideas, and effective delivery.

There are occasions, however, that demand more than the application of fundamental principles. For example, if you are called upon to speak at some gathering without benefit of extensive preparation, it will be necessary for you to gather your thoughts immediately. Making an announcement, presenting a guest speaker to your club members, nominating a candidate for office, giving a speech to offer a token of honor to one who is leaving the community, accepting an award for service to your school, speaking as official host to a visiting delegation—all such events have special peculiarities to which you must adapt. At some time during your life you will have occasion to deliver one of these speeches.

THE IMPROMPTU SPEECH

The impromptu speech is a short talk given on the spur of the moment. Does the thought of making such a talk frighten you? Actually, the main difference between the requirements of impromptu speaking and other types is the amount of preparation time. We shall not attempt to convince you that this difference is insignificant because that would not be accurate. Yet, every speech that you have made can be thought of as a preparatory experience for making future impromptu speeches. In all of your speaking you have been getting ready to give speeches of limited preparation. Since much of the groundwork has been laid, the job now is to carry over to a special occasion what you have learned about composition and delivery. You will find this less difficult than you now think.

The following instructions will help you to implement your knowledge of speaking and be successful in the impromptu situation:

1. *Give thought to your subject.* On some occasions you may be allowed to choose your own subject while at other times you will be expected to adhere to an imposed subject. When the choice is yours, it is always wise to choose a significant subject. Speak about the occasion: its purposes, high points, or humorous aspects. Speak about the people assembled: their successes, future plans, or other group interests. Current events can offer impromptu topics such as popular fads or recent happenings in the community. Do not attempt to cover a wide area; limit your scope.

2. *Plan your course.* Decide immediately upon your proposition or theme, and select two or three main heads for developing it. The proposition might suggest that the main heads be topical, spatial, or chronological; or they may be set up as reasons or in a problem-solution pattern. Pairs of opposites are frequently quite handy "pillars of thought": for example, East and West, ups and downs, right and wrong, or past and future.

3. *Select materials as you speak.* During the time that it

takes you to push back your chair and assume your speaking position you can be gathering together a few introductory words. Make no apologies about "being unaccustomed to giving impromptu speeches." At a banquet you can refer to the beautiful table decorations, to a timely conversation that you had a minute ago, possibly to the committee's excellent work in arranging the program, or you can tell an appropriate story.

After leading into your proposition, state it. Present your first main idea, and elaborate on it with a story or example, some statistics, or a quotation if one should come to you at the time. Available visual aids might be used as means of development. One person, in fact, used a knife, fork, and spoon upon which to base his entire talk. He discussed "cutting through red tape" (with his knife), "spearing the main facts" (with his fork), and "scooping out details" (with his spoon). Use your imagination; capitalize on the tone of the occasion and factors related to it.

Before sitting down, perhaps you should summarize, make an appeal, or work both in together. In speaking before an organization, it is often appropriate to close with pertinent comments about the group's goals and aspirations, their unsolved problems, future gatherings, or noteworthy efforts of the officers and members.

4. *Guard against speciousness.* Reference is made here to a danger that may present itself to a person who has had enough impromptu speaking experience to give him a feeling of overconfidence but not enough to give him a respect for having a significant message. Glibness and smoothness do not necessarily indicate effectiveness. If the impromptu speaker has a worthy message and presents it sincerely, he will avoid becoming "inebriated with the exuberance of his own verbosity."

THE ANNOUNCEMENT

Whether given as an impromptu speech or based upon extensive planning, the announcement speech is often poorly made. This is probably due to its not being thought of as a "speech"; some persons seem to think that only formal public addresses require careful preparation.

What are the "rules" for making announcements?

1. Plan your talk.
2. Open with an attention-getting sentence.
3. Succinctly and clearly relate all of the essential information: who, what, when, where, and how much.
4. Be enthusiastic; make the subject inviting; emphasize its importance.
5. Repeat the essential information briefly.
6. Be seated!

Below is a sample outline:

I. *Introduction*
   A. Don't save your money.
   B. Bring it with you next Wednesday, and throw it away.
II. *Proposition:* Throw it away at the Jester Club's Annual Candy Sale to be held all day Wednesday along the arcade.
III. *Body*
   A. We will have creamy homemade fudge.
   B. We will have heavenly divinity.
   C. We will have mouth-watering peanut brittle.
IV. *Conclusion*
   A. Each generously filled bag will cost you a mere twenty-five cents.
   B. Remember that Wednesday is candy day along the arcade.

THE SPEECH OF INTRODUCTION

If you have had the uncomfortable experience of being thrown into a group at a party without benefit of introduction, you certainly appreciate the fact that guest speakers deserve appropriate speeches of introduction. The loneliest and most anxious time in a speaker's experience can be that period during which he waits to become acquainted with the audience. He may wonder what they have heard about him, what they think of him, or if they have heard of him at all. These typical thoughts of concern may pass through his mind: "Will my ideas be accepted? Can I get across to them? I wish I were more familiar with them and they with me."

Speeches of introduction are important. They help to create a friendly relationship between the speaker and his audience, to dispel fear, and to effect a "shaking of hands." Vital though they are, such talks often are mishandled. When you have the opportunity to acquaint a speaker with an audience and help him to get started, follow these suggestions:

1. *Know your function.* You are to make a speech; however, you are not the *main* speaker. Like the waiter in a restaurant, you provide a service, but like the waiter, again, what you introduce is the more important element. Subordinate yourself on this occasion like a good host, and give the main speaker his rightful position of prominence. Rarely would you be justified in speaking longer than two or three minutes. In fact, the introduction of a very well-known person might be accomplished in a few seconds with, "Ladies and Gentlemen, our president, Dr. Wagner."

2. *Learn about the speaker.* Study his background by consulting printed sources and people who know him. If possible, arrange to have a personal talk with him well ahead of the speaking time. Be certain that all of your information is accurate, including, of course, his proper title and the pronunciation of his name.

3. *Include appropriate data.* Remember now, that *he* is the speaker. Avoid trespassing very far into his subject area. General comments that show how the subject relates to the occasion or that summarize the speaker's work in his field are appropriate. Your knowledge or personal philosophy of the subject normally should not be included.

Specifically, what information is to be presented? Though occasions vary, usually you would summarize his qualifications, why everyone anticipates his speech. Capitalize on the background data that are especially meaningful to the audience.

Point out primary accomplishments of the speaker, yet do not overburden your introduction with many statistics and facts. Use humor if you wish, but use care and good taste in so doing. Build him up, yet not to an embarrassing extent. You can sympathize certainly with a person who is introduced as "the greatest speaker in Ohio." You may envy his announced reputation, but you would not want to be in his position of having to live up to it.

On the other hand, if he is your second choice, you should not embarrass him by revealing the fact. It would be most uncomplimentary to say, for instance, that you had tried to get Mr. Wilson but that Mr. Rogers, here, will surely give a good speech.

4. *Organize your remarks.* Like any other oral effort, the speech of introduction should be properly arranged. Many people like to use the inductive or upside-down plan. It involves making a brief opening to get attention and interest, developing two or three main heads, and finishing with a combination Proposition-Conclusion. Here is a sample outline:

I. *Introduction*
   A. Some people say that television has killed radio.
   B. Those of us who enjoy popular music would, indeed, debate that point.
   C. The point would be debated also by the prominent man who is to speak to us today.
II. *Body*
   A. He has fourteen years of experience in broadcasting.
      1. He started out as a script writer for KRRL.
      2. He worked for them as a disc jockey for three years.
      3. After extended experience in other capacities, he became manager of KRRL.
   B. Our speaker believes that radio has more potential today than it ever had.

    1. He has proven this in our community.

    2. He has more new ideas about the future of radio, some of which he will describe to us today.

III. *Proposition-Conclusion*

Ladies and gentlemen, I present, speaking on the topic "Radio and You," the man who makes of air a tangible commodity—the manager of KRRL, Tom Barber.

5. *Present the speaker.* As indicated in the sample outline, you should make an appropriate statement to tell him that *his* time has come. Sometimes a speaker is embarrassed because the introducer fails to present him properly to the audience. After the presentation, turn his way, and lead the applause.

NOMINATING SPEECHES

Most of the recommendations for giving speeches of introduction apply to speeches designed to nominate a candidate for office. You should, however, pay special attention to the following points:

    1. Mention the requirements of the office and how your candidate is qualified to meet them.

    2. Be positive in your approach; avoid sarcasm and ridicule if you must refer to other candidates running for the office.

    3. You might include a memory point, a catchy phrase or slogan that the voters will be likely to remember. The famous "I like Ike" was enormously helpful to Dwight Eisenhower during his first campaign for the Presidency.

    4. Deliver the speech with conviction and enthusiasm.

SPEECHES OF PRESENTATION

Many organizations, communities, and businesses have established the practice of presenting symbols of acknowledgment to praiseworthy persons or institutions. Such presentations may be made to recognize publicly long or exemplary service, scholarship, or athletic accomplishment, or to commemorate an event.

Since the occasion is of considerable importance, the accompanying speech should serve to carry it off in the proper spirit. If this speaking opportunity ever devolves upon you, what should you do?

1. Do not use notes.
2. Discuss reasons for the presentation and what the symbol being offered represents.
3. Discuss the characteristics and qualifications of the recipient.
4. Be sincere in expressing the genuine pleasure felt by those giving the award or gift.
5. Maintain the proper spirit of bestowing an honor, yet avoid making embarrassing exaggerations.

SPEECHES OF ACCEPTANCE

A speech given to accept an award or gift is usually an impromptu effort. Even though the recipient may have advance notice of the event, he must adapt his remarks to those of the presenter. The nature of the occasion, the type of symbol offered, and the preceding formalities will influence your response. However, there are certain general guideposts which apply to most speeches of acceptance:

1. Speak briefly, unless a long speech is expected.
2. Discuss the importance of the award to you; show your appreciation.
3. Modestly discuss significant and relevant facts which led to the honor being paid to you; discuss the roles played by other persons.
4. Pay tribute to those responsible for the presentation.

SPEECHES OF WELCOME

Noted groups or individuals who visit your school, community, church gathering, or club should be accorded the courtesy of a welcoming speech. Similarly, new members of a professional or social organization ought to be so treated. Allow these suggestions to guide you in handling this type of speaking assignment:

1. Do not use notes.
2. Discuss the nature of the occasion.
3. Discuss complimentary and interesting traits or characteristics of your visitor(s) or new member(s).
4. Discuss pertinent features of the welcoming group, your group.
5. Be a genial and cordial ambassador of good will; put out the welcome mat.

The Response to a Speech of Welcome

Occasionally when welcomed, you are expected to respond briefly. You ought to consider the following recommendations:

1. Graciously acknowledge the host's extended courtesy.
2. Bring greetings from the group that you represent (if you are a representative), and point up common bonds.
3. Sincerely praise the welcoming organization.

LET US SUMMARIZE

We have discussed specific pecularities of several varying speech types: the impromptu speech, the announcement, the speech to introduce a speaker, the nomination speech, along with speeches of presentation and acceptance, welcome speeches, and response to speeches of welcome. There is a type of speech for nearly every special occasion, and realistically we could not consider all of them in this chapter. When making any speech for a special occasion, remember three governing principles:

1. Know the demands of the occasion.
2. Employ sound speaking fundamentals.
3. Adapt the speech to the occasion.

FOR FURTHER STUDY

Gilman, Wilbur E., Aly, Bower, and Reid, Loren D., *Fundamentals of Speaking* (New York, The Macmillan Co., 1954), Ch. 25, "Public Address."

Monroe, Alan H., *Principles of Speech,* 4th ed. (Chicago, Scott, Foresman, 1958), Ch. 9, "Speeches for Special Occasions."

Norvelle, Lee, Smith, Raymond G., and Larson, Orvin, *Speaking Effectively* (New York, Holt-Dryden, 1957), Ch. 8, "Speeches for Special Occasions."

White, Eugene E., and Henderlider, Clair R., *Practical Public Speaking* (New York, The Macmillan Co., 1954), Ch. 15, "Speeches of Special Types."

SUGGESTED EXERCISE A

Arrange to have a series of impromptu talks in your class. The instructor may ask you to suggest some topics or areas of general knowledge from which topics can be drawn.

SUGGESTED EXERCISE B

Prepare a brief announcement about a subject of special importance to you—a dance to be held soon, an interesting television program, motion picture, or book, a cake sale, formation of a new club, or an athletic or speech contest, and so forth.

SUGGESTED EXERCISE C

Arrange to introduce a speaker in your class during the next series of assigned speeches.

SUGGESTED EXERCISE D

Divide the class into two equal sections. One section is to make speeches of presentation for hypothetical (but serious) occasions, and the other section is to respond with speeches of acceptance.

SUGGESTED EXERCISE E

Arrange to have a friend visit your class. Receive him with a short welcoming speech.

SUGGESTED EXERCISE F

Attend an event where one of the speeches discussed in this chapter is likely to be made. Analyze the effectiveness of the speech.
1. Did the speaker employ sound speaking fundamentals? Explain.
2. Did he adapt to the occasion? Explain.

SUGGESTED EXERCISE G

Attend the next assembly held to nominate student body officers. If you were a speech consultant for the speakers, what "do's" and "don'ts" would you offer them for future consideration?

14

Reading Aloud

OPPORTUNITIES TO READ ALOUD

"I plead for more reading aloud. It is a friendly, quiet and thoroughly refreshing thing to do. It makes us participants rather than spectators. Instead of sitting by to let the professionals amuse or enlighten us, *we* can get into the act, make contact with new ideas, exercise our imaginations."[1] These are the words of Charles Laughton, a recognized authority on the art of reading aloud.

Oral reading is an art—and a practical skill. The experience it offers can help one to become not only a better reader but also a better speaker. Have you ever noted how much actual reading is necessary in some types of speech making? Many speeches call for the use of abundant quoted material such as poetry, statistics, and prose passages. For accuracy and convenience, material of this kind is usually read.

Perhaps you have also observed that speakers frequently do not handle their quoted content to full advantage. If the material were used to full advantage, there would always be

---

[1] Charles Laughton, *This Week Magazine*, November 19, 1950.

evidence of careful preparation. We would not hear, as we do occasionally, the distracting contrast between the delivery of what is read and what is presented extemporaneously. Too, we as listeners would not be disturbed by lack of eye contact, monotony, mispronunciations, and embarrassing stumblings. All too common is the speaker who does not attend to this phase of his job. As a result of neglecting to prepare those portions of the speech that are to be read, he limits his total effectiveness.

In addition to the many opportunities for one to apply reading ability in typical speaking situations, there are scores of practical and artistic uses not associated with speech making as such. Consider, for instance, the variety of reading experiences that one person may have during one week. On Monday morning, let us say, Frank read a newspaper article to his family at breakfast. Later in the morning at work, he read a safety bulletin to his staff, and at three o'clock that afternoon, his superintendent listened to his oral presentation of a written report on plant operations. Before his two children went to bed that night, he amused them with a reading from *Winnie-the-Pooh*. He read some new regulations to his platoon at the Naval Reserve meeting Tuesday night. Wednesday evening, as secretary of the Men's Club, he reviewed the minutes of the last meeting. Late Thursday afternoon, Frank was called upon to read a policy statement to new employees at the plant. Friday night he came upon a familiar Robert Frost poem, and he read it to his wife; he knew that she would enjoy it. On Saturday, the Cub Scouts were delighted with his rendition of a Huck Finn episode. The next morning he read to his Sunday School class.

Frank's experiences are hypothetical, but they are not unusual. They are typical of those engaged in by thousands of people everywhere, for all of us have opportunities to read aloud.

What types of reading aloud will be required of you in your future life? Are you a good oral reader? Consider these questions as you study this chapter.

THE READER'S ROLE

Your reading assignments in this class are designed to help you gain increased reading skill and develop an appreciation for the art. Your role in some ways will be similar to your role as a speech maker. The two activities overlap at points: (1) Both original speaking and oral reading require thoughtful subject matter selection; (2) both demand that you determine a purpose or central idea and that you analyze; (3) attention to organization is a key factor in both activities; (4) the use of introductions and transitions can apply to both; (5) the same instruments of delivery are utilized in each case, of course, and (6) both require ample practice before actual presentation.

The major difference between the roles of the original speaker and the oral reader is that in the first type of speaking you develop your own thoughts and feelings while in the second you *interpret* the thoughts and feelings of someone else. As a speech maker, you speak for yourself; as a reader, you speak for the author who wrote what you are reading. You orally interpret what he has written. You attempt to convey to your listeners the content of his work. We might think of the oral interpreter as a translator who deciphers the alphabetical symbols on a printed page and relays the message to his listeners. From his familiarity with the author's work, he is able to bring out the ideas and feelings contained therein.

The interpreter has three instruments at his command to use in presenting his reading: personality, voice, and body. The voice is the primary means by which the essence of a selection is communicated. Heavy reliance upon only one instrument limits the reader, yet reading is a limited speech form. It is quite different from impersonating or acting on the stage. No costumes, properties, or make-up are employed in true oral interpretation. It is not acting. It is a unique type of activity. You can imagine how ridiculous it would be for a left-fielder in a baseball game to play in a football uniform or for a couple to attempt dancing a tango when the band plays a waltz. Those things are not done, except possibly in humorous stunts. Baseball is baseball, and waltzing is waltzing. The same holds true for reading aloud. Reading is reading. It is not acting or dancing, and the reader is himself, not a character in a play or skit.

In Chapter 8 we discussed the vocal characteristics: pitch, loudness, duration, and quality. It is, to a great degree, in the variation of these four factors that the reader is able to interpret his selected material for his audience. Here is essentially what happens: The reader studies his selection thoroughly in order to master the meaning and grasp the feeling. With this knowledge and understanding of the material, he reads it orally. While reading, the pitch, loudness, duration, and quality of his voice vary as his mind and "heart" respond to the content of the selection. Please note, however, that he does not consciously vary his pitch in certain places or add extra loudness in other places. He allows his knowledge and inward feelings for the material to inspire the appropriate vocal variation. Thus the oral interpreter avoids a mechanical recital of the author's words, and he is assured that his expression will be natural and true, a salutary response to the author's work.

The reader's bodily actions, too, must stem from an inner relationship with the material. If the content is humorous, the interpreter will surely be moved to smile; on the other hand, a sad story will provoke a facial response which reflects the mood. The expressions, head movements, and gestures that *naturally* accompany faithful interpretations of literature can help the audience to understand the selection.

In summary, at this point we should say that the role of the oral reader is to communicate the author's ideas and emotions to his listeners. He must do it sincerely and naturally by allowing his personality, voice, and body to reveal what he feels and what he has learned about the selection.

In other words, his job is to act as the author's faithful representative and to do so within the limitations of the specialized activity.

FINDING AN APPROPRIATE SELECTION

Not every piece of literature can be read aloud well, and material that may be appropriate for one person may not be appropriate for you. In situations where you have a choice of materials, you should choose a selection because you *want* to read it and not because you feel duty-bound to tackle a work that is accepted as great writing. If the poetry of T. S. Eliot, for example, does not appeal to you, try the work of another author. In literature there are selections for everyone; make a search, and you will find some which are suitable to you. Here are specific suggestions to assist you in making your decision:

1. Choose material that you appreciate and desire to study.
2. Choose material that you can cause your audience to appreciate and understand.
3. Choose material that has inherent human appeal—warmth, feeling, and interesting development.
4. Choose material that is worthy of being read aloud, material which makes you feel that it ought to be passed on to others.

PROSE AND POETRY

Most of the reading that you have done since acquiring the skill was written in prose form. Newspaper and magazine articles, short stories, novels, and textbooks are written in prose form. But what about the other form of written expression? Have you avoided poetry? Are you poetry shy? Has fear caused you to miss one of the most pleasurable human experiences? If you have a genuine desire to increase your appreciation of poetry, you can do it. Many students quite like yourself have gained their first respect for poetry by reading it orally. Others who were once quietly tolerant of such literature are now ardent enthusiasts.

How would you define poetry? Arriving at a succinct and acceptable definition is one of the most perplexing problems in the study of literature. Even such a poet as Edwin Arlington Robinson is unable to offer an exact definition. He says, "Poetry is a language that tells us, through a more or less emotional reaction, something that cannot be said."

Though poetry may defy definition, it can be understood better when compared to prose. Prose does not have a rhyme scheme nor obvious meter; poetry frequently includes rhyme and a noticeable meter. Prose is set up in paragraph units while poetry is organized in stanzas. Finally, it has been said that while some prose has a degree of poetic appeal, it speaks mainly to our heads. Poetry speaks "to our heads through ideas, to our hearts through feelings, to our ears through music, to our eyes through pictures, and to our bodies through rhythm." With such a diverse appeal, it is no wonder that poetry has been recognized as the highest form of literary expression.

Let us now examine several types of prose and poetry which are suited particularly to our purpose of studying oral reading. Though the classifications may overlap in some cases, certain essential distinctions justify our studying them separately. As an oral interpreter, you should have some experience in reading each of these types.

Narrative Literature

Narrative literature tells a story. If it is poetry, it is a story in verse form. Here are some examples:

RICHARD CORY

Whenever Richard Cory went down town,
We people on the pavement looked at him:
He was a gentleman from sole to crown,
Clean favored, and imperially slim.

And he was always quietly arrayed,
And he was always human when he talked;

But still he fluttered pulses when he said,
"Good morning," and he glittered when he walked.

And he was rich—yes, richer than a king—
And admirably schooled in every grace:
In fine, we thought that he was every thing
To make us wish that we were in his place.

So on we worked, and waited for the light,
And went without the meat, and cursed the bread;
And Richard Cory, one calm summer night,
Went home and put a bullet through his head.

—EDWIN ARLINGTON ROBINSON, *The Children
of the Night* (New York, Scribner's).

THE BALLAD OF THE OYSTERMAN

It was a tall young oysterman lived by the riverside,
His shop was just upon the bank, his boat was on the tide;
The daughter of a fisherman, that was so straight and slim,
Lived over on the other bank, right opposite to him.

It was the pensive oysterman that saw a lovely maid,
Upon a moonlight evening, a-sitting in the shade;
He saw her wave a handkerchief, as much as if to say,
"I'm wide awake, young oysterman, and all the folks away."

Then up arose the oysterman, and to himself said he,
"I guess I'll leave the skiff at home, for fear that folks should see;
I read it in the story book, that, for to kiss his dear,
Leander swam the Hellespont—and I will swim this here."

And he has leaped into the waves, and crossed the shining stream,
And he has clambered up the bank, all in the moonlight gleam;
Oh, there are kisses sweet as dew, and words as soft as rain—
But they have heard her father's steps, and in he leaps again!

Out spoke the ancient fisherman: "Oh, what was that, my daughter?"
" 'Twas nothing but a pebble, sir, I threw into the water."
"And what is that, pray tell me, love, that paddles off so fast?"
"It's nothing but a porpoise, sir, that's been a-swimming past."

Out spoke the ancient fisherman: "Now bring me my harpoon!
I'll get into my fishing boat, and fix the fellow soon."
Down fell the pretty innocent, as falls a snow-white lamb;
Her hair drooped round her pallid cheeks, like seaweed on a clam.

Alas for those two loving ones! she waked not from her swound,
And he was taken with the cramp, and in the waves was drowned;
But Fate has metamorphosed them, in pity of their woe,
And now they keep an oyster shop for mermaids down below.

—OLIVER WENDELL HOLMES,
The Poetical Works of Oliver Wendell Holmes
(Boston, Houghton Mifflin, 1927).

COME UP FROM THE FIELDS, FATHER

Come up from the fields, father, here's a letter from our Pete,
And come to the front door, mother, here's a letter from thy dear son.

Lo, 'tis autumn,
Lo, where the trees, deeper green, yellower and redder,
Cool and sweeten Ohio's villages with leaves fluttering in the
    moderate wind,
Where apples ripe in the orchards hang and grapes on the
    trellis'd vines.
(Smell you the smell of the grapes on the vines?
Smell you the buckwheat where the bees were lately buzzing?)

Above all, lo, the sky so calm, so transparent after the rain,
    and with wondrous clouds,
Below too, all calm, all vital and beautiful, and the farm prospers
    well.

Down in the fields all prospers well,
But now from the fields come, father, come at the daughter's call,
And come to the entry, mother, to the front door come right away.

Fast as she can she hurries, something ominous, her steps trembling,
She does not tarry to smooth her hair nor adjust her cap.

Open the envelope quickly,
O this is not our son's writing, yet his name is sign'd,

O a strange hand writes for our dear son, O stricken mother's soul!
All swims before her eyes, flashes with black, she catches the
     main words only,
Sentences broken, *gunshot wound in the breast, cavalry skirmish,*
     taken to hospital,
At present low, but will soon be better.

Ah now the single figure to me,
Amid all teeming and wealthy Ohio with all its cities and farms,
Sickly white in the face and dull in the head, very faint,
By the jamb of a door leans.

Grieve not so, dear mother, (the just-grown daughter speaks
     through her sobs,
The little sisters huddle around speechless and dismay'd,)
See, dearest mother, the letter says Pete will soon be better.

Alas poor boy, he will never be better, (nor may-be needs to be
     better, that brave and simple soul,)
While they stand at home at the door he is dead already,
The only son is dead.

But the mother needs to be better,
She with thin form presently drest in black
By day her meals untouch'd, then at night fitfully sleeping,
     often waking,
In the midnight waking, weeping, longing with one deep longing,
O that she might withdraw unnoticed, silent from life escape
     and withdraw,
To follow, to seek, to be with her dear dead son.

                    —WALT WHITMAN, *Leaves of Grass*
                       (Philadelphia, David McKay, 1900)

Folklore and Dialect

     Our second category, folklore and dialect literature, in
cludes stories, legends, and songs that tell the customs, belief
and experiences of distinctive individuals or groups. Suc

material is suggested for reading aloud because its frankness, openness, and spontaneity should inspire the reader to respond in kind, to let go.

Then, too, there is something about reading a folk tale or dialect selection which gives one a feeling of respect for the people whom the piece represents. One learns that all men have like feelings even though certain of their cultural, language, or physical features may differ. One learns that we are all human. "Dialect is the language of the heart and of the emotions, and we react naturally to its appeal."[2] Such an appeal cannot be ignored as an aid in the improvement of oral reading and as a delight to listeners. The following selections are representative.

MIA CARLOTTA

Giuseppe, da barber, ees greata for "mash,"
He gotta da bigga, da blacka mustache,
Good clo'es an' good styla an' playnta good cash.

W'enevra Giuseppe ees walk on da street,
Da peopla dey talka, "How nobby! how neat!
How softa da handa, how smalla da feet."

He raisa hees hat an' he shaka hees curls,
An' smila weeth teetha so shiny like pearls;
O! many da heart of da seelly young girls
   He gotta.
  Yes playnta he gotta—
   But notta
   Carlotta!

Giuseppe, da barber, he maka da eye,
An' lika da steam engine puffa an' sigh,
For catcha Carlotta w'en she ees go by.

Carlotta she walks weeth nose in da air,
An' look through Giuseppe weeth far-away stare,
As eef she no see dere ees som'body dere.

---

[2] Gertrude E. Johnson, *Studies in the Art of Interpretation*, New York, Appleton-Century, 1940.

Giuseppe, da barber, he gotta da cash,
He gotta da clo'es an' da bigga mustache,
He gotta da seelly young girls for da "mash,"
But notta—
You bat my life, notta—
Carlotta.
I gotta!

—T. A. DALY, from *Selected Poems of T. A. Daly*,
copyright, 1936, by Harcourt, Brace and Company,
Inc., and reprinted with their permission.

LULLABY

Kiver up yo' haid, my little lady,
Hyeah de win' a-blowin' out o' do's;
Don' you kick, ner projick wid de comfo't,
Less'n fros' 'll bite yo' little toes.
Shut yo' eyes an' snuggle up to mammy;
Gi' me bofe yo' han's, I hol' 'em tight;
Don' you be afeard an' 'mence to trimble
Des ez soon ez I blows out de light.

Angels is a-mindin' you, my baby,
Keepin' off de Bad Man in de night.
Whut de use o' bein' skeered o' nuffin'?
You don' fink de da'kness gwine to bite?
Whut de crackin' soun' you hyeah erroun' you?—
Lawsy, chile, you tickles me to def!—
Dat's de man what brings de fros', a-paintin'
Picters on de winder wid his bref.

Mammy ain' afeard, you hyeah huh laughin'?
Go 'way, Mistah Fros', you can't come in;
Baby ain' erceivin' folks dis evenin',
Reckon dat you'll have to call ag'in.
Curl yo' little toes up so, my 'possum—
Umph, but you's a cunnin' one fu' true!—

Go to sleep, de angels is a-watchin',
An' yo' mammy's mindin' of you, too.

—Paul Laurence Dunbar, reprinted by permission
of Dodd, Mead & Company from *The Collected
Poems of Paul Laurence Dunbar.*

JOHN HENRY AND THE MACHINE

At the time the race was to start, the blacksmiths had sharpened piles of drills, the steam drill had its steam up, and the carriers
were ready with pads on their shoulders to carry the sharpened
steels from the shop and the dull ones back to be sharpened. When
there was one minute to go, the steam drill whistled, and John
Henry lifted one of his twenty-pound hammers. Then Captain
Tommy dropped his hat, and the race started.

Says John Henry to Li'l Bill, the shaker, "Boy, you'd better
pray. Cause if I miss this piece of steel, tomorrow be your buryin'
day, sure as you born."

Then the steam drill was chugging, and John Henry was
swinging and singing—singing "Oh, My Hammer," "Water Boy,
Where Is You Hidin'," "If I Die a Railroad Man," and other hammer
songs he could keep time to. The steel rang like silver, the carriers
trotted to and from the blacksmith shops, and the crowd watched
with all its might and main.

It wasn't long after the start that John Henry took the lead.
The steam drill salesman wasn't worried though—or if he was his
talk didn't show it. "That man's a mighty man," he said. "But when
he hits the hard rock, he'll weaken." Then when John Henry hit
the hard rock, and kept driving fast as ever, the salesman said, "He
can't keep it up."

John Henry did keep it up, though, swinging those two hammers and driving down the steel, stopping only once an hour, may-
be, to take a drink of water from the dipper Polly Ann had carried
in her slender little hands. Six hours—seven hours—eight hours of
that nine-hour race, he made his hammer ring like gold. And
though Li'l Bill got plumb played out and a new shaker had to take
his place, all through the eighth hour John Henry was going strong

as ever, with the rhythm in every muscle and joint helping him wham the steel.

It wasn't until the ninth hour that John Henry showed any signs of getting tired. Then, when Captain Tommy came up to ask him how things were going, he answered him back, "This rock is so hard and this steel is so tough, I feel my muscles givin' way. But," he went on to say, "before I let that machine beat me, I'll die with my hammer in my hand."

After that, the crowd that was watching could see signs that John Henry was a weary man—very, very tired and weary.

And John Henry wasn't singing any more. All you could hear was the ring of the hammer on the steel and the chug-chug of the steam drill.

When Captain Tommy, at the end of the ninth hour, looked at his watch and yelled, "The race is over," and when the drills stopped going down, everything was as still as a graveyard. Captain Tommy was looking at the holes. Then, when Captain Tommy said, John Henry won—three holes ahead of the steam drill," everybody cheered—everybody, that is, excepting the salesman and the steam drill crew—and John Henry.

When the crowd looked at John Henry they saw the great man was lying on the ground, and his loving Polly Ann was holding his head. John Henry was moaning, and he sort of mumbled, "Before I let that steam drill beat me, I'll die with my hammer in my hand." (Sure enough, he had two hammers in his big hands.)

Then he said, "Give me a cool drink of water fore I die."

Polly Ann was crying when she gave him the water.

Then John Henry kissed his hammer and he kissed his loving Polly Ann. She had to stoop down so he could kiss her. Then he lay very still, and Polly Ann cried harder than ever—sounded mighty loud in that quiet quarry.

Just at that minute there was a sound of hoofs, and a preacher came riding up on a gray mule. "You got troubles, sister?" he said to Polly Ann. "Can I help you?"

"Only way you can help," she answered him back, "is to read the buryin' service for my lovin' John Henry. Cause his home ain' here no more."

So the preacher read the burying services. They buried John Henry on a hillside—with a hammer in each hand, a rod of steel across his breast, and a pick and shovel at his head and feet. And a great black cloud came out of the southwest to cover the copper sun.

—from WALTER BLAIR, *Tall Tale America*

(New York, Coward-McCann, 1944).

THE SOCIETY UPON THE STANISLAUS

I reside at Table Mountain, and my name is Truthful James;
I am not up to small deceit or any sinful games;
And I'll tell in simple language what I know about the row
That broke up our Society upon the Stanislow.

But first I would remark, that it is not a proper plan
For any scientific gent to whale his fellow-man,
And, if a member don't agree with his peculiar whim,
To lay for that same member for to "put a head" on him.

Now nothing could be finer or more beautiful to see
Than the first six months' proceedings of that same Society,
Till Brown of Calaveras brought a lot of fossil bones
That he found within a tunnel near the tenement of Jones.

Then Brown he read a paper, and he reconstructed there,
From those same bones, an animal that was extremely rare;
And Jones then asked the Chair for a suspension of the rules,
Till he could prove that those same bones was one of his lost mules.

Then Brown he smiled a bitter smile, and said he was at fault.
It seemed he had been trespassing on Jones's family vault;
He was a most sarcastic man, this quiet Mr. Brown,
And on several occasions he had cleaned out the town.

Now I hold it is not decent for a scientific gent
To say another is an ass,—at least, to all intent;
Nor should the individual who happens to be meant
Reply by heaving rocks at him, to any great extent.

Then Abner Dean of Angel's raised a point of order, when
A chunk of old red sandstone took him in the abdomen,

And he smiled a kind of sickly smile, and curled up on the floor,
And the subsequent proceedings interested him no more.

For, in less time than I write it, every member did engage
In a warfare with the remnants of a palaeozoic age;
And the way they heaved those fossils in their anger was a sin,
Till the skull of an old mammoth caved the head of Thompson in.

And this is all I have to say of these improper games,
For I live at Table Mountain, and my name is Truthful James;
And I've told in simple language what I know about the row
That broke up our Society upon the Stanislow.

—BRET HARTE, *The Poetical Works of Bret Harte*
(Boston, Houghton Mifflin).

Children's Literature

Children's literature is included here not only because most people have occasion to read to youngsters but also because this type of material facilitates the development of oral reading skills. There is feeling and life in a good children's selection, and the reader is impelled to respond accordingly.

THE ELEPHANT'S CHILD

" 'Scuse me," said the Elephant's Child most politely, "but do you happen to have seen a Crocodile in these promiscuous parts?"

Then the Crocodile winked the other eye, and lifted half his tail out of the mud; and the Elephant's Child stepped back most politely, because he did not wish to be spanked again.

"Come hither, Little One," said the Crocodile. "Why do you ask such things?"

" 'Scuse me," said the Elephant's Child most politely, "but my father has spanked me, my mother has spanked me, not to mention my tall aunt, the Ostrich, and my tall uncle, the Giraffe, who can kick ever so hard, as well as my broad aunt, the Hippopotamus, and my hairy uncle, the Baboon, *and* including the Bi-Coloured-Python Rock-Snake, with the scalesome, flailsome tail, just up the bank who spanks harder than any of them; and *so* if it's quite all the same to you, I don't want to be spanked any more."

"Come hither, Little One," said the Crocodile, "for I am the Crocodile," and he wept crocodile-tears to show it was quite true.

Then the Elephant's Child grew all breathless, and panted, and kneeled down on the bank and said, "You are the very person I have been looking for all these long days. Will you please tell me what you have for dinner?"

"Come hither, Little One," said the Crocodile, "and I'll whisper."

Then the Elephant's Child put his head down close to the Crocodile's musky, tusky mouth, and the Crocodile caught him by his little nose, which up to that very week, day, hour, and minute, had been no bigger than a boot, though much more useful.

"I think," said the Crocodile—and he said it between his teeth, like this—"I think to-day I will begin with Elephant's Child!"

—RUDYARD KIPLING, *The Elephant's Child,*
from *Just So Stories.*

BAMBI

Round about grew hazel bushes, dogwoods, blackthorns and young elders. Tall maples, beeches, and oaks wove a green roof over the thicket and from the firm, darkbrown earth sprang fern fronds, wood-vetch and sage. Underneath, the leaves of the violets, which had already bloomed, and of the strawberries, which were just beginning, clung to the ground. Through the thick foliage, the early sunlight filtered in a golden web. The whole forest resounded with myriad voices, was penetrated by them in a joyous agitation. The wood-thrush rejoiced incessantly, the doves cooed without stopping, the blackbirds whistled, finches warbled, the tit-mice chirped. Through the midst of these songs the jay flew, uttering its quarrelsome cry, the magpie mocked them, and the pheasants cackled loud and high. At times the shrill exulting of a woodpecker rose above all the other voices. The call of the falcon shrilled, light and piercing, over the tree-tops, and the hoarse crow chorus was heard continuously.

The little fawn understood not one of the many songs and calls, not a word of the conversations. He did not even listen to them. Nor did he heed any of the odors which blew through the woods. He only heard the soft licking against his coat that washed him and warmed him and kissed him. And he smelled nothing but his mother's body near him. She smelled good to him and, snuggling closer to her, he hunted eagerly around and found nourishment for his life.

While he suckled, the mother continued to caress her little one. "Bambi," she whispered. Every little while she raised her head and, listening, snuffed the wind. Then she kissed her fawn again, reassured and happy.

"Bambi," she repeated. "My little Bambi."

—Felix Salten, *Bambi* (New York, Simon and Schuster, Publishers, 1928).

HIDING

I'm hiding, I'm hiding,
And no one knows where;
For all they can see is my
Toes and my hair.

And I just heard my father
Say to my mother—
"But, darling, he must be
Somewhere or other;

"Have you looked in the ink well?"
And Mother said, "Where?"
"In the INK WELL," said Father. But
I was not there.

Then, "Wait!" cried my mother—
"I think that I see
Him under the carpet." But
It was not me.

"Inside the mirror's
A pretty good place,"
Said Father and looked, but saw
only his face.

"We've hunted," sighed Mother,
"As hard as we could
And I AM so afraid that we've
Lost him for good."

Then I laughed out aloud
And I wiggled my toes
And Father said—"Look, dear,
I wonder if those

Toes could be Benny's.
There are ten of them. See?"
And they WERE so surprised to find
Out it was me!

> —DOROTHY ALDIS, *Hiding, Everywhere and Anything* (New York, G. P. Putnam's Sons, 1927).

Lyric Poetry

Lyric poetry differs from narrative poetry in that it unfolds feelings and moods more than it tells a story. Such poetry gives us the collected impressions of the author on certain aspects of life; it is an expression of the poet's mood or viewpoint and often corresponds to our own unexpressed emotions. In reading lyric poems, particular emphasis should be placed upon the beauty, music, and color latent in the poem.

LINES FOR AN INTERMENT

Now it is fifteen years you have lain in the meadow:
The boards at your face have gone through: the earth is
Packed down and the sound of the rain is fainter:
The roots of the first grass are dead:

It's a long time to lie in the earth with your honor:
The world, Soldier, the world has been moving on:

The girls wouldn't look at you twice in the cloth cap:
Six years old they were when it happened:

It bores them even in books: "Soissons besieged!"
As for the gents they have joined the American Legion:

Belts and a brass band and the ladies' auxiliaries:
The Californians march in the OD silk:

We are all acting again like civilized beings:
People mention it at tea . . .

The Facts of Life we have learned are Economic:
You were deceived by the detonations of bombs:

You thought of courage and death when you thought of warfare:
Hadn't they taught you the fine words were unfortunate?

Now that we understand we judge without bias:
We feel of course for those who had to die:

Women have written us novels of great passion
Proving the useless death of the dead was a tragedy:

Nevertheless it is foolish to chew gall:
The foremost writers on both sides have apologized:

The Germans are back in the Midi with cropped hair:
The English are drinking the better beer in Bavaria:

You can rest now in the rain in the Belgian meadow—
Now that it's all explained away and forgotten:
Now that the earth is hard and the wood rots:

Now you are dead . . .

> —ARCHIBALD MACLEISH, from *Collected Poems*
> (Boston, Houghton Mifflin, 1952), reprinted by per-
> mission of and arrangement with Houghton Mifflin
> Company, the authorized publishers.

MENDING WALL

Something there is that doesn't love a wall,
That sends the frozen-ground-swell under it,
And spills the upper boulders in the sun;
And makes gaps even two can pass abreast.

The work of hunters is another thing:
I have come after them and made repair
Where they have left not one stone on a stone,
But they would have the rabbit out of hiding,
To please the yelping dogs. The gaps I mean,
No one has seen them made or heard them made,
But at spring mending-time we find them there.
I let my neighbor know beyond the hill;
And on a day we meet to walk the line
And set the wall between us once again.
We keep the wall between us as we go.
To each the boulders that have fallen to each.
And some are loaves and some so nearly balls
We have to use a spell to make them balance:
"Stay where you are until our backs are turned!"
We wear our fingers rough with handling them.
Oh, just another kind of out-door game,
One on a side. It comes to little more:
There where it is we do not need the wall:
He is all pine and I am apple orchard.
My apple trees will never get across
And eat the cones under his pines, I tell him.
He only says, "Good fences make good neighbors."
Spring is the mischief in me, and I wonder
If I could put a notion in his head:
"*Why* do they make good neighbors? Isn't it
Where there are cows? But here there are no cows.
Before I built a wall I'd ask to know
What I was walling in or walling out,
And to whom I was like to give offence.
Something there is that doesn't love a wall,
That wants it down." I could say "Elves" to him,
But it's not elves exactly, and I'd rather
He said it for himself. I see him there
Bringing a stone grasped firmly by the top
In each hand, like an old-stone savage armed.
He moves in darkness as it seems to me,

Not of woods only and the shade of trees.
He will not go behind his father's saying,
And he likes having thought of it so well
He says again, "Good fences make good neighbors."

SPRING NIGHT

The park is filled with night and fog,
    The veils are drawn about the world,
The drowsy lights along the paths
    Are dim and pearled.

Gold and gleaming the empty streets,
    Gold and gleaming the misty lake,
The mirrored lights like sunken swords,
    Glimmer and shake.

Oh, is it not enough to be
Here with this beauty over me?
My throat should ache with praise, and I
Should kneel in joy beneath the sky.
O beauty, are you not enough?
Why am I crying after love
With youth, a singing voice, and eyes
To take earth's wonder with surprise?
Why have I put off my pride,
Why am I unsatisfied,—
I, for whom the pensive night
Binds her cloudy hair with light,—
I, for whom all beauty burns
Like incense in a million urns?
O beauty, are you not enough?
Why am I crying after love?

Literature of High Resolve

Literature of a high resolve, though it may overlap with other types, can be considered individually here. Into this category we put public addresses, editorials, Biblical selections, inspirational poems, serious essays, and patriotic and biographical selections that reflect a spirit of moral or ethical values.

LETTER TO MRS. BIXBY

Dear Madam:

I have been shown in the files of the War Department a statement of the Adjutant General that you are the mother of five sons who have died gloriously on the field of battle. I feel how weak and fruitless must be any words of mine which should attempt to beguile you from the grief of a loss so overwhelming. But I cannot refrain from tendering to you the consolation that may be found in the thanks of the Republic they died to save. I pray that our heavenly Father may assuage the anguish of your bereavement and leave you only the cherished memory of the loved and lost and the solemn pride that must be yours to have laid so costly a sacrifice upon the altar of freedom.

Yours very sincerely and respectfully,

Abraham Lincoln

But I want first of all—in fact, as an end to these other desires—to be at peace with myself. I want a singleness of eye, a purity of intention, a central core to my life that will enable me to carry out these obligations and activities as well as I can. I want, in fact—to borrow from the language of the saints—to live "in grace" as much of the time as possible. I am not using this term in a strictly theological sense. By grace I mean an inner harmony, essentially spiritual, which can be translated into outward harmony. I am seeking perhaps what Socrates asked for in the prayer from the *Phaedrus* when he said, "May the outward and inward man be at one." I would like to achieve a state of inner spiritual grace from which I could function and give as I was meant to in the eye of God.

Vague as this definition may be, I believe most people are aware of periods in their lives when they seem to be "in grace" and other periods when they feel "out of grace," even though they may use different words to describe these states. In the first happy condition, one seems to carry all one's tasks before one lightly, as if borne along on a great tide; and in the opposite state one can hardly tie a shoe-string. It is true that a large part of life consists in learning a technique of tying the shoe-string, whether one is in grace or not. But there are techniques of living too; there are even techniques in the search for grace. And techniques can be cultivated. I have learned by some experience, by many examples, and by the writings of countless others before me, also occupied in the search, that certain environments, certain modes of life, certain rules of conduct are more conducive to inner and outer harmony than others. There are, in fact, certain roads that one may follow. Simplification of life is one of them.

—ANNE MORROW LINDBERGH, *Gift From the Sea*
(New York, Pantheon Books, 1955)

About to enter, fellow-citizens, on the exercise of duties which comprehend everything dear and valuable to you, it is proper you should understand what I deem the essential principles of our Government, and consequently those which ought to shape its Administration. I will compress them within the narrowest compass they will bear, stating the general principles, but not all its limitations. Equal and exact justice to all men, of whatever state of persuasion, religious or political; peace, commerce, and honest friendship with all nations, entangling alliances with none; the support of the State governments in all their rights, as the most competent administrations for our domestic concerns and the surest bulwarks against antirepublican tendencies; the preservation of the General Government in its whole constitutional vigor, as the sheet anchor of our peace at home and safety abroad; a jealous care of the right of election by the people—a mild and safe corrective of abuses which are lopped by the sword of revolution where peaceable remedies are unprovided; absolute acquiescence in the decisions of the ma jority, the vital principle of republics, from which is no appeal but to force, the vital principle and immediate parent of despotism; a well-disciplined militia, our best reliance in peace and for the first moments of war, till regulars may relieve them; the supremacy of the civil over the military authority; economy in the public expense, that labor may be lightly burthened; the honest payment of our debts and sacred preservation of the public faith; encouragement of agriculture, and of commerce as its handmaid; the diffusion of information and arraignment of all abuses at the bar of the public reason; freedom of religion; freedom of the press, and freedom of person under the protection of the habeas corpus, and trial by juries impartially selected. These principles form the bright con-stellation which has gone before us and guided our steps through an age of revolution and reformation. The wisdom of our sages and blood of our heroes have been devoted to their attainment. They should be the creed of our political faith, the text of civic instruction, the touchstone by which to try the services of those we trust; and should we wander from them in moments of error or of alarm, let us hasten to retrace our steps and to regain the road which alone leads to peace, liberty and safety.

—THOMAS JEFFERSON, First Inaugural Address, 1801

A COWBOY'S PRAYER

Oh Lord. I've never lived where churches grow.
    I love creation better as it stood
That day You finished it so long ago
    And looked upon Your work and called it good.
I know that others find You in the light
    That's sifted down through tinted window panes,
And yet I seem to feel You near tonight
    In this dim, quiet starlight on the plains.

I thank You, Lord, that I am placed so well,
    That You have made my freedom so complete;
That I'm no slave of whistle, clock or bell,
    Nor weak-eyed prisoner of wall and street.
Just let me live my life as I've begun

And give me work that's open to the sky;
Make me a pardner of the wind and sun,
And I won't ask a life that's soft or high.

Let me be easy on the man that's down;
Let me be square and generous with all.
I'm careless sometimes, Lord, when I'm in town,
But never let 'em say I'm mean or small!
Make me as big and open as the plains,
As honest as the hawse between my knees,
Clean as the wind that blows behind the rains,
Free as the hawk that circles down the breeze!

Forgive me, Lord, if sometimes I forget.
You know about the reasons that are hid.
You understand the things that gall and fret;
You know me better than my mother did.
Just keep an eye on all that's done and said
And right me, sometimes, when I turn aside,
And guide me on the long, dim trail ahead
That stretches upward toward the Great Divide.

> —BADGER CLARK, *Sun and Saddle Leather* (Boston,
> Chapman and Grimes, 1915), by permission of The
> Westerners Foundation, College of the Pacific.

STUDYING THE SELECTION

After choosing a piece of prose or poetry, you must become better acquainted with it; you cannot interpret the material for your audience unless you understand it thoroughly. First, it is necessary to discover the essential thoughts and feelings, what the author is saying. Next break the selection down and analyze its smaller components.

The analysis, then, is our present object of consideration. At another point in the chapter, under the heading "Practicing the Selection," we will discuss the synthesis: the selection in its whole form with all the parts functioning together as a unit.

Discovering the Thoughts and Feelings

1. *What is the central idea or theme?* Look for the author's main point by reading the selection silently. Do not despair if you are unable to grasp the central idea during the first reading. Go over it again, and do not be satisfied until you can state it in one or two sentences. Seeking the central idea may take you into a study of the background or setting related to the material. To understand the theme of Tom Paine's essay, *The Crisis*, for instance, it is necessary to know the chain of historical events that led to its publication.

2. *Can you express the content in your own words?* Paraphrase the selection. Write it out in *your* language. This is one of the surest ways to teach yourself the meaning of difficult prose or poetry.

3. *What is the author's purpose?* Does he wish to arouse and cause his "audience" to act? Is it his design to give information, to entertain, to point out the beauty or ugliness of life, to eulogize a person, or to poke fun? Did Jonathan Swift write *Gulliver's Travels* to entertain children? Parts may appear to be for young people, but the book basically is a satire on the stupidity of human behavior. To interpret an author's work faithfully, you need to know his aim.

4. *What are the author's attitudes?* What feelings does he express in his work? A reader who is not sensitive to the author's attitudes will present little more than an uninteresting pile of words. Oral interpretation entails communication of feeling as well as thought. Neither should be neglected. If you know when the author's mood suggests contentedness and when it is one of bitterness or jealousy or fear or anger or contempt or love, you will be able to suggest such emotions in your interpretative reading.

5. *What is the author's background?* Find out about the elements that have influenced his writing: where he has lived, his character and personality, his associates, his family. There is good reason for this investigation, for his writing will reflect his personality, philosophy of life, and general rearing. Is it

not logical that a study of an author will help you to gain a better understanding of and appreciation for his works? When you read *The Raven* knowing that Edgar Allan Poe led a turbulent life filled with disappointment, grief, and illness, it is very likely that you will be able to communicate to your listeners considerably more of the "Poe in Poe." The more that you know of what lies behind the material, the better you will be able to convey its meaning.

6. *What moved him to write the selection?* Can you determine a specific motivating factor? Edwin Markham's *The Man with the Hoe* was inspired by Millet's classic painting of a French peasant "bowed by the weight of centuries." To understand Alfred Tennyson's *In Memoriam*, one must know that this long series of lyrics was motivated by grief over the death of Arthur Hallam, Tennyson's closest friend.

Analyzing the Details

After discovering the essential thoughts and feelings latent in your selection, you will need to study certain relevant details.

1. *Do you know the meanings of all the words and phrases?* We become overconfident at times and occasionally choose to ignore details. The result can prove embarrassing. Take the case of Marilyn who was reading a short story about football to a class. It was quite evident that she had not prepared adequately. One thing was certain; she had not bothered to define questionable words. How did the class know? Well, whenever she read "offensive lineman" or "offensive half-back," she did so with an obvious indication of disgust. To her, she later confessed, *offensive* had but one meaning—*obnoxious*.

We color our expression of words naturally according to our knowledge of their meanings and our feelings about them. Words have at least two meanings in most cases, perhaps in all cases. First, there is the dictionary definition. Then there is the meaning that an author implies by the way he uses the word or by the setting into which he puts it. That is, a word in each context carries a different *connotation* or signification. The reader must be alert to the author's intent, what he wants his words to say. *Love,* for example, may connote *fondness* in one place and *rapture* in another. You should be able to interpret each faithfully.

2. *Can you explain all figures of speech?* We referred to figures of speech in Chapter 7. They are the language symbols used by speakers and writers to beautify and strengthen their thoughts. What does William Hamilton Hayne in his *A Sea Lyric* mean to say with this metaphor?

> For the sea is a harp, and the winds of God
> Play over his rhythmic breast,

Explain the meaning of this beautiful simile from Byron's *Childe Harold.*

> Parting day
> Dies like the dolphin, whom each pang imbues
> With a new colour as it gasps away,

Literature is full of figures of speech, and the oral reader must be able to translate them if he is to be effective in communication.

3. *Can you pronounce all the words?* When in doubt, check the dictionary; do not guess. Our language can play tricks on us, especially when words are not pronounced as they are spelled. It is hard for many to understand how the people in Massachusetts can get something sounding like *wurster* out of *Worcester* or how *quay* is pronounced *key.*

INTRODUCING THE SELECTION

To set the scene and put your audience in a receptive mood, you should prepare an introduction to your reading.

Plan your remarks carefully, and present them extemporaneously. One or more of the following topics could be covered:
1. Reasons for reading the selection.
2. A biographical sketch of the author.
3. Background elements of the selection such as time, place, and setting.
4. Explanation of the theme.

PRACTICING THE SELECTION

When you are satisfied that you have discovered the essential thought and feeling, analyzed the smaller parts, and composed a fitting introduction, you are ready for the final phase of preparation. You will need to practice the material to insure communication of what the author has put into it.

Find a place where you can practice aloud without being disturbed. Practice purposefully, with your goal of transmitting the meaning firmly in mind. Expressiveness in oral interpretation comes primarily from a desire to share with others what you know and feel about a selection. Without the urge to communicate, without a willing and enthusiastic attitude, it is difficult to make printed words on a page come alive.

Knowledge of content and willingness to express it make conscious concern for such factors as pitch and rate variation unnecessary. Reading is not a mechanical activity. You do not succeed in communication by "pulling levers" or "pushing buttons" as you reach prescribed points on the page. It cannot be overemphasized that success in oral reading is achieved by responding fully to the facts and inward feelings that you have accumulated from a comprehensive study of the material.

Be conscious of the need for eye contact as you practice. During rehearsal sessions you will learn that you can let your eyes leave the page from time to time without losing your place and breaking the continuity. Hold the book or manuscript high enough for ease in reading and low enough to allow visual contact.

When practicing a selection of poetry, do not be hindered by its unique form. Be careful not to let rhyme or meter push thought into the background. Undue emphasis of these elements can result in a singsong kind of reading.

Do not stop at the end of each line of poetry. Let the meaning tell you when to pause or drop your voice. Punctuation marks will help you to understand the poem, and in most cases you should treat them as though they were being used in prose writing. If the punctuation and sense of the poem suggest that you should read on, then read on. Carry the thought naturally and expressively along, and stop only when the meaning dictates a pause.

Read to convey the beauty and melody of a poem. Beyond thought content, poetry has emotion and music which must be communicated if the reader is to be faithful to the author. Release yourself. Do not be afraid to let yourself respond. You may find that for the first time in your life you are *truly* expressing yourself.

And always remember that audiences are made up of *real people* who can be moved by your interpretation of a selection of literature. By thinking of your reading as an opportunity to share a worthwhile piece of writing with them, you can make them forget that you are completing an assignment for class credit. Read to them. Read directly to them. Read sincerely, naturally, and willingly to them.

LET US SUMMARIZE

Again and again during your life, occasions for reading aloud will arise, and now is the time to prepare for those eventualities. Such preparation will help you also in making original speeches since many speeches include quoted material. Then, too, the expressiveness that one acquires from training in oral reading is carried over to other forms of speech communication.

Before beginning the first assignment, reconsider the suggestions we have made:
1. Appreciate the reader's role.
2. Find an appropriate selection.
3. Study the selection.
4. Introduce the selection.
5. Practice the selection.

Clarence T. Simon, professor of speech at Northwestern University, has a bit of sound advice:

> If the student wishes to develop and deepen his appreciation, he must be willing to surrender himself to the reactions which are prompted. He must allow the responses to sweep through him. There must be no undue holding back; there must be a forgetfulness of self.[3]

FOR FURTHER STUDY

Crocker, Lionel, and Eich, Louis M., *Oral Reading*, 2d ed. (Englewood Cliffs, N. J., Prentice-Hall, 1955).

Henneke, Ben G., *Reading Aloud Effectively* (New York, Rinehart, 1955).

Lee, Charlotte I., *Oral Interpretation* (Boston, Houghton Mifflin, 1952).

Lowrey, Sara, and Johnson, Gertrude E., *Interpretative Reading*, rev. ed. (New York, Appleton-Century-Crofts, 1953).

Woolbert, C. H., and Nelson, Severina E., *The Art of Interpretative Speech*, 4th ed. (New York, Appleton-Century-Crofts, 1956).

FOR READING SELECTION

Barnes, Ruth. ed., *I Hear America Singing* (Philadelphia, Winston, 1937).

---

[3] Clarence T. Simon, "Appreciation in Reading," *Studies in the Art of Interpretation*, ed. by Gertrude E. Johnson, New York, Appleton-Century, 1940, p. 27.

Blair, Walter, ed., *Native American Humor* (New York, American Book, 1937).

Burnett, Whit, ed., *The World's Best* (New York, Dial, 1950).

Compere, Moiree, *Living Literature for Oral Interpretation* (New York, Appleton-Century-Crofts, 1949).

Daly, T. A., *Late Lark Singing* (New York, Harcourt, Brace, 1946).

Johnson, Gertrude E., ed., *Dialects for Oral Interpretation* (New York, Appleton-Century-Crofts, 1920).

Parrish, Wayland Maxfield, and Hochmuth, Marie K., eds., *American Speeches* (New York, Longmans, Green, 1954).

Teter, George, ed., *A Book of Humorous Poems* (Chicago, Scott, Foresman, 1931).

Untermeyer, Louis, ed., *Modern American Poetry* (New York, Harcourt, Brace, 1950).

———, *A Treasury of Laughter* (New York, Simon and Schuster, 1946).

Wallace, Douglas, Lamson, Roy, and Smith, Hallett, eds., *The Critical Reader* (New York, Norton, 1949).

Wells, Henry W., ed., *One Thousand and One Poems of Mankind* (New York, Mackay, 1953).

White, E. B., and White, Katherine S., eds., *A Subtreasury of American Humor* (New York, Coward-McCann, 1941).

Woods, Ralph L., ed., *A Second Treasury of the Familiar* (New York, The Macmillan Co., 1955).

———, *A Treasury of Friendship* (New York, McKay, 1957).

SUGGESTED EXERCISE A

Find a two-minute selection of prose or poetry that you would *like* to read. The purpose of this exercise is to help you to become accustomed to reading aloud before an audience. Strive to do your best. Study the selection carefully and practice aloud conscientiously.

SUGGESTED EXERCISE B

For future use, make a bibliography of ten library references which contain information about authors.

SUGGESTED EXERCISE C

Compile a bibliography of ten anthologies of prose and poetry that are to be found in your library.

SUGGESTED EXERCISE D

Choose a narrative poem of two to four minutes which you would like to read. Submit to your instructor an analysis of the meaning, covering these points:

1. The central idea.
2. A short paraphrase of the selection.
3. The author's purpose.
4. The author's attitudes.
5. The author's background.
6. The author's reasons for writing the selection.

Prepare an appropriate introduction, and practice with a desire to communicate.

SUGGESTED EXERCISE E

Repeat Suggested Exercise D, substituting a folklore, dialect, or children's selection of prose or poetry.

SUGGESTED EXERCISE F

Repeat Suggested Exercise D, substituting a lyric poem. Bring out the feeling and melody along with the meaning.

SUGGESTED EXERCISE G

Repeat Suggested Exercise D, substituting a literary selection of high resolve (printed speech, Biblical selection, essay, editorial, inspirational poem, or so forth). Convey to your audience the high principles and moral or ethical values contained in the selection.

SUGGESTED EXERCISE H

Prepare a four-to-seven-minute lecture-recital type of program, either alone or with other members of the class. This is an exercise in which you develop a certain theme with two or more selections of prose and/or poetry. Choose a theme of special interest to you.

It may be concerned with characteristics of people, sports, the seasons, love, death, patriotism, places, children, adventure, or so forth. Introduce the selections and connect them with meaningful transitions.

Submit analyses of the selections to your instructor.

SUGGESTED EXERCISE I

Prepare a speech in which you use quotations as your main supporting material. Use lengthy quotations in the introduction, in developing each main head, and in the conclusion.

IV

APPENDIXES

IV

APPENDIXES

Appendix A

Practical Methods Applied: Model Speeches

REMARKS ON JEFFERSON DAY

BOWER ALY

University of Missouri, April 13, 1955

Mr. Chairman: We have come this morning to do honor to Thomas Jefferson, author of the Declaration of American Independence, and of the Statute of Virginia for Religious Freedom, and Father of the University of Virginia. We have come to honor him, even though we realize that his fame has long since passed beyond our power to praise. Indeed, this morning it behooves us to ask ourselves the searching question whether we are worthy to praise him.

Thomas Jefferson declared eternal warfare against every form of tyranny over the minds of men. In this generation we have quietly witnessed an onslaught on our liberties by those whose plan of attack on Russian tyranny begins with the destruction of American liberty. Are we worthy to praise Thomas Jefferson?

Thomas Jefferson believed in the Constitution, under which he served, and in the Bill of Rights, in which were embodied his ideas of liberty under law. Today we sit complacently while those who would destroy our Bill of Rights slander the precious Fifth Amendment by attaching to it the epithet "Communist." Are we worthy to praise Thomas Jefferson?

Thomas Jefferson welcomed honest dissent boldly expressed as the surest evidence of liberty prevailing. Today we see timid men fleeing to conform; and we witness citizens as yet unconvicted of any crime harried by government informers and suborners of perjury who gain their fees, without our protest, from taxes we have paid. Are we worthy to praise Thomas Jefferson?

In an age which, like our own, knew grave danger, Thomas Jefferson and his contemporaries cast out fear and stood unafraid. Americans today, though rich and powerful, stand irresolute and fearful when they should be confident and strong. Are we worthy to praise Thomas Jefferson?

Mr. Chairman: We Americans of this generation did not earn our liberties. We merely inherited them. We inherited them with our Constitution, our Bill of Rights, and our government of free men established by Washington, Hamilton, and Jefferson. We stand in present danger of being disinherited. No less a person than the Chief Justice of the Supreme Court of the United States has recently warned us of the grave and growing dangers to our ancient liberties. We shall be disinherited unless we learn how to defend the values handed down to us by Jefferson and his compatriots.

Mr. Chairman: I submit that we Americans today have not kept faith with Thomas Jefferson. Since we have not kept true faith with him in our deeds we have no right to praise him with our words. I propose, therefore, that we offer as our tribute today a solemn and inward determination so to live in protest against every form of tyranny that our actions may earn for us the right to praise Jefferson in happier days to come.

—A. Craig Baird, ed., *Representative American Speeches:* *1955-1956* (New York, H. W. Wilson), pp. 59-61.

NO. 2

THE FUNCTION OF DEMOCRACY

JUSTICE WILLIAM O. DOUGLAS

Given before the Commonwealth Club in San Francisco,
June 20, 1941

There probably have been but few generations which have felt as poignantly as ours the challenge in the poet's dictum that—
Each age is a dream that is dying
Or one that is coming to birth.
We know that we are more than mere spectators on a world revolutionary scene. We know that those revolutionary forces are infections in the world bloodstream and that we shall be profoundly affected even though that disease will not ultimately triumph.

For these reasons we are all thinking deeply and profoundly about our responsibilities in this present world crisis.

Not so long ago I heard a professional group cheer the boast of a speaker that he had not mentioned once in his address the word "democracy."

Democracy, however, is no empty word, no mere shibboleth. It is a word to fill the heart with pride.

It reflects the faith of nations in the common sense of the common man.

It carries the precious cargo of equal justice under the law, the right freely to speak and write and to worship God, the right of free assembly, and equality of political and social opportunity.

It is the way of life which respects the dignity of man, which recognizes no special class of citizenship based on wealth or poverty, or color, race, or creed.

These are commonplaces to us. We are inclined to take them for granted as we are the sun, and moon, and stars. But in these days of world upheaval unguarded assumption of the permanency of any institution is hazardous.

For these reasons, now is the time for open avowal of our faith, not for silence. Now is the time to utilize vigorously our constitutional rights so as to preach and practice incessantly the truths of democracy.

As Francis Hackett has put it, "We, the democrats, have not supposed that we must assert ourselves aggressively. Our faith has been sapped because of that." (*I Chose Denmark*, 1940.) Aggressive assertion of an unbounded devotion to this way of life not only replenishes the people's faith—it helps create the alertness in thought and action necessary to transform that faith into a work-a-day creed.

With the world on fire we know it is not enough for us to vote and pay taxes and earn a living. Fifty years ago the thought was current that the nation could afford the luxury of having little skill in government because it required the use of its best brains and talents in the development of the country. But we know that we can ill afford any such diversions from active participation in this current campaign.

The needs of democracy cannot be filled merely by service within the normal orbit of our daily lives. Those needs must also be satisfied through civic, municipal, county, state, and national activities. And, somehow or other, our contributions must be made through those channels by devoting at least a part of our reserves of energy to public enterprises.

We have it in our power, by giving only a part of our lives, to provide a leadership in thought and action which will create a genuine—a spiritual—renaissance of the democratic faith. Those millions of Americans who have a real appreciation of the blood and sweat and sacrifice which through the centuries have ingrained into our present society the noblest ideals of mankind are the strongest sort of bulwark against those forces which would dislodge society from its moorings.

1. We must make sure that our citizens retain their old tradition of participating in the important decisions which affect their lives, their property, their ideals. The gap between local democracy and national representative government must not be allowed to widen. The people must remain part of an integrated national system, so that they feel an intimate contact with their government so that it does not become a thing apart—removed and remote from

them. One of the ways of maintaining that bridge is through the many articulate but unofficial groups concerned with some aspect of our social, economic, or governmental problems. Through them many a citizen can become an active participant in the body politic and actually share in the decisions which affect his own welfare. Such groups help make democratic government the imperishable possession of each citizen. Hence they are strong underpinning for an aroused and alert democracy. May the leaders of community thought, devoted to democratic ideals, assume responsibility for making them effective agencies through which the people may undertake active daily roles of citizenship.

2. The function of democracy, unlike totalitarian governments, is to train men—little men as well as big men—not for subjugation but for independence. We know that therein lies the great strength of democracy. We know that only in that way can the great spiritual values of a whole people be cultivated and preserved. Yet we also know that that requires great skills in view of the complexities of a technological age. It means that every citizen must have a stake in his country adequate to justify in his eyes the sacrifices which any contingency may entail. It means that some way or other big men and little men must work as partners in our national endeavors. It means that powerful men and weak men must be joint ventures in preserving America in its own image. It means that government must serve a whole people—regardless of lines of wealth or poverty, strength, or weakness. And our endeavor must be not the detection of motes in each other's eyes but an objective, united assault on common problems.

To integrate the energies of little men and big men, share and share alike, into all local, state, and national undertakings is a task which requires continuous statesmanship. But success in that effort is a permanent achievement. It means that no caste system takes root. It mean that equality and fraternity are given practical recognition. It means that men from all walks of life will find common adventure and thrills in serving jointly a great cause. It means that the eyes of men will be lifted from mean objectives to lofty ideals.

The sense of fraternity, the desire for service, the adventurous instinct are deep in the soul of America. They have been successfully appealed to before by offer of far less noble causes than the democracies now tender.

3. There must not grow up in this country any second or third or fourth class of citizenship.

There is only one class of citizenship in this nation. There is no room for any inferior grade. Where one has been allowed, the result has been the downward spiral of disunity. Then hate and intolerance have been incorporated. Under those conditions the enemies of democracy invariably have risen to power. Under those conditions there is an insistence on a conformity which is the beginning of a disintegrating process.

Every nonconformist who is beaten, every practitioner of the right of free speech who is jailed, every unpopular exponent of a religious faith who is deprived of his constitutional rights bring every free man a step closer to incarceration or punishment, or discreet and frightened conformity. Infraction of the Bill of Rights knows no terminal points. We know from the experience of other peoples that what starts as suppression of an unpopular minority swings as easily to persecutions on the right or on the left, until few can afford to be nonconformists. Those who started as instigators of oppression of a minority often turned out to be the next victims. We know that the concentration camps of Europe are not operated on racial, economic, social, or intellectual lines.

We should ever be mindful that all the battles for freedom are not won in the courts. "Only a persistent, positive translation of the liberal faith into the thoughts and acts of the community is the real reliance against the unabated temptation to straitjacket the human mind." (Frankfurter, *Law and Politics*, p. 197.) Vigilant patrol of the domestic scene against infraction of these fundamental constitutional rights will guarantee that the American sense of fair play will carry the day.

4. A contemporary observer has said that as a result of the incredible sophistries and the brutal and ruthless attacks by totalitarian leaders on the democratic processes, "The Declaration of Independence may now be referred to without apology, and even policemen on the beat are becoming dimly aware that there is such a thing as the Bill of Rights."

Certainly, those assaults have made us all realize more keenly than ever before that there is only one liberty, and that is liberty within the law. Without that cementing element there can never be confidence in order—the real basis of all security. And without a common sense of security there can be no effective compact among men based on conceptions of equality and fraternity. That entails, as a practical necessity, a constant recognition of the responsibilities as well as the rights of citizenship. There will be some who will be willing to exploit the Bill of Rights in order to destroy or mutilate the system which makes the Bill of Rights possible. But the defense against them is vigorous assertion by millions of Americans of their constitutional rights so as to preserve our basic freedoms, not to defile them. It is to be found in an alert and aroused citizenry intent on making the democratic processes function in any and all crises and resolved not to permit the forces of discord, fear, hesitation, or inaction to paralyze the operations of government.

Those who appreciate the human sacrifices which have made our free institutions possible know that rights are accompanied by responsibilities. They know that recognition of those responsibilities is the certain method of preserving and nurturing those rights. When rights and responsibilities go hand in hand, there is the strongest guaranty possible that liberty within the law is not mere temporary luxury but a permanent necessity for a free people. When the energies of the people are absorbed in that common endeavor the whisperers of hate and intolerance loom no more important than the occupants of psychiatric wards.

Whatever may be the specific ways and means, whatever the effort, the pole star will always be the ingredients of the democratic faith. These have recently been stated by an eminent American, Carl Becker, as follows:

To have faith in the dignity and worth of the individual man as an end in himself, to believe that it is better to be governed by persuasion that by coercion, to believe that fraternal good will is more worthy than a selfish and contentious spirit, to believe that in the long run all values are inseparable from the love of truth and the disinterested search for it, to believe that knowledge and the power it confers should be used to promote the welfare and happiness of all men rather than to serve the interests of those individuals and classes whom fortune and intelligence endow with temporary advantage— these are the values which are affirmed by the traditional democratic ideology.

In final analysis our individual and joint efforts must have as their end product the way of life which underwrites those eternal truths.

In 1775, when this nation was uniting against the tyranny of that age, a great patriot said, "We are not weak if we make a proper use of those means which the god of nature hath placed in our power." Today those words ring as true as they did then.

The means which God has placed in our power embrace not only material resources but also great inner spiritual strength, an abiding sense of fair play, an abundance of common sense, a deep sense of fraternity, a great reserve of ingenuity, a desire for service. To evoke these qualities from all the people in times of peace as well as war will mean that our rich heritage of freedom will remain imperishable. Utilization of those tremendous reserves of strength will guarantee that this age is not a dream that is dying but one that is coming to glorious birth.

—A. Craig Baird, ed., *Representative American Speeches: 1940-1941* (New York, H. W. Wilson), pp. 225-231.

NO. 3

SOCIAL RESPONSIBILITY OF SCIENCE

HARRISON S. BROWN

Delivered before a teen-age audience at the Waldorf-Astoria Hotel New York City, March 5, 1949

Whenever I am asked to speak before a group of young me and women, my thoughts drift back to the days when I was grad uated from high school and a prominent business man in my hom town spoke at our commencement. "The world is in a sorry plight he told us, "it is up to you—the citizens of tomorrow—to mold the world into a globe fit for human habitation. It is up to you to abolish war and to see to it that the necessities of life are made available to all mankind."

Such graduation speeches were given that year throughout the United States and throughout the world, and for all I know they are still being given.

But what happens when the high school graduate goes out into the world and attempts to change things for the better? He suddenly finds himself called "naive," "rash," "inexperienced." He learns that the oldsters really don't want the youngsters to remake the world after all. The soreness of the tops of many young heads (resulting from much battering against stone walls) testifies amply to the resistance that confronts them.

Yet if we look back a few years we find that the majority of the soldiers who fought and died in the last war were in their early twenties and younger. The majority of the scientists who contributed actively toward the development of the atomic bomb were in their twenties. Youngsters, we are told, are old enough to fight and die; they are old enough to help figure out how to make atomic bombs—but they are too young to have anything to say about what to do about the frightening problems that face the modern world and threaten to destroy it.

In speaking today about the social responsibilities of science, I will speak of things which are relatively easy for young people, but difficult for older persons, to understand. This is because young people possess a quality that in general diminishes with years: the quality of imagination. Imagination is a quality which is an integral part of science, and naturally endowed to young people. It is a quality which sadly enough evaporates with advancing age, yet it is a quality which our unhappy world needs in abundance at the present time.

For the last three centuries the findings of science have had marked impact upon society, but people on the whole have not understood just how our world has been affected, nor have they cared. From the time of Newton men began to realize that through technology, which is based upon the findings of science, substantial comforts and profits could be gained. From the time of Pasteur men began to realize that through the application of science to medicine they might be able to live longer.

From the time of Leonardo da Vinci, men appreciated that science could materially aid in winning wars. As years went by a technological materialism was developed; demands for new technical knowledge became greater and greater; more and more men became scientists and technologists. The scientist came to be looked upon as the creator of a new and abundant life. To make substantial profits, to work less, to live longer, to win wars—what more could the people of a nation desire? In the valor of its ignorance humanity accepted science and technology as its benefactors seldom questioning, seldom asking where it was leading.

And where has it led? To a large part of the world it has brought unprecedented comfort. To an even larger part of the world it has brought unprecedented agony.

To the world of the future (the world in which you young people must live) technological expansion may bring total catastrophe, or it may aid in the moulding of a balanced world in which men may have the opportunity to live in reasonable harmony with their environment and with each other. The end result will depend upon the wisdom and imagination with which we plan for the future—upon the wisdom and imagination with which we integrate our scientific and technical knowledge from other fields of human endeavor, into a pattern for a peaceful and stable world.

Let's look at the record. It is not a happy one! Science and technology have placed in the hands of the rulers of nations tools of coercion and persuasion of unprecedented effectiveness. Modern implements of war make it possible for small groups of men to enforce their rule over large groups of people. In modern totalitarian states, the weapons in the hands of rulers make impossible successful popular revolts.

In the past, uprisings against despotism by masses of people armed only with crude weapons were possible. Today, applied science makes despotism invulnerable to internal overthrow by violent means.

Improvements in transportation and communications have increased the effectiveness of police action. Revolutionary method of mass communication, rotary presses, radio and motion pictures provide powerful tools for persuasion. Today, when propaganda can be spread to millions of people, when the governed can be unknowingly fed with untruths and kept in ignorance of the truth by government control of communications outlets, the people become powerless.

It would be pleasant to believe that by creating new techniques in transportation and communication, thus making the world effectively smaller, some sort of a dent might have been made in minimizing the concept of intense nationalism. But the reverse has been true. The creation of vast industrial nations, competing with one another, and the creation of centralized national authorities of ever-increasing power have more than overbalanced the effect upon nationalism of increasing communication and education.

History has taught us that intense nationalism sooner or later results in wars between nations. Today wars are, more than ever before, wars of competing technologies. The first half of the twentieth century will go down in history as the period within which technological developments took place which converted destruction from a difficult operation into a fantastically easy one. But as yet, we have seen only the crude beginnings of what can be done, should circumstances dictate. Now that nations, each in the interest of its own military security, have mobilized science, we can expect developments in the technology of war to proceed at an accelerated pace.

Even our good intentions have brought trouble. The spread of sanitation measures and the control of disease to ever-increasing bodies of humanity has created the problem of overpopulation. With the population check of disease removed, we are now confronted with the gigantic task of finding ways to feed people and to keep populations in check.

Increased populations and wars have, in turn, placed tremendous drains upon our natural resources, upon our power reserve, upon our arable land.

Indeed, it is not a pretty picture that confronts us. It has caused many persons to say that perhaps, like the dinosaur, mankind is doomed to extinction.

But fortunately our position is somewhat different from that of the dinosaur, whose size, which once permitted him to survive, destroyed him when his environment changed. The dinosaur did not create the environment that destroyed him. Man, through his thoughtless misuse of science, has created his. The dinosaur had no control over his environment. Man, if he wishes and if he is willing to apply science and technology properly, may have control over his.

Science and technology offer man important tools that may enable him better to control his environment and as a result enable him to control his destiny. Man must learn how to use those tools properly and he must apply his imagination to the task of devising the social and political institutions that will permit him to utilize the tools with maximum effectiveness.

As we have not thought sufficiently far into the future, the net result of our haphazard and unplanned use of science and technology has been disastrous to society. We should now, realizing the danger that confronts us, study the future, plan accordingly and utilize those aspects of science that can aid us in moulding a more hopeful destiny than that which now confronts us.

The first social responsibility of science is to shout from the housetops whenever it sees science and technology being used in the dangerous ways in which they have been used in the past.

The second responsibility is to develop wherever possible constructive solutions to the political problems that now confront mankind: the production of food, clothing and shelter.

A third, and in many respects an even more important responsibility exists, and that is to disseminate far and wide an attitude that I like to call the "scientific attitude."

The scientific attitude is at once a way of thought, a way of conduct and a way of life. It is an attitude that has been found essential for constructive scientific progress—an attitude which, if it were to be more widely disseminated, accepted, appreciated and used, would go a long way toward helping mankind resolve the many dilemmas that now confront it. A scientific attitude has many component parts, the most important of which are straightforward and easy to understand:

The scientist must avoid dogmatism. He must always insist upon valid argument. He must proceed cautiously, yet he must be ready for change. He must insist upon the truth. He cannot permit national fetishisms to influence his judgment. And above all, he must insist upon complete, undistorted and uncompromising freedom of speech.

The assimilation of a scientific attitude will enable all of you to build the kind of world you want to live in—a world free of fear, free of war and free of want.

> —A. Craig Baird, ed., *Representative American Speeches: 1948-1949* (New York, H. W. Wilson), pp. 140-144.

NO. 4

THE INTELLECTUAL AND THE POLITICIAN

SENATOR JOHN F. KENNEDY

Commencement address, Harvard University, June 14, 1956

It is a pleasure to join with my fellow alumni in this pilgrimage to the second home of our youth.

Prince Bismarck once remarked that one third of the students of German universities broke down from overwork; another third broke down from dissipation; and the other third ruled Germany. As I look about this campus today, I would hesitate to predict which third attends reunions (although I have some suspicion), but I am confident I am looking at "rulers" of America in the sense that all active informed citizens rule.

I can think of nothing more reassuring for all of us than to come again to this institution whose whole purpose is dedicated to the advancement of knowledge and the dissemination of truth.

I belong to a profession where the emphasis is somewhat different. Our political parties, our politicians are interested, of necessity, in winning popular support—a majority, and only indirectly truth is the object of our controversy. From this polemic of contending factions, the general public is expected to make a discriminating judgment. As the problems have become more complex, as our role as a chief defender of Western civilization has become enlarged, the responsibility of the electorate as a court of last resort has become almost too great. The people desperately seek objectivity and a university such as this fulfills that function.

And the political profession needs to have its temperature lowered in the cooling waters of the scholastic pool. We need both the technical judgment and the disinterested viewpoint of the scholar, to prevent us from becoming imprisoned by our own slogans.

Therefore, it is regrettable that the gap between the intellectual and politician seems to be growing. Instead of synthesis, clash and discord now characterizes the relations between the two groups much of the time. Authors, scholars and intellectuals can praise every aspect of American society but the political. My desk is flooded with books, articles and pamphlets criticizing Congress. But, rarely if ever, have I seen any intellectual bestow praise on either the political profession or any political body for its accomplishments, its ability or its integrity—much less for its intelligence. To many universities and scholars we rear nothing but censors, investigators and perpetrators of what has been called "the swinish cult of anti-intellectualism."

James Russell Lowell's satiric attack more than a hundred years ago on Caleb Cushing, a celebrated attorney general and member of Congress, sets the tone:

> Gineral C is a dreffle smart man,
> He's ben on all sides that give places or pelf,
> But consistency still wuz a part of his plan—
> He's ben true to one party, that is himself.

But in fairness, the way of the intellectual is not altogether serene; in fact so great has become popular suspicion that a recent survey of American intellectuals by a national magazine elicited from one of our foremost literary figures the guarded response, "I ain't no intellectual."

Both sides in this battle, it seems to me, are motivated by largely unfounded feelings of distrust. The politican, whose authority rests upon the mandate of the popular will, is resentful of the scholar who can, with dexterity, slip from position to position without dragging the anchor of public opinion. It was this skill that caused Lord Melbourne to say of the youthful historian Macaulay that he wished he was as sure of anything as Macaulay was of everything. The intellectual, on the other hand, finds it difficult to accept the difference between the laboratory and the legislature. In the former, the goal is truth, pure and simple, without regard to changing currents of public opinion; in the latter, compromises and majorities and procedural customs and rights affect the ultimate decision as to what is right or just or good. And even when they realize this difference, most intellectuals consider their chief function that of the critic—and politicians are sensitive to critics (possibly because we have so many of them). "Many intellectuals," Sidney Hook has said, "would rather 'die' than agree with the majority, even on the rare occasions when the majority is right."

It seems to me that the time has come for intellectuals and politicians alike to put aside those horrible weapons of modern internecine warfare, the barbed thrust, the acid pen, and—most sinister of all—the rhetorical blast. Let us not emphasize all on which we differ but all we have in common. Let us consider not what we fear separately but what we share together.

First, I would ask both groups to recall that the American politician of today and the American intellectual of today are descended from a common ancestry. Our nation's first great politicians were also among the nation's first great writers and scholars. The founders of the American Constitution were also the founders of American scholarship. The works of Jefferson, Madison, Hamilton, Franklin, Paine and John Adams—to name but a few—influenced the literature of the world as well as its geography. Books were their tools, not their enemies. Locke, Milton, Sydney, Montesquieu, Coke and Bolingbroke were among those widely read in political circles and frequently quoted in political pamphlets. Our political leaders traded in the free commerce of ideas with lasting results both here and abroad.

In these golden years, our political leaders moved from one field to another with amazing versatility and vitality. Jefferson and Franklin still throw long shadows over many fields of learning. A contemporary described Jefferson, "A gentleman of thirty-two, who could calculate an eclipse, survey an estate, tie an artery, plan an edifice, try a cause, break a horse, dance a minuet, and play the violin."

Daniel Webster could throw thunderbolts at Hayne on the Senate floor, and then stroll a few steps down the corridor and dominate the Supreme Court as the foremost lawyer of his time. John Quincy Adams, after being summarily dismissed from the Senate for a notable display of independence, could become Boylston Professor of Rhetoric and Oratory at Harvard and then become a great Secretary of State. (Those were the happy days when Harvard professors had no difficulty getting Senate confirmation.)

The versatility also existed on the frontier. An obituary of Missouri's first senator, Thomas Hart Benton, the man whose tavern brawl with Jackson in Tennessee caused him to flee the state, said:

> With a readiness that was often surprising, he could quote from a Roman law or a Greek philosopher, from Virgil's *Georgics*, the *Arabian Nights*, Herodotus or Sancho Panza, from the Sacred Carpets, the German reformers or Adam Smith; from *Fénelon* or *Hudibras*, from the financial reports of Necca or the doings of the Council of Trent, from the debates on the adoption of the Constitution or intrigues of the Kitchen Cabinet or from some forgotten speech of a deceased member of Congress.

This link between the American scholarship and the American politician remained for more than a century. Just one hundred years ago today in the Presidential campaign of 1856, the Republicans sent three brilliant orators around the campaign circuit: William Cullen Bryant, Henry Wadsworth Longfellow and Ralph Waldo Emerson. Those were the carefree days when the "egg-heads" were all Republicans.

I would hope that both groups, recalling their common heritage, might once again forge a link between the intellectual and political professions. I know that scholars may prefer the mysteries of pure scholarship or the delights of abstract discourse. But "Would you have counted him a friend of ancient Greece," as

George William Curtis asked a century ago during the Kansas-Nebraska controversy, "who quietly discussed of patriotism on that Greek summer day through whose hopeless and immortal hours Leonidas and his three hundred stood at Thermopylae for liberty? Was John Milton to conjugate Greek verbs in his library or talk of the liberty of the ancient Shunammites when the liberty of Englishmen was imperiled?" No, the duty of the scholar—particularly in a republic such as ours—is to contribute his objective views and his sense of liberty to the affairs of his state and nation.

Secondly, I would remind both groups that the American politician and the American intellectual operate within a common framework—a framework we call liberty. Freedom of expression is not divisible into political expression and intellectual expression. The lock on the door of the Legislature, the Parliament or the Assembly Hall—by order of the King, the Commissar or the Fuehrer—has historically been followed or preceded by a lock on the door of the university, the library or the printer's. And if the first blow for freedom in any subjugated land is struck by a political leader, the second is struck by a book, a newspaper or a pamphlet.

Unfortunately, in more recent times, politicians and intellectuals have quarreled bitterly—too bitterly in some cases—over how each group has met the modern challenge to freedom both at home and abroad. Politicans have questioned the discernment with which intellectuals have reacted to the siren call of the extreme left; and intellectuals have tended to accuse politicians of not always being aware, especially here at home, of the toxic effects of freedom restrained.

While differences in judgment where freedom is endangered are perhaps inevitable, there should nevertheless be more basic agreement on fundamentals. In this field we should be natural allies, working more closely together for the common cause, against the common enemy.

Third and finally, I would stress the great potential gain for both groups resulting from increased political cooperation.

The American intellectual and scholar today must decide, as Goethe put it, whether he is to be an anvil—or a hammer. Today, for many, the stage of the anvil, at least in its formal phases, is complete. The question he faces is whether he is to be a hammer—whether he is to give the world in which he was reared and educated the broadest possible benefits of his learning. As one who is familiar with the political world, I can testify that we need it.

For example: The password for all legislation, promoted by either party, is progress. But how do we tell what is progress and what is retreat? Those of us who may be too close to the issue, or too politically or emotionally involved in it, look for the objective world of the scholar. Indeed, the operation of our political life is such that we may not even be debating the real issues.

In foreign affairs, for example, the parties dispute over which is best fitted to implement the long-accepted policies of collective security and Soviet containment. But perhaps these policies are no longer adequate, perhaps these goals are no longer meaningful—the debate goes on nevertheless, for neither party is in a position to undertake the reappraisal necessary, particularly if the solutions presented are more complex to, and less popular with, the electorate.

Or take our agricultural program, for another example. Republicans and Democrats debate long over whether flexible or rigid price supports should be in effect. But this may not be the real issue at all—and in fact I am convinced that it is not, that neither program offers any long-range solution to our many real farm problems. The scholars and the universities might re-examine this whole area and come up with some real answers—the political parties and their conventions rarely will.

Other examples could be given indefinitely—where do we draw the line between free trade and protection, when does taxation become prohibitive, what is the most effective use we can make of our present nuclear potential? The intellectuals who can draw upon their rational disinterested approach and their fund of learning to help reshape our political life can make a tremendous contribution to their society while gaining new respect for their own group.

I do not say that our political and public life should be turned over to experts who ignore public opinion. Nor would I adopt from the Belgian Constitution of 1893 the provision giving three votes instead of one to college graduates; or give Harvard a sea in the Congress as William and Mary was once represented in the Virginia House of Burgesses.

But, I would urge that our political parties and our universities recognize the need for greater cooperation and understanding between politicians and intellectuals. We do not need scholars or politicians like Lord John Russell, of whom Queen Victoria remarked, he would be a better man if he knew a third subject—but he was interested in nothing but the Constitution of 1688 and himself. What we need are men who can ride easily over broad fields of knowledge and recognize the mutual dependence of our two worlds.

"Don't teach my boy poetry," an English mother recently wrote the Provost of Harrow. "Don't teach my boy poetry; he is going to stand for Parliament." Well, perhaps she was right—but if more politicians knew poetry, and more poets knew politics, I am convinced the world would be a little better place to live on this Commencement Day of 1956.

—A. Craig Baird, ed., *Representative American Speeches: 1956-1957* (New York, H. W. Wilson), pp. 166-172.

NO. 5

THE KOREAN CRISIS

PRESIDENT HARRY S TRUMAN

Radio and television address, April 11, 1951 (the day he ordered General Douglas MacArthur to turn over the various Far East commands to General Matthew B. Ridgway)

I want to talk plainly to you tonight about what we are doing in Korea and about our policy in the Far East.

In the simplest terms, what we are doing in Korea is this: We are trying to prevent a third world war.

I think most people in this country recognized that fact last June. And they warmly supported the decision of the government to help the Republic of Korea against the Communist aggressors.

Now, many persons, even some who applauded our decision to defend Korea, have forgotten the basic reason for our action.

It is right for us to be in Korea. It was right last June. It is right today.

I want to remind you why this is true.

The Communists in the Kremlin are engaged in a monstrous conspiracy to stamp out freedom all over the world. If they were to succeed, the United States would be numbered among their principal victims. It must be clear to everyone that the United States cannot—and will not—sit idly by and await foreign conquest. The only question is: When is the best time to meet the threat and how?

The best time to meet the threat is in the beginning. It is easier to put out a fire in the beginning when it is small than after it has become a roaring blaze.

And the best way to meet the threat of aggression is for the peace-loving nations to act together. If they don't act together, they are likely to be picked off, one by one.

If they had followed the right policies in the 1930's—if the free countries had acted together, to crush the aggression of the dictators, and if they had acted in the beginning, when the aggression was small—there probably would have been no World War II.

If history has taught us anything, it is that aggression anywhere in the world is a threat to peace everywhere in the world. When that aggression is supported by the cruel and selfish rulers of a powerful nation who are bent on conquest, it becomes a clear and present danger to the security and independence of every free nation.

This is a lesson that most people in this country have learned thoroughly. This is the basic reason why we joined in creating the United Nations. And since the end of World War II we have been putting that lesson into practice—we have been working with other free nations to check the aggressive designs of the Soviet Union before they can result in a third world war.

That is what we did in Greece, when that nation was threatened by the aggression of international Communism.

The attack against Greece could have led to general war. Bu

this country came to the aid of Greece. The United Nations supported Greek resistance. With our help, the determination and efforts of the Greek people defeated the attack on the spot.

Another big Communist threat to peace was the Berlin blockade. That too could have led to war. But again it was settled because free men would not back down in an emergency.

The aggression against Korea is the boldest and most dangerous move the Communists have yet made.

The attack on Korea was part of a greater plan for conquering all of Asia.

I would like to read to you from a secret intelligence report which came to us after the attack. It is a report of a speech a Communist army officer in North Korea gave to a group of spies and saboteurs last May, one month before South Korea was invaded. The report shows in great detail how this invasion was part of a carefully prepared plot. Here is part of what the Communist officer, who had been trained in Moscow, told his men: "Our forces," he said, "are scheduled to attack South Korean forces about the middle of June. . . . The coming attack on South Korea marks the first step toward the liberation of Asia."

Notice that he used the word "liberation." That is Communist double talk meaning "conquest."

I have another secret intelligence report here. This one tells what another Communist officer in the Far East told his men several months before the invasion of Korea. Here is what he said: "In order to successfully undertake the long awaited world revolution, we must first unify Asia. . . . Java, Indochina, Malaya, India, Tibet, Thailand, Philippines, and Japan are our ultimate targets. . . . The United States is the only obstacle on our road for the liberation of all countries in southeast Asia. In other words, we must unify the people of Asia and crush the United States."

That is what the Communist leaders are telling their people, and that is what they have been trying to do.

They want to control all Asia from the Kremlin.

This plan of conquest is in flat contradiction to what we believe. We believe that Korea belongs to the Koreans, that India belongs to the Indians—that all the nations of Asia should be free to work out their affairs in their own way. This is the basis of peace in the Far East and everywhere else.

The whole Communist imperialism is back of the attack on peace in the Far East. It was the Soviet Union that trained and equipped the North Koreans for aggression. The Chinese Communists massed 44 well-trained and well-equipped divisions on the Korean frontier. These were the troops they threw into battle when the North Korean Communists were beaten.

The question we have had to face is whether the Communist plan of conquest can be stopped without general war. Our government and other countries associated with us in the United Nations believe that the best chance of stopping it without general war is to meet the attack in Korea and defeat it there.

That is what we have been doing. It is a difficult and bitter task.

But so far it has been successful.

So far, we have prevented World War III.

So far, by fighting a limited war in Korea, we have prevented aggression from succeeding and bringing on a general war. And the ability of the whole free world to resist Communist aggression has been greatly improved.

We have taught the enemy a lesson. He has found out that aggression is not cheap or easy. Moreover, men all over the world who want to remain free have been given new courage and new hope. They know now that the champions of freedom can stand up and fight and that they will stand up and fight.

Our resolute stand in Korea is helping the forces of freedom now fighting in Indochina and other countries in that part of the world. It has already slowed down the timetable of conquest.

In Korea itself, there are signs that the enemy is building up his ground forces for a new mass offensive. We also know that there have been large increases in the enemy's available air forces.

If a new attack comes, I feel confident it will be turned back. The United Nations fighting forces are tough and able and well equipped. They are fighting for a just cause. They are proving to all the world that the principle of collective security will work. We are proud of all these forces for the magnificent job they have done against heavy odds. We pray that their efforts may succeed, for upon their success may hinge the peace of the world.

The Communist side must now choose its course of action. The Communist rulers may press the attack against us. They may take further action which will spread the conflict. They have that choice, and with it the awful responsibility for what may follow. The Communists also have the choice of a peaceful settlement which could lead to a general relaxation of tensions in the Far East. The decision is theirs, because the forces of the United Nations will strive to limit the conflict if possible.

We do not want to see the conflict in Korea extended. We are trying to prevent a world war—not to start one. The best way to do that is to make it plain that we and the other free countries will continue to resist the attack.

But you may ask: Why can't we take other steps to punish the aggressor? Why don't we bomb Manchuria and China itself? Why don't we assist Chinese Nationalist troops to land on the mainland of China?

If we were to do these things we would be running a very grave risk of starting a general war. If that were to happen, we would have brought about the exact situation we are trying to prevent.

If we were to do these things, we would become entangled in a vast conflict on the continent of Asia and our task would become immeasurably more difficult all over the world.

What would suit the ambitions of the Kremlin better than for our military forces to be committed to a full-scale war with Red China?

It may well be that, in spite of our best efforts, the Communists may spread the war. But it would be wrong—tragically wrong—for us to take the initiative in extending the war.

The dangers are great. Make no mistake about it. Behind the North Koreans and Chinese Communists in the front lines stand additional millions of Chinese soldiers. And behind the Chinese stand the tanks, the planes, the submarines, the soldiers, and the scheming rulers of the Soviet Union.

Our aim is to avoid the spread of the conflict.

The course we have been following is the one best calculated to avoid an all-out war. It is the course consistent with our obligation to do all we can to maintain international peace and security. Our experience in Greece and Berlin shows that it is the most effective course of action we can follow.

First of all, it is clear that our efforts in Korea can blunt the will of the Chinese Communists to continue the struggle. The United Nations forces have put up a tremendous fight in Korea and have inflicted very heavy casualties on the enemy. Our forces are stronger now than they have been before. These are plain facts which may discourage the Chinese Communists from continuing their attack.

Second, the free world as a whole is growing in military strength every day. In the United States, in Western Europe, and throughout the world, free men are alert to the Soviet threat and are building their defenses. This may discourage the Communist rulers from continuing the war in Korea—and from undertaking new acts of aggression elsewhere.

If the Communist authorities realize that they cannot defeat us in Korea, if they realize it would be foolhardy to widen the hostilities beyond Korea, then they may recognize the folly of continuing their aggression. A peaceful settlement may then be possible. The door is always open.

Then we may achieve a settlement in Korea which will not compromise the principles and purposes of the United Nations.

I have thought long and hard about this question of extending the war in Asia. I have discussed it many times with the ablest military advisers in the country. I believe with all my heart that the course we are following is the best course.

I believe that we must try to limit the war to Korea for these vital reasons: To make sure that the precious lives of our fighting men are not wasted; to see that the security of our country and the free world is not needlessly jeopardized; and to prevent a third world war.

A number of events have made it evident that General Mac-Arthur did not agree with that policy. I have therefore considered it essential to relieve General MacArthur so that there would be no doubt or confusion as to the real purpose and aim of our policy.

It was with the deepest personal regret that I found myself compelled to take this action. General MacArthur is one of our greatest military commanders. But the cause of world peace is more important than any individual.

The change in commands in the Far East means no change whatever in the policy of the United States. We will carry on the fight in Korea with vigor and determination in an effort to bring the war to a speedy and successful conclusion.

The new commander, Lieutenant General Matthew Ridgway, has already demonstrated that he has the great qualities of military leadership needed for this task.

We are ready, at any time, to negotiate for a restoration of peace in the area. But we will not engage in appeasement. We are only interested in real peace.

Real peace can be achieved through a settlement based on the following factors:

One: the fighting must stop.

Two: concrete steps must be taken to insure that the fighting will not break out again.

Three: there must be an end to the aggression.

A settlement founded upon these elements would open the way for the unification of Korea and the withdrawal of all foreign forces.

In the meantime, I want to be clear about our military objective. We are fighting to resist an outrageous aggression in Korea. We are trying to keep the Korean conflict from spreading to other areas. But at the same time we must conduct our military activities so as to insure the security of our forces. This is essential if they are to continue the fight until the enemy abandons its ruthless attempt to destroy the Republic of Korea.

That is our military objective—to repel attack and to restore peace.

In the hard fighting in Korea, we are proving that collective action among nations is not only a high principle but a workable means of resisting aggression. Defeat of aggression in Korea may be the turning point in the world's search for a practical way of achieving peace and security.

The struggle of the United Nations in Korea is a struggle for peace.

The free nations have united their strength in an effort to prevent a third world war.

That war can come if the Communist rulers want it to come. But this nation and its allies will not be responsible for its coming.

We do not want to widen the conflict. We will use every effort to prevent that disaster. And in so doing we know that we are following the great principles of peace, freedom, and justice.

NO. 6

NOMINATING CALVIN COOLIDGE

WILL ROGERS

Written in political jest as a newspaper report during the time of the drawn-out Democratic Nominating Convention of 1924. Although never given as a speech, it is included here to illustrate the use of gentle satire (Calvin Coolidge was a Republican) and of the inductive organizational plan which calls for placing the proposition near the end.

Oh, my friends, I am too good a Democrat not to be appreciative of what the party has done for me, not to try and warn you while there is yet time.

We are not gathered here just to name a nominee of the next election, but we are here to name the next President of the grand and glorious United States, of which this party today is the sole refuge for the true patriot.

In naming a man for this high and lofty office there are certain traditions and specifications which we must hold in mind, if we want to reach a successful victory in November.

The man we name must be a man who is not now connected with those intersectional fights and feuds here on the floor. The man I am about to name is absolutely aloof from them.

The man we name to carry us to victory must be geographically strong enough to carry a majority of New England. The man I am about to name knows these mysterious canny people.

The man we name must be able to go into the far Westland and reap a majority. The man I am about to name possesses the attributes to do that very deed.

The man we name must be able to remove any doubtful States into the realm of certainty. The man I am about to name can give you a majority that will look like a census report.

The man we name here must be a man who never earned outside of public life a fee of over $10. The man I am about to name has that honorable reputation.

The man we name here must have no taint of Morgan or Wall Street. The man I am about to name never saw Wall Street.

The man we name here must have absolutely no affiliation with the Klan. The man I am about to name is not a member of the Klan.

The man we name must be of no minority religious creed. The man I am about to name belongs to the creed whose voters are in the majority.

On account of the present length of the convention, the man we name must not be of too many score years of age. The man I am about to name has many useful and unworried years of public service ahead of him.

The man we name must have had no connection with oil. The man I am about to name never used oil, except at Government or State expense.

Oh, gentlemen of the grand and glorious Democratic party, let us not make a mistake. We have our greatest chance this year to bring home victory. That great scandal in our opponents' party and their close affiliation with predatory wealth has given us an unbounded opportunity.

Don't let us disrupt the party when we can win. We will go to a sure Democratic defeat if we name the wrong man. Oh, my friends, let us be connected with a victory in this glorious year of 1924. Why court defeat?

The man I am about to name is the only man in these grand and glorious United States who, if we nominate, we can go home and have no worry as to the outcome. Don't, oh, my Democratic Colleagues, listen to my friend Bryan. He named ten candidates; ten men can't win! Only one man can win. Oh, my newly made friends, have confidence in me. Trust me just this once and I will lead you out of this darkened wilderness into the gates of the White House. Oh, my tired and worn friends, there is only one man. That man I am about to name to you is Calvin Coolidge.

—From Donald Day, ed., *Sanity Is Where You Find It* (Boston, Houghton Mifflin, 1955), pp. 30-32.

```
┌─────────────────────────────────────────────┐
│                                             │
│                                             │
│      Appendix  B                            │
│                                             │
│                                             │
│                                             │
│      Readings  In  Speech                   │
│                                             │
│                                             │
│                                             │
└─────────────────────────────────────────────┘
```

This section contains a variety of selected writings, most of them excerpts, which refer to varying facets of man-and-speech. They are included here to provide a number of possible services. The following are a few suggested uses:

1. For oral reading
2. To motivate study and research activities
3. To suggest case-study projects
4. To stimulate group discussion
5. To stimulate selection of speech subjects
6. To stimulate reflection on our heritage and on our ethical responsibilities.

NO. 1

STOLEN THUNDER

CHARLES HEBER CLARK

The chairman began with a short speech in which he went over almost precisely the ground covered by my introduction; and as that portion of my oration was . . . reduced to a fragment . . . I quietly resolved to begin, when my turn came, with point number two.

The chairman introduced to the crowd Mr. Keyser, who was received with cheers. He was a ready speaker, and he began, to my deep regret, by telling in capital style my story number three, after which he used up some of my number six arguments, and concluded with the remark that it was not his purpose to occupy the attention of the meeting for any length of time, because the executive committee in Wilmington had sent an eloquent orator who was now upon the platform and would present the cause of the party in a manner which he could not hope to approach.

Mr. Keyser then sat down, and Mr. Schwartz was introduced. Mr. Schwartz observed that it was hardly worth while for him to attempt to make anything like a speech, because the gentleman from New Castle had come down on purpose to discuss the issues of the campaign, and the audience, of course, was anxious to hear him. Mr. Schwartz would only tell a little story which seemed to illustrate a point he wished to make, and he thereupon related my anecdote number seven. . . . The point illustrated I was shocked to find was almost precisely that which I had attached to my story number seven. The situation began to have a serious appearance. Here, at one fell swoop, two of my best stories and three of my sets of arguments were swept off into utter uselessness.

When Schwartz withdrew, a man named Krumbauer was brought forward. Krumbauer was a German, and the chairman announced that he would speak in that language for the benefit of those persons in the audience to whom the tongue was pleasantly familiar. Krumbauer went ahead, and the crowd received his remarks with roars of laughter. After one particularly exuberant outburst of merriment, I asked the man who sat next to me, and who seemed deeply interested in the story,

"What was that little joke of Krumbauer's? It must have been first rate."

"So it was," he said. "It was about a Dutchman up in Berks county, Penn., who got mixed up in his dates."

"What dates?" I gasped, in awful apprehension.

"Why, his Fourths of July, you know. Got seven or eight years in arrears and tried to make them all up at once. Good, wasn't it?"

"Good? I should think so; ha! ha! My very best story, as I'm a sinner!"

It was awfully bad. I could have strangled Krumbauer and then chopped him into bits. The ground seemed slipping away beneath me; there was the merest skeleton of a speech left. But I determined to take that and do my best, trusting to luck for a happy result.

But my turn had not yet come. Mr. Wilson was dragged out next, and I thought I perceived a demoniac smile steal over the countenance of the cymbal player as Wilson said he was too hoarse to say much; he would leave the heavy work for the brilliant young orator who was here from New Castle. He would skim rapidly over the ground and then retire. He did. Wilson rapidly skimmed all the cream off of my arguments numbers two, five, and six, and wound up by offering the whole of my number four argument. My hair fairly stood on end when Wilson bowed and left the stand. What on earth was I to do now? Not an argument left to stand upon; all my anecdotes gone but two, and my mind in such a condition of frenzied bewilderment that it seemed as if there was not another available argument or suggestion or hint or anecdote remaining in the entire universe. In an agony of despair, I turned to the man next to me and asked him if I would have to follow Wilson.

He said it was his turn now.

"And what are you going to say?" I demanded, suspiciously.

"Oh, nothing," he replied—"nothing at all. I want to leave room for you. I'll just tell a little story or so, to amuse them, and then sit down."

"What story, for instance?" I asked.

"Oh, nothing, nothing; only a little yarn I happen to remember about a farmer who married a woman who said she could cut four cords of wood, when she couldn't."

My worst fears were realized. I turned to the man next to me, and said, with suppressed emotion.

"May I ask your name, my friend?"

He said his name was Gumbs.

"May I inquire what your Christian name is?"

He said it was William Henry.

"Well, William Henry Gumbs," I exclaimed, "gaze at me! Do I look like a man who would slay a human being in cold blood?"

"Hm-m-m, n-no; you don't," he replied, with an air of critical consideration.

"But I AM!" said I, fiercely—"I AM; and I tell you now that if you undertake to relate that anecdote about the farmer's wife I will blow you into eternity without a moment's warning; I will, by George!"

Mr. Gumbs instantly jumped up, placed his hand on the railing of the porch, and got over suddenly into the crowd. He stood there pointing me out to the bystanders, and doubtless advancing the theory that I was an original kind of a lunatic, who might be expected to have at any moment a fit which would be interesting when studied from a distance.

The chairman looked around, intending to call upon my friend Mr. Gumbs; but not perceiving him, he came to me and said:

"Now is your chance, sir; splendid opportunity; crowd worked up to just the proper pitch. We have paved the way for you; go in and do your best."

"Oh yes; but hold on for a few moments, will you? I can't speak now; the fact is I am not quite ready. Run out some other man."

"Haven't got another man. Kept you for the last purposely, and the crowd is waiting. Come ahead and pitch in, and give it to 'em hot and heavy."

It was very easy for him to say "give it to them," but I had nothing to give. Beautifully they paved the way for me! Nicely they had worked up the crowd to the proper pitch! Here I was in a condition of frantic despair, with a crowd of one thousand people expecting a brilliant oration from me who had not a thing in my mind but a beggarly story about a fire extinguisher and a worse one about a farmer's wife. I groaned in spirit and wished I had been born far away in some distant clime among savages who knew not of mass meetings, and whose language contained such a small number of words that speech-making was impossible.

But the chairman was determined. He seized me by the arm and fairly dragged me to the front. He introduced me to the crowd in flattering, and I may say outrageously ridiculous, terms, and then whispering in my ear, "Hit 'em hard, old fellow, hit 'em hard," he sat down. The crowd received me with three hearty cheers. As I heard them I began to feel dizzy. The audience seemed to swim around and to increase tenfold in size. By a resolute effort I recovered my self-possession partially, and determined to begin. I could not think of anything but the two stories, and I resolved to tell them as well as I could. I said,

"Fellow-citizens: It is so late now that I will not attempt to make a speech to you." (Cries of "Yes!" "Go ahead!" "Never mind the time!" etc., etc.) Elevating my voice, I repeated: "I say it is so late now that I can't make a speech as I intended on account of its being so late that the speech which I intended to make would keep you here too late if I made it as I intended to. So I will tell you a story about a man who bought a patent fire-extinguisher which was warranted to split four cords of wood a day; so he set fire to his house to try her, and—No, it was his wife who was warranted to split four cords of wood—I got it wrong; and when the flames obtained full headway, he found she could only split two cords and a half, and it made him—What I mean is that the farmer, when he bought the exting—courted her, that is, she said she could set fire to the house, and when he tried her, she collapsed the first time—the extinguisher did, and he wanted a divorce because his house—Oh, hang it, fellow-citizens, you understand that this man, or farmer, rather, bought a—I should say courted a—that is, a fire-ex—" (Desperately.) "Fellow-citizens IF ANY MAN SHOOTS THE AMERICAN FLAG, PULL HIM DOWN UPON THE SPOT; BUT AS FOR ME, GIVE ME LIBERTY OR GIVE ME DEATH!"

As I shouted this out at the top of my voice, in an ecstasy of confusion, a wild, tumultuous yell of laughter came up from the crowd. I paused for a second beneath the spell of that cold eye in the band, and then, dashing through the throng at the back of the porch, I rushed down the street to the depot, with the shouts of the crowd and the uproarious music of the band ringing in my ears.

I got upon a freight train, gave the engineer five dollars to take me along on the locomotive, and spent the night riding to New Castle.

–From *Out of the Hurly-Burly*
(Philadelphia, "Today" Publishing Co., 1874).

NO. 2

HOW TO TELL A STORY

MARK TWAIN

I do not claim that I can tell a story as it ought to be told. I only claim to know how a story ought to be told, for I have been almost daily in the company of the most expert story-tellers for many years.

There are several kinds of stories, but only one difficult kind— the humorous. I will talk mainly about that one. The humorous story is American, the comic story is English, the witty story is French. The humorous story depends for its effect upon the *manner* of the telling; the comic story and the witty story upon the *matter*.

The humorous story may be spun out to great length, and may wander around as much as it pleases, and arrive nowhere in particular; but the comic and witty stories must be brief and end with a point. The humorous story bubbles gently along, the others burst.

The humorous story is strictly a work of art—high and delicate art—and only an artist can tell it; but no art is necessary in telling the comic and the witty story; anybody can do it. The art of telling a humorous story—understand, I mean by word of mouth, not print —was created in America, and has remained at home.

The humorous story is told gravely; the teller does his best to conceal the fact that he even dimly suspects that there is anything funny about it; but the teller of the comic story tells you beforehand that it is one of the funniest things he has ever heard, then tells it with eager delight, and is the first person to laugh when he gets through. And sometimes, if he has had good success, he is so glad and happy that he will repeat the "nub" of it and glance around from face to face collecting applause, and then repeat it again. It is a pathetic thing to see.

Very often, of course, the rambling and disjointed humorous story finishes with a nub, point, snapper, or whatever you like to call it. Then the listener must be alert, for in many cases the teller will divert attention from that nub by dropping it in a carefully casual and indifferent way, with the pretense that he does not know it is a nub.

Artemus Ward used that trick a good deal; then when the belated audience presently caught the joke he would look up with innocent surprise, as if wondering what they had found to laugh at. Dan Setchell used it before him. Nye and Riley and others use it today.

But the teller of the comic story does not slur the nub; he shouts it at you—every time. And when he prints it, in England, France, Germany, and Italy, he italicizes it, puts some whooping exclamation-points after it, and sometimes explains it in a parenthesis. All of which is very depressing and makes one want to renounce joking and lead a better life.

NO. 3

MAN GETS LANGUAGE

GEORGE R. STEWART

Naturally, language did not start all at once. Most animals obviously can communicate in some degree by sounds. Gesture also can be very eloquent indeed, as when a skunk raises his tail.

My language, however, goes much further, and no one is sure just how it developed. In fact, its origin is one of those delightful subjects in which one theory is still as good as another. So I might as well rush in with the one I prefer.

Language, I think, may well have sprung from two sources, of which the one produced the verb and the other the noun. I, more than many animals, was full of grunts, groans, howls, and snorts, and there was little restraint on my giving vent to them. I was not required, like the cow, to spend long hours in silent cud-chewing; or, like the panther, to range the forest in soft-footed stealth; or, like the rabbit, to nibble silently for fear of being pounced on. Most of my noises expressed in some manner the way I was feeling at the moment. Therefore, each yelp or squeal or burble was really a vague sentence beginning with the words, "I feel. . . ." Some half-formed cry like "Ouch!" might be translated, "I feel sudden pain!" After a while, when a creature had as good a brain as mine, the sounds would be more standardized, and their meanings fitted to the situation. Thus "Ouch!" might be used playfully, when the individual felt no real pain, or it might warn a child not to pick up a bee.

The noun-idea was more difficult, and probably followed long after. But it too was necessary for real language.

Just how it developed is harder to suggest. Yet the tendency of speech is to begin with the special and concrete nouns before working over to the general and abstract. Certainly the most special and concrete of them all are proper names, and for this reason the first nouns may have been the names of individuals. One person, it might happen, would often snore. Possibly at first in fun, others would make the same sound to refer to him. Once started, the habit of individual names might quickly spread to all the members of the band, for to have a name is to have a bit of very flattering personal property; each individual might like to have one, and each mother to have one for her child.

Again, something which could start more for playfulness than for "use" might soon come to be of value in other ways. When the band was foraging, one of them might signal his position by calling "Coo" like a dove, to let the others know where he was.

Eventually came the union of the noun-idea and the verb-idea. It may be that a woman came back without her companion and much troubled. All attempts at gesture failed to tell what had happened. In desperation, naturally enough and yet with a stroke of genius, she cried, "Coo-ouch!" Then they knew that he who was called Coo had been taken with a sudden pain. Such a combination of two ideas was more than mere expression of personal feeling, and more also than mere pointing-out of an individual. It was the setting of two ideas into a new relation, and thus the beginning of real language.

I like to think that the mothers may first have made and practiced language, and that for some generations the fathers still sat around merely grunting while the mothers chattered happily. At least I notice that girl-babies are still quicker to speak than boy-babies, and that they grow up in general to be the more apt talkers. Besides, there has always been in language a great deal of an illogical and emotional quality. I might say, "Women invented language, but men invented grammar."

The discovery of language was as great an event as anything that had happened. Its obvious uses, as anyone can recognize, were social—for all kinds of working and playing together. But perhaps it was greatest as a tool which more than any stick or stone gave me power over the world. For not only is language an instrument for telling thought, but it is also an instrument for thought itself. I do not want to raise that old argument of whether thought is possible without speech; but at least I am sure that thought cannot go very far without language, any more than mathematics can go very far without its symbols.

> —From *Man: An Autobiography,* by GEORGE R. STEWART, pp. 31-33. Copyright 1946 by George R. Stewart. Reprinted by permission of Random House, Inc.

NO. 4

THE GIFT OF THE POWER OF SPEECH

NORBERT WIENER

Speech is such a peculiarly human activity that it is not even approached by man's closest relatives and his most active imitators. The few sounds emitted by chimpanzees have, it is true, a great deal of emotional content, but they have not the fineness of clear and repeated accuracy of organization needed to make them into a code much more accurate than the yowlings of a cat. Moreover (and this differentiates them still more from human speech), at times they belong to the chimpanzee as an unlearned inborn manifestation, rather than as the learned behavior of a member of a given social community.

The fact that speech belongs in general to man as man, but that a particular form of speech belongs to man as a member of a particular social community, is most remarkable. In the first place, taking the whole wide range of man as we know him today, it is safe to say that there is no community of individuals, not mutilated by an auditory or a mental defect, which does not have its own mode of speech. In the second place, all modes of speech are learned, and notwithstanding the attempts of the nineteenth century to formulate a genetic evolutionistic theory of languages, there is not the slightest general reason to postulate any single native form of speech from which all the present forms are originated. It is quite clear that if left alone, babies will make attempts at speech. These attempts, however, show their own inclinations to utter something, and do not follow any existing form of language. It is almost equally clear that if a community of children were left out of contact with the language of their seniors through the critical speech-forming years, they would emerge with something, which crude as it might be, would be unmistakably a language.

Why is it then that chimpanzees cannot be forced to talk, and that human children cannot be forced not to? Why is it then that the general tendencies to speak and the general visual and psychological aspects of language are so uniform over large groups of people, while the particular linguistic manifestation of these aspects is varied? At least partial understanding of these matters is essential to any comprehension of the language-based community. We merely state the fundamental facts by saying that in man, unlike the apes, the impulse to use some sort of language is overwhelming; but that the particular language used is a matter which has to be learned in each special case. It apparently is built into the brain itself, that we are to have a preoccupation with codes and with the sounds of speech, and that the preoccupation with codes can be extended from those dealing with speech to those that concern themselves with visual stimuli. However, there is not one fragment of these codes which is born into us as a pre-established ritual, like the courting dances of many of the birds, or the system by which ants recognize and exclude intruders into the nest. The gift of speech does not go back to a universal Adamite language disrupted in the Tower of Babel. It is strictly a psychological impulse, and is not the gift of speech, but the gift of the power of speech.

—NORBERT WIENER, *The Human Use of Human Beings* (Boston, Houghton Mifflin, 1950), pp. 82-84.

NO. 5

A HIGH DEGREE OF PROBABILITY

RUDOLF FLESCH

Or take another recent study by Dr. Sheldon Glueck of Harvard University and his wife, Dr. Eleanor Glueck. They tried to find the causes of juvenile delinquency. More scientifically speaking, they tried to isolate certain factors that distinguish delinquent boys from those who are not.

Dr. and Mrs. Glueck devoted ten years to their study. Being scientists, they began by making certain guesses. They assembled mountains of data on five hundred delinquent and five hundred nondelinquent boys. When they had collected all the statistics on the factors they were interested in, they looked for differences in the degree of correlation.

They found, among other things, that the parents of delinquent boys were often more erratic than those of other boys; that between-children are more likely to become delinquent than either first or last children; that delinquent boys are usually more muscular than others and scored higher in certain parts of intelligence tests. On the whole, they found that delinquency is connected with a boy's home life, with his temperament and character, and with his ability to get along with people. In fact, Dr. and Mrs. Glueck drew up a "prediction table" by which six-year-olds can be spotted as future delinquents if a long list of factors is known. But, of course, they didn't say that this prediction was infallible or that they had found once and for all the causes of juvenile delinquency. They just reported what they gingerly called "a tentative causal formula or law."

Now this is exactly the kind of thing people are apt to explain by "fate" or "bad blood" or "slum conditions" or whatever pet explanation they are fond of. The Glueck study is a beautiful example of the scientific approach. The Gluecks didn't look for a single cause; in fact, they didn't look for "a cause" at all. They looked for certain factors that were to a certain degree connected with delinquency. And they concluded, *not* that juvenile delinquency was due to this or that, but that if a combination of factors was present to a certain degree, the result would probably be a tendency to delinquency.

Of course I don't mean to say that in everyday life you shouldn't decide anything before you have made a ten-year statistical study. But you can use the scientific approach as a model. Instead of the black-and-white, single-track, everyone-knows-that-this-is-due-to-that approach, get used to the idea that this is a world of multiple causes, imperfect correlations, and sheer, unpredictable chance.

It is true that the scientists, with their statistics and their probabilities, have made a stab at the harnessing of chance. But they know very well that certainty is unattainable. A high degree of probability is the best we can ever get.

–RUDOLF FLESCH, *The Art of Clear Thinking*
(New York, Harper, 1951), pp. 136-137.
Copyright, 1951, by Rudolph Flesch.

NO. 6

LET THERE BE UNLICENSED EXPRESSION

JOHN MILTON

And now the time in special is, by privilege to write and speak what may help to the further discussing of matters in agitation The temple of Janus with his two controversial faces might now not unsignificantly be set open. And though all the winds of doc trine were let loose to play upon the earth, so Truth be in the field, we do injuriously, by licensing and prohibiting, to misdoubt her strength. Let her and Falsehood grapple; who ever knew Truth put to the worse, in a free and open encounter? Her confuting is the best and surest suppressing. He who hears what praying there is for light and clearer knowledge to be sent down among us, would think of other matters to be constituted beyond the discipline of Geneva, framed and fabricked already to our hands. Yet when the new light which we beg for shines in upon us, there be who envy and oppose, if it come not first in at their casements. What a collusion is this, whenas we are exhorted by the wise man to use diligence, to seek for wisdom as for hidden treasures early and late, that another order shall enjoin us to know nothing but by statute? When a man hath been laboring the hardest labour in the deep mines of knowledge; hath furnished out his findings in all their equipage; drawn forth his reasons as it were a battle ranged; scattered and defeated all objections in his way; calls out his adversary into the plain, offers him the advantage of wind and sun, if he please, only that he may try the matter by dint of argument; for his opponents then to skulk, to lay ambushments, to keep a narrow bridge of licensing where the challenger should pass, though it be valour enough in soldiership, is but weakness and cowardice in the wars of Truth.

For who knows not that Truth is strong, next to the Almighty? She needs no policies, nor statagems, nor licensings to make her victorious; those are the shifts and the defences that error uses against her power.

—JOHN MILTON, *Areopagitica.*

NO. 7

THE GOLDEN MEAN

ARISTOTLE

We must premise that every excellence or virtue perfects that thing of which it is the virtue, and causes it to discharge its especial function well. The special excellence of the eye, for example, makes the eye good, and perfects it function; for it is only by the virtue of the eye that we can see well. So, too, the excellence of the horse makes it a good horse, swift, and strong to carry its rider, and bold to face his enemies. And if this be true, as it is in all cases, it follows that the virtue of man will be such a habit as will make him a good man, and enable him to discharge his especial function well. And how this is to be brought about we have already said: but we shall make the matter yet clearer if we consider wherein exactly it is that the nature of moral virtue consists. In everything that is continuous, and consequently capable of division, we can mark off an amount which will be either more than, or less than, or equal to the remainder; and can do so either objectively, that is to say with reference to the matter in question, or subjectively, that is to say with reference to ourselves. Now that which is equal is a mean between excess and defect. And by the mean of the matter I understand that which, as is the point of bisection in a line, is equally distant from either extreme, and which is for all persons alike one and the same. But by the mean with reference to ourselves I understand that which is neither too much for us nor too little, and which consequently is not any one fixed point which for all alike remains the same. If, for example, ten pounds be too much and two pounds be too little, we take as the mean with reference to the matter six pounds, which itself exceed two pounds by as much as they are exceeded by ten. This is what is called a mean in arithmetical progression. But the mean with reference to ourselves must not be thus fixed. For it does not follow that, if ten pounds of meat be too much to eat, and two pounds be too little, our trainer will therefore order us six pounds. This may be either too little for him who is to take it, or too much. For Milo, for example, it would be too little, while for one who is to begin training it would be too much. And in running, and in wrestling, the same rule holds good. And so, too, all skilled artists avoid the excess and the defect, while they seek and choose the mean, that is to say not the absolute but the relative mean. And since it is thus that all skilled knowledge perfects its results, by keeping the mean steadily in view, and by modeling its work upon it, whence it comes that we are wont to say, at the termination of any good work, that neither to it can anything be added, nor from it can anything be taken away; inasmuch as excess and defect destroy perfection, while moderation preserves it; since, then, all good artists, as we have said, always work with the mean in view, and since virtue is, as also is nature, more exact and higher than is any art, it follows that virtue also will aim at the mean. And when I say virtue I mean moral virtue, for moral virtue is concerned with our emotions, that is to say with our actions; and in these excess and defect are to be found, and also moderation. Fear, for example, and confidence, and desire, and anger, and pity, and, generally, any pleasure or pain, we can feel both more and less than we ought, and in either case we feel them not well. But to feel them when we ought, and at what we ought, and towards whom we ought, and for the right motive, and as we ought—in all this lies the mean, and, with the mean, perfection; and these are the characteristics of virtue. And so, too, with reference to our actions, no less than our emotions, excess and defect are possible, and with them consequently moderation. Now virtue is concerned with our emotions and with our actions. It is in these that excess is an error, and that defect is blamed as a fault; while moderation meets with praise and with success, both of which things are marks of virtue. And hence it is that all virtue is a mean, in that it aims at that which is the mean. Moreover the forms of wrong are manifold (for evil is of the infinite, as said the allegory of the Pythagoreans, and good of the finite), while of right the form is but one. Hence the one is easy, the other hard; easy is it to miss, hard to hit our aim. And from this again it follows that to vice belong excess and defect, and to virtue belongs moderation.

—ROBERT WILLIAMS, translator, *Nichomachean Ethics* (New York, Longmans, Green, 1879).

NO. 8

THE ALL-PURPOSE SPEECH

ROBERT H. DAVIS

Mr. Chairman, Ladies and Gentlemen: It is indeed a great and undeserved privilege to address such an audience as I see before me. At no previous time in the history of human civilization have greater problems confronted and challenged the ingenuity of man's intellect than now. Let us look around us. What do we see on the horizon? What forces are at work? Whither are we drifting? Under what mist of clouds does the future stand obscured? My friends, casting aside the raiment of all human speech, the crucial test for the solution of all these intricate problems to which I have just alluded is the sheer and forceful application of those immutable laws which down the corridor of Time have always guided the hand of man, groping, as it were, for some faint beacon light for his hopes and aspirations. Without these great vital principles we are but puppets responding to whim and fancy, failing entirely to grasp the hidden meaning of it all. We must readdress ourselves to these questions which press for answer and solution. The issue cannot be avoided. There they stand. It is upon you—and you—and yet even upon me that the yoke of responsibility falls.

What, then, is our duty? Shall we continue to drift? No! With all the emphasis of my being I hurl back the message No! Drifting must stop. We must press onward and upward toward the ultimate good to which all must aspire. But I cannot conclude my remarks, dear friends, without touching briefly upon a subject which I know is steeped in your very consciousness. I refer to that spirit which gleams from the eyes of a new-born babe; that animates the toiling masses; that sways all the hosts of humanity past and present. Without this energizing principle all commerce, trade and industry are hushed and will perish from this earth as surely as the crimson sunset follows the golden sunshine. Mark you, I do not seek to unduly alarm or distress the mothers, fathers, sons and daughters gathered before me in this vast assemblage, but I would indeed be recreant to a high resolve which I made as a youth if I did not at this time and in this place and with the full realizing sense of responsibility which I assume publicly declare and affirm my dedication and my concentration to the eternal principles and receipts of simple, ordinary, commonplace JUSTICE.

For what, in the last analysis, is justice? Whence does it come? Where does it go? Is it tangible? It is not. Is it ponderable? It is not. It is all of these things combined. While I cannot tell you wha justice is, this much I can tell you: That without the encircling arms of justice, without her shield, without her guardianship, the ship of state will sail through uncharted seas, narrowly avoiding rocks and shoals, headed inevitably to the harbor of calamity.

Justice! Justice! Justice! To thee we pay homage. To thee we dedicate our laurels of hope. Before thee we kneel in adoration, mindful of thy great power, mute before thy inscrutable destiny!

—From HOMER D. LINDGREN, *Modern Speeches*
(New York, Appleton-Century-Crofts, 1930), pp. 66-67.

NO. 9

THE GOOD MAN

QUINTILIAN

Let the orator, then, whom I propose to form, be such a one as is characterized by the definition of Marcus Cato, a good man skilled in speaking.

My judgment carries me still further; for I not only say that he who would answer my idea of an orator, must be a good man, but that no man, unless he be good, can ever be an orator. To an orator discernment and prudence are necessary; but we can certainly not allow discernment to those, who, when the ways of virtue and vice are set before them, prefer to follow that of vice; nor can we allow them prudence, since they subject themselves, by the unforeseen consequences of their actions, often to the heaviest penalty of the law, and always to that of an evil conscience. But if it be not only truly said by the wise, but always justly believed by the vulgar, that no man is vicious who is not also foolish, a fool, assuredly, will never become an orator.

Since an orator, then, is a good man, and a good man cannot be conceived to exist without virtuous inclinations and virtue, though it receives certain impulses from nature, requires notwithstanding to be brought to maturity by instruction, the orator must above all things study morality, and must obtain a thorough knowledge of all that is just and honourable, without which no one can either be a good man or an able speaker.

—LESTER THONSSEN, ed., Selected Readings in
Rhetoric and Public Speaking
(New York, Wilson, 1942), pp. 156 and 157.

NO. 10

THE MODES OF PERSUASION

ARISTOTLE

Of the modes of persuasion furnished by the spoken word there are three kinds. The first kind depends on the personal character of the speaker; the second on putting the audience into a certain frame of mind; the third on the proof, or apparent proof, provided by the words of the speech itself. Persuasion is achieved by the speaker's personal character when the speech is so spoken as to make us think him credible. We believe good men more fully and more readily than others: this is true generally whatever the question is, and absolutely true where exact certainty is impossible and opinions are divided. This kind of persuasion, like the others, should be achieved by what the speaker says, not by what people think of this character before he begins to speak. It is not true, as some writers assume in their treatises on rhetoric, that the personal goodness revealed by the speaker contributes nothing to his power of persuasion; on the contrary, his character may almost be called the most effective means of persuasion he possesses. Secondly, persuasion may come through the hearers, when the speech stirs their emotions. Our judgments when we are pleased and friendly are not the same as when we are pained and hostile. It is towards producing these effects, as we maintain, that present-day writers of rhetoric direct the whole of their efforts. This subject shall be treated in detail when we come to speak of the emotions. Thirdly, persuasion is effected through the speech itself when we have proved a truth or an apparent truth by means of the persuasive arguments suitable to the case in question.

There are, then, these three means of effecting persuasion. The man who is to be in command of them must, it is clear, be able (1) to reason logically, (2) to understand human character and goodness in their various forms, and (3) to understand the emotions—that is, to name them and describe them, to know their causes and the way in which they are excited.

—From Aristotle's *Rhetoric*, trans. by W. Rhys Roberts, in Vol. XI of *The Works of Aristotle*, translated into English under the editorship of W. D. Ross. By permission of the Clarendon Press, Oxford.

NO. 11

PERSUASION

ABRAHAM LINCOLN

When the conduct of man is designed to be influenced, persuasion, kind, unassuming persuasion, should ever be adopted. It is an old and true maxim "that a drop of honey catches more flies than a gallon of gall." So with men. If you would win a man to your cause, first, convince him that you are his sincere friend.

Therein is a drop of honey that catches his heart, which, say what he will, is the great highroad to his reason, and which, when once gained, you will find but little trouble in convincing his judgment of the justice of your cause, if indeed that cause really be a just one.

On the contrary, assume to dictate to his judgment, or to command his action, or to mark him as one to be shunned and despised, and he will retreat within himself, close all the avenues to his head and his heart; and though your cause be naked truth itself, transformed to the heaviest lance, harder than steel, and sharper than steel can be made, and tho' you throw it with more than Herculean force and precision, you shall be no more able to pierce him than to penetrate the hard shell of a tortoise with a rye straw.

Such is man, and so must he be understood by those who would lead him, even to his own best interest.

Index

acceptance, speech of, 232
adapting ideas
  adequate material for, 95
  importance of, 121-122
Address to Foreign-born Citizens, 139-140
adjustment, to speech environment, 8
Adler, Mortimer J., quoted, 8
Aldis, Dorothy, poem, 252-253
All-purpose Speech, The, 315-317
Ally, Bower, quoted, 273-274
Ameil, Henri Frédéric, quoted, 31
analogy, types and uses of, 88-89
analysis, as a listening technique, 150
announcement, 227-228
appearance, importance of in persuasion, 212-213
Aristotle, 8, 123; quoted, 313-315, 318-319
articulation, 131-134
  improvement of, 134
  as related to pronunciation, 132
  as a step in speech production, 128
articulators, function of, 131-132
Atlanta Exposition Address, 140-141
attention, holding, in persuasion, 208-209
audience
  analysis of in early stages, 18-19

analysis of for persuasion, 199-200
considering welfare of, 135
dynamics of, 55
as a factor in choosing a subject, 18-19
keeping contact with, 74-75, 208-209
participation of in group discussion, 170-171
showing respect for, 213
audio aids, 75-76

Bacon, Francis, quoted, 88
Ballad of the Oysterman, The, 242-243
Bambi, 251-252
Barkley, Alben, quoted, 213
Bartlett's Familiar Quotations, 96
Blair, Hugh, quoted, 20
Blair, Walter, quoted, 247-249
bodily action
  control of, 123-124
  in reading aloud, 239
body, of the speech, 37-43
breathing, as a step in speech production, 125-126
Brown, Harrison S., quoted, 280-285
Byron, Lord, quoted, 22, 263

Campbell, George, quoted, 20
Carlyle, Thomas, quoted, 136

Carroll, Lewis, quoted, 96
Childe Harold, 263
children's literature, 250-253
Churchill, Winston, quoted, 109
Clark, Badger, poem, 259-260
Clark, Charles Heber, quoted, 301-306
Cicero, 8
Come up from the Fields, Father, 243-244
communication, definition of, 6
conclusion, requirements of, 43-44
connotation, 262-263
consonants, voice production of, 128
constitution, sample, 194-196
Coolidge, Calvin, quoted, 145
Cowboy's Prayer, A, 259-260
Cowper, William, quoted, 113
criticism, 10

Daly, T. A., poem, 245-246
data, general and specific, defined, 71
Davis, Robert H., quoted, 315-317
deduction
  definition of, 203-204
  in organizing persuasive speeches, 209-210
definition
  methods of, 62-63
  need for in speaking, 61-62
delivery, 121-136
  adapting ideas for, 121-122
  eye contact in, 124
  freedom of, 123-124
  instruments used in, 122-131; *see also* articulation; bodily action; personality; voice
  suggestions for being effective in, 135-136
Dewey, John, problem-solving plan, 162-163, 209-210
diaphragm, 126
discussion, *see* group discussion
distractions
  as barriers to listening, 149-150

as caused by faulty language, 115
  in the environment, 56
  removing from delivery, 135-136
divisions of a speech, 24, 35ff
  body, 37-43
  conclusion, 43-44
  introduction, 35-36
  proposition, 36-37
Donne, John, 6
Douglas, William O., quoted, 275-280
Dryden, John, quoted, 32
Dunbar, Paul Laurence, poem, 246-247
duration, of sound, 130

Elephant's Child, The, 250-251
Emerson, Ralph Waldo, quoted, 108
emotions, as barriers to listening, 149
environment, of speaking situation
  adjustment to, 8
  control of in listening, 148
  emotional, 56
  physical, 56
ethics
  and delivery, 135
  in persuasion, 199, 207-208
  as a social responsibility, 11-12
  in using quotations, 94
  in using statistics, 92
evidence, as used in persuasion, 201
example
  comparison, 88-89; *see also* analogy
  contrast, 89
  definition of, 83
  forms of, 84-88
  hypothetical, 89-90
extemporaneous style, 26-28; *see also* delivery
eye contact, 124
  in reading aloud, 264

fallacies, in reasoning, 204-205
Farewell Address, 139

fear, in speaking, 5-6
  reducing by use of physical materials, 73
  and subject choice, 17
figures of speech, 112-113
  study of in reading aloud, 263
First Inaugural Address, 258-259
Flesch, Rudolph, quoted, 311-312
folklore, 244-250
forum, as a phase of group discussion, 170-171
Franklin, Benjamin, quoted, 32
Frost, Robert, poem, 254-256
Function of Democracy, The, 275-280

Gift from the Sea, 257-258
Gift of the Power of Speech, The, 309-311
goals, of speech training, 7-9
Golden Mean, The, 313-315
Good Man, The, 317-318
Grady, Henry, quoted, 111
group discussion, 157ff
  audience participation in, 170-171
  choosing a subject for, 159-160
  forms of, 163-170
  importance of, 157-158
  leadership of, 176-177
  materials for, 171-174
  organization of, 162-163
  participating in, 174-176
  process of, 158-159
  timing of, 168-170
  topics for, 178-179
  wording the question for, 160-162
  see also parliamentary procedure

Harte, Bret, quoted, 249-250
Hayne, William Hamilton, 263
Hazlitt, William C., quoted, 214
Hiding, 252-253
High Degree of Probability, A, 311-312
Holmes, Oliver Wendell, poem, 242-243

How to Tell a Story, 306-307
Hughes, Charles Evans, quoted, 19

illustration, definition and use of, 84-88
impromptu speech, requirements of, 226-227
individuality, as an asset, 9
induction, 201-202
  use of for persuasion, 210-212
insertion, as a fault of articulation, 133
instance, use of, 85-88
Intellectual and the Politician, The, 285-291
introduction
  for oral reading, 263-264
  for original speech, 35-36
introduction, speech of, 228-231
irony, 113

Jefferson, Thomas, quoted, 258-259
John Henry and the Machine, 247-249
Johnson, Gertrude E., quoted, 245

Kennedy, John F., quoted, 285-291
Kipling, Rudyard, quoted, 250-251
Korean Crisis, The, 291-298

language, 107-117
  clarity in use of, 108-110
  figurative, 112-113
  in group discussion, 175-176
  improving use of, 115-116
  sense-appealing, 111
  variety in, 113-115
larynx, 126-127
Laughton, Charles, quoted, 236
lecture panel, 169-170
Leibman, Joshua Loth, quoted, 123
Let there Be Unlicensed Expression, 312-313
Letter to Mrs. Bixby, 257
Lewis, Thomas R., quoted, 147
library, use of, 96, 171-172

Lincoln, Abraham, quoted, 94, 139, 257, 319-320
Lindbergh, Anne Morrow, quoted, 257-258
Lines for an Interment, 253-254
lips, as articulators, 128-129
listening skills, 144ff
  goals of, 145-146
  in group discussion, 176
  guides to, 148-150
  importance of, 144-145, 146-147
  improving, 8, 147-150
  nature of, 145-147
  and the speaker, 147-148
literature
  analyzing, 261-263
  children's, 250-253
  folklore, 244-250
  of high resolve, 257-260
  narrative, 241-244
  see also poetry; reading aloud
logic, in persuasion, *see* persuasion, logical elements
Lullaby, 246-247

McCall, Roy C., quoted, 130
MacLeish, Archibald, poem, 253-254
Macaulay, Thomas, quoted, 178
Man Gets Language, 307-309
materials, physical, 71-73
materials, verbal, 82ff
  criteria for selecting, 94
  definition of, 82
  finding a supply of, 95-96
  usefulness of, 72, 83
memorization, 26-27
Mending Wall, 254-256
Message to Congress, 140
metaphor, 112
Mia Carlotta, 245-246
Milton, John, quoted, 312-313
Mizner, Wilson, quoted, 144
Modes of Persuasion, The, 318-319
motions, in parliamentary procedure, 185-193
  to amend, 187, 189
  handling of, 185, 188

incidental, 189-190
main, 185-186
privileged, 190-191
subsidiary, 186-189
table of, 193
unclassified, 191-192
mouth, as a resonator, 128

narrative literature, 241-244
nasal passages, as resonators, 128
New South, The, 111
Nichols, Ralph G., quoted, 147
Nominating Calvin Coolidge, 298-300
nomination, speech of, 231
notecards, use of, 172-173
notes, in speech delivery, 124

occasion
  meeting demands of, 225ff
  and subject choice, 19, 95
omission, as a fault of expression, 133
organization of speeches, 31ff
  in group discussion, 162-163
  outlining for, 33-34
  patterns of, 41-43
  in persuasion, 209-212
outlines, sample
  deductive, 46-48, 64-67, 70-71, 77-79, 97-101
  for discussion panel, 165-168
  for group discussion, 164
  for persuasive speeches, 216ff
outlining, 33-34

palate, as an articulator, 128-129
panel, as a discussion form, 163-168
parliamentary procedure, 182ff
  chairman, 183-184
  importance of, 182-183
  participating under, 184-185
  voting, 192
  see also motions
Patterson, Grove, 27-28
Peace of Mind, 123
personal element

in persuasion, 212-213
in speaking, 28
personality
definition of, 122
growth of, 5-6
persuasion, 198-215
logical elements of, 201-205
nature of, 198-199
organization in, 209-212
personal element in, 212-213
psychological elements of, 205-209
sample outlines of speeches for, 216-221
topics for, 214-215
use of evidence in, 201
Persuasion, 319-320
Phaedrus, 35
pharynx, as a resonator, 128
phonation step in speech production, 126-127
pitch, as voice characteristic, 129-130
Plato, 35
poetry
for children, 252-253
folklore, 244-247, 249-250
lyric, 253-256
and prose, compared, 240-241
narrative, 241-244
suggestions for reading aloud, 265
practice
for reading aloud, 264-265
removing distracting elements in, 135-136
presentation, speech of, 231-232
problem-solution order, 42-43
pronunciation, 132-134
in reading aloud, 263
problem words in, 141-143
proposition, 24-26, 36-37
prose, compared with poetry, 240-241; *see also* literature
purpose, general, 19-22

questions, for group discussion, 178-179

Quintilian, 8, 135; quoted, 13, 317-318
quotations, use of, 92-94

Rankin, Paul, 144
rate of speaking, 131
reading aloud, 236ff
bibliography of materials for, 266-267
bodily action in, 239
finding a selection for, 240ff
introducing a selection for, 263-264
opportunities for, 236-237
preparing for, 259-265
reader's role in, 238-239
vocal characteristics in, 239
readings in speech, 301-320
reason, as a speech arrangement, 41-42
reasoning, fallacies in, 204-205
Remarks on Jefferson Day, 273-274
resonation step in speech production, 128
response, to a speech of welcome, 233
restatement, 60-61
Richard Cory, 241-242
Robert, Henry M., quoted, 182
Robinson, Edwin Arlington, poem, 241-242
Rogers, Will, quoted, 11, 123, 298-300
Roget's Thesaurus, 83
Roosevelt, Franklin D., quoted, 140

Salten, Felix, quoted, 251-252
Sea Lyric, A, 263
seating
as a factor in listening, 149
for a discussion panel, 164
Second Inaugural Address, 139
sentence, variety in construction of, 113-114
Shakespeare, William, quoted, 11
simile, 112

Simon, Clarence T., quoted, 266
slang, cautions in use of, 114-115
Smith, Eugene, quoted, 26
speech
   definition of, 54
   nature of a class in, 3-4
   production of, 125-129
   see also specific entries
speeches, model, 273ff; see also divisions of a speech
Spring Night, 256
statistics, nature and use of, 90-92
Stewart, George R., quoted, 307-309
Stolen Thunder, 301-306
style, 8, 26-28; see also language
subject
   factors in selecting, 15-19
   for group discussion, 159-160
   narrowing of, 22-24
   see also topics
subordination, in outlining, 33-34
substitution, as a fault of articulation, 132-133
summary, preparation of, 43-44
Sutherland, George, quoted, 44
syllogism, 203
symposium, 168-169

Teasdale, Sara, poem, 256
teeth, as articulators, 128-129
tongue, as an articulator, 128-129
topics
   for group discussion, 178-179
   for persuasive speeches, 214-215
   suggested list of, 16-17, 45
trachea, in speech production, 126
transitions, types and uses of, 57-60

Truman, Harry S, quoted, 291-298
Twain, Mark, quoted, 110, 306-307

variety
   in sentence construction, 113-114
   in using quotations, 94
   in vocal expression, 130, 134
   in word choice, 59, 114-115
   in wording the summary, 43-44
visual aids, 73-75
vocal characteristics, in reading aloud, 239
vocal cords, 127, 129-130
voice, characteristics of, 129-131
volume, as a characteristic of voice, 130
voting, in parliamentary procedure, 192
vowels, formation of, 128

Washington, Booker T., quoted, 140-141
Washington, George, quoted, 139
Webster, Daniel, quoted, 213
Webster's Collegiate Dictionary, 121
welcome, speech of, 233
Whitman, Walt, quoted, 3, 243-244
Wiener, Norbert, quoted, 54, 309-311
Wilson, Woodrow, quoted, 139-140
word choice, variety in, 59, 114-115
words, see language